I0823016

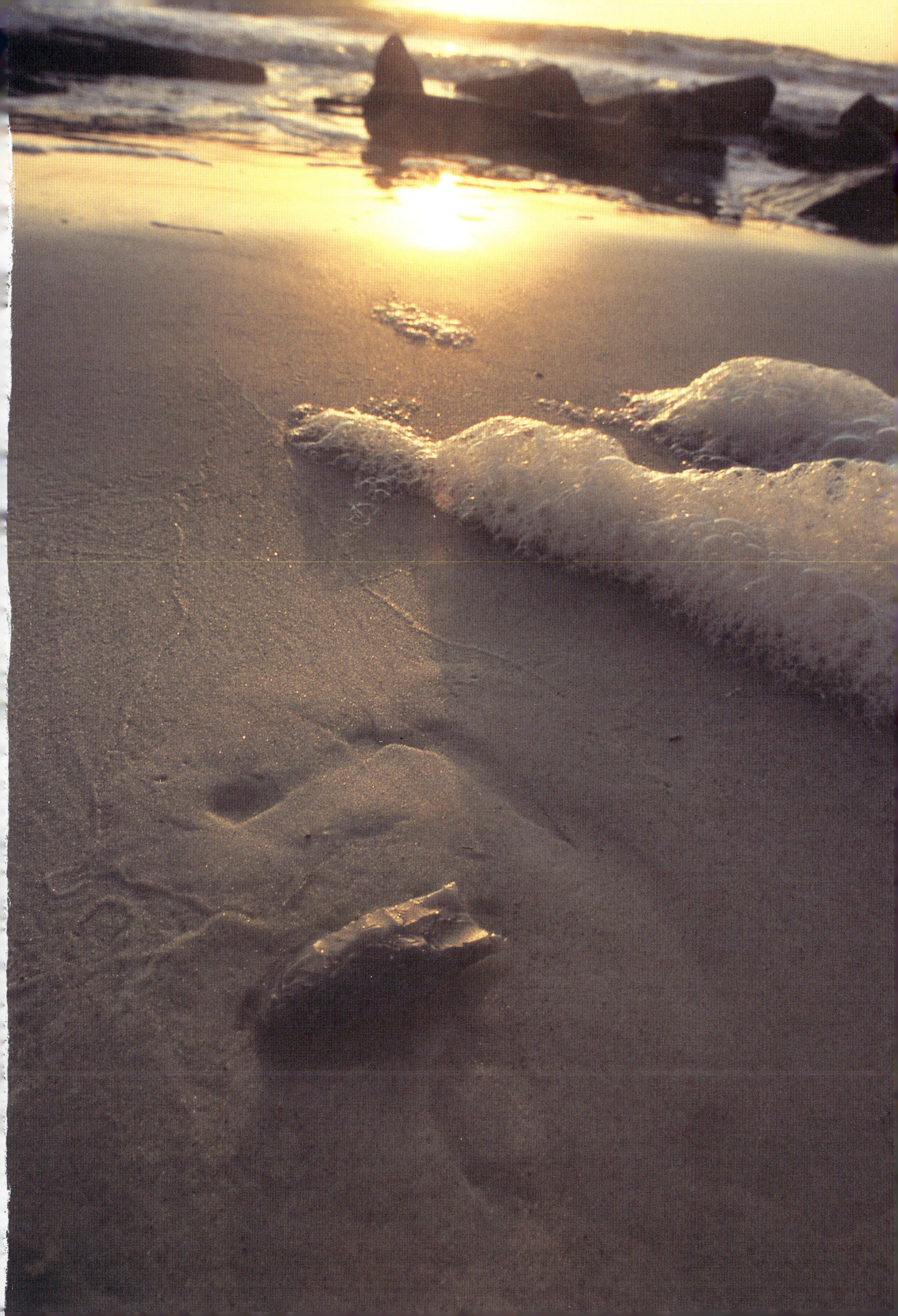

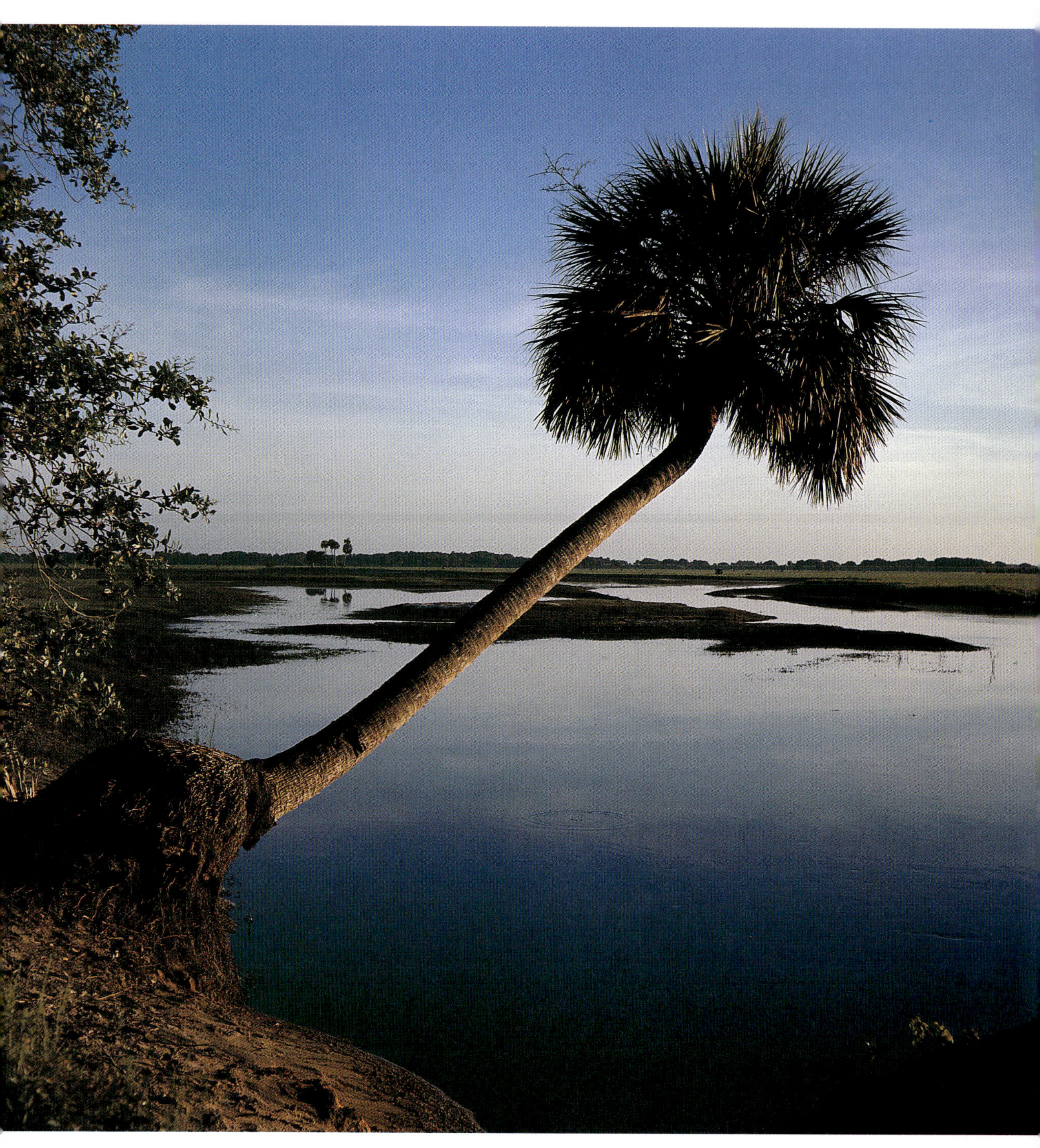

Leaning palms, Fort Center
(overleaf) Clovis point, St. Augustine

INDIAN ART OF ANCIENT FLORIDA

by Barbara A. Purdy
Photographs by Roy C. Craven, Jr.

University Press of Florida
GAINESVILLE TALLAHASSEE TAMPA BOCA RATON
PENSACOLA ORLANDO MIAMI JACKSONVILLE

Printed in Hong Kong on acid-free paper

02 01 00 99 98 97 6 5 4 3 2 1

LIBRARY OF CONGRESS CATALOGING-IN-PUBLICATION DATA
Purdy, Barbara A.
Indian art of ancient Florida / by Barbara A. Purdy;
photographs by Roy C. Craven, Jr.
p. cm.
Includes bibliographical references.
ISBN 0-8130-1462-X (alk. paper)
1. Indian art—Florida. 2. Indians of North America—Florida—Material culture. 3. Indians of North America—Florida—Antiquities.
4. Florida—Antiquities. I. Title.
E78.F6P89 1996
704'.03970759—dc20 96-7798

The University Press of Florida is the scholarly publishing agency for the State University System of Florida, comprised of Florida A & M University, Florida Atlantic University, Florida International University, Florida State University, University of Central Florida, University of Florida, University of North Florida, University of South Florida, and University of West Florida.

University Press of Florida
15 Northwest 15th Street
Gainesville, FL 32611

This work is respectfully dedicated to the memory of the native peoples of Florida

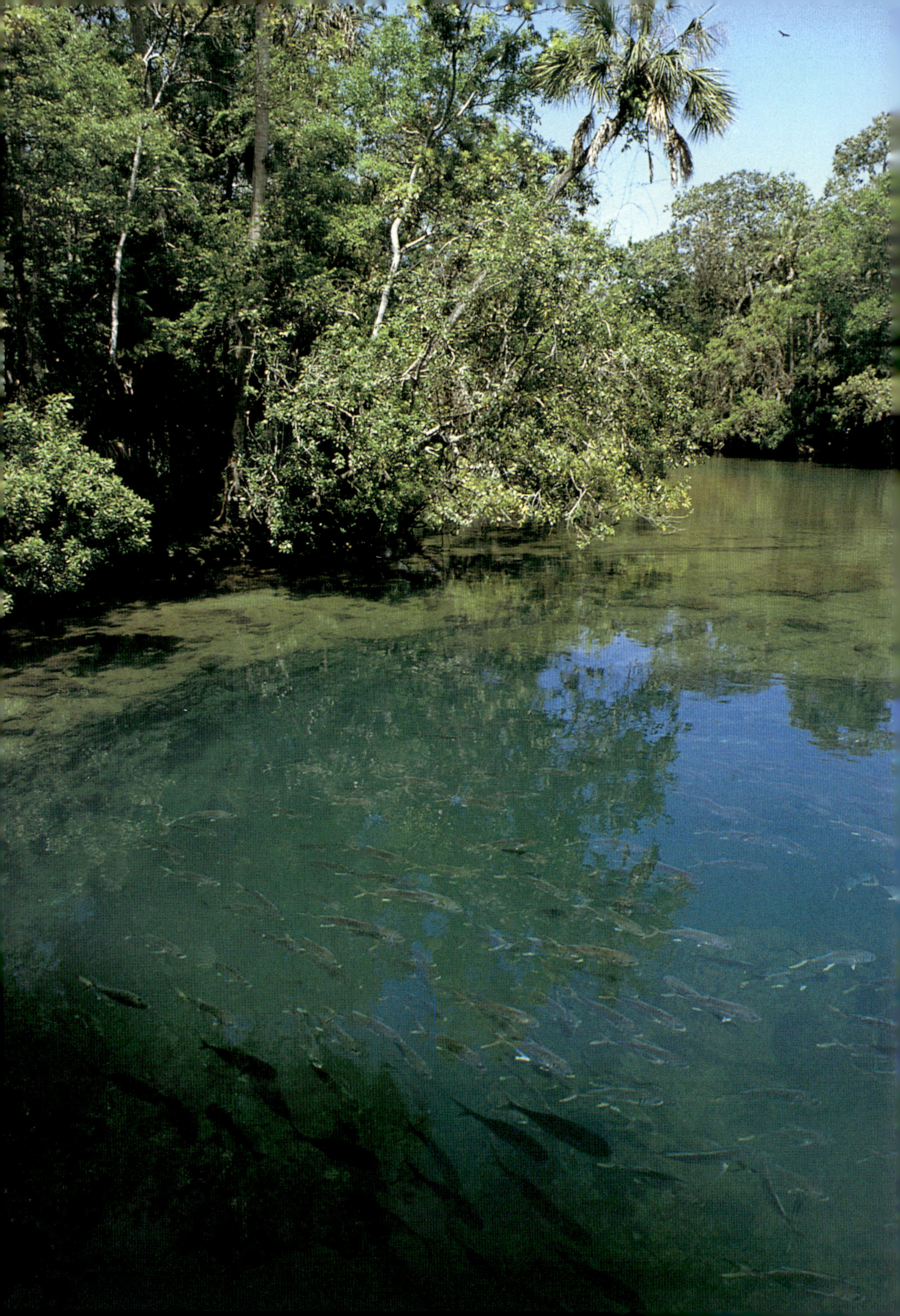

CONTENTS

FOREWORD

THIS IS A SUPERB BOOK—and one that is long overdue. Quite rightly, Barbara Purdy states in her introduction that while "every schoolchild can identify King Tut . . . not a single one of them recognizes the images shown here." Many of these images—the artistic creations of ancient Indian Florida—have been known to archaeologists for more than a century, but this knowledge rarely has been spread beyond our limited circle. Therefore this volume is especially important because it presents these works of art to a wider audience.

The native peoples themselves are long gone, but the artworks they left behind, as Roy Craven writes in his prologue, are "wrought with a passion that, though dimmed by the passage of time, still excites us with its inventive beauty." This is the place to say that Craven's sensitivity to this "inventive beauty" is admirably expressed in his skilled and imaginative photographs.

The archaeological settings of this ancient Florida art are clearly and briefly set out by Purdy. The Florida peninsula was occupied as early as what archaeologists designate as Paleoindian period (ca. 9500–8000 B.C.), a late glacial era characterized by a big-game-hunting way of life. This was followed by a long Archaic period (8000–4000 B.C.), in which post-Pleistocene hunters, fishers, and food collectors subsisted on the natural resources of Florida's semitropical environment. It was in this Archaic-period context, especially from 5000 B.C. onward, that the first works of art were fashioned in Florida. Many of these are fascinating pieces of carved wood or bone that have been preserved in wetlands. Some ground-and-polished stone implements also originate from the Archaic period. I am often amazed at the care that was given to the fashioning of utilitarian objects such as throwing-stick weights (also referred to as a bannerstones) into objects of art.

Pottery appears in the Florida archaeological sequence at about 2000 B.C.. It is probably the earliest pottery in native North America; whether it was invented locally or whether the idea was introduced from elsewhere is still an open question among archaeologists. Gradually these ceramics became more elaborate in form and decoration, in response to contacts with other native societies in the southeastern United States. The Weeden Island pottery style, which flourished between about A.D. 400 and 1000, represents a climactic expression of this Floridian ceramic art. Many Weeden Island vessels were made especially for mortuary or ritual purposes and are found in burial mounds. The wider cultural relationships of Weeden Island pertain to the Middle Woodland period of the eastern United States; however, the culture's special flamboyance is unique to Florida.

Subsequent native Florida cultures and ceramics, especially those of the Gulf Coast regions, were influenced in Late Prehistoric times (A.D. 1000–1500) by the Mississippian cultures of the areas to the north. Some of the most fascinating and appealing objects of art from Prehistoric Florida date to those late centuries and come from the Glades region in the south. A prime example is the exquisite carved wooden seated feline figure (plate 24) that was recovered from the Key Marco site.

Even after the arrival of the first Spaniards in the early sixteenth century, Florida Indians continued their creative work, sometimes refashioning European-introduced metals (gold and silver ornaments and coins) into objects that expressed their own ideas and beliefs.

All of this and more—a fine sampling of a unique native American artistic heritage—is laid out before you, in text and in pictures, in this exciting book.

GORDON R. WILLEY
Harvard University

PREFACE

THE NATIVE PEOPLES who inhabited Florida prior to the arrival of Europeans in the sixteenth century created exquisite works of art in wood, bone, shell, and ceramics. Although Florida has no naturally occurring metals or stone suitable for carving, a few objects of copper and polished stone were imported from areas to the north. When precious metals became available early in the Historic period, the Indians transferred some of their traditional styles to these new media.

Most of the beautiful objects shown in this volume have been described and illustrated in numerous, but often obscure, publications for more than a century. Their importance has been diminished, however, because until now no book has been devoted exclusively to the artistic achievements of the Florida Indians. Because of this neglect we have cheated the memory of these early inhabitants. The richness of Florida's past is as exciting as that of other places and should be treasured even more because it is ours. The diverse natural environments still remaining in the state are also featured in this book. These scenes are probably identical to those enjoyed and exploited by the native peoples.

We had hoped to show only perfect pieces, in the condition known by the people who made them. This has not always been possible. Also, some specimens were not available to us, and others have been lost. Undoubtedly, many spectacular pieces are in private collections and remain unknown. We have attempted, however, to include representative objects from all cultural periods, geographic areas, and media and from all of the environmental settings in which Florida Indians lived.

Most art historians do not believe that the twentieth-century concept of "art for art's sake" is valid for preindustrial societies. The objects that we present here were probably made in order to objectify the relationships of people to the natural and supernatural worlds. This conclusion is supported by the presence of recurring themes in the art of both egalitarian and hierarchical cultures in various times and locations. In Florida, for example, similar patterns have been identified on artifacts recovered at 6000- to 8000-year-old sites that are separated by great distances. It is tempting sometimes to conclude that a one-of-a-kind object was made by an individual with an uninhibited imagination. The uniqueness of the object is probably more apparent than real, however, simply because others like it have not been found or have not survived.

It is important to consider the materials that were available to produce the tools, weapons, ornaments, statues, and buildings that Florida Indians used. The advantages of a warm climate and abundant aquatic species were not lost on the Indians, but, as mentioned above, Florida lacks materials such as volcanic and metamorphic rocks, soapstone, and metal ores. Small numbers of imported objects have been found in the state, but, for the most part, chipped stone, bone, wood, shell, and ceramic industries were developed using local resources. It is sad to realize that basketry, furs, leather goods (particularly painted deer skins), musical instruments, feather work, tattoos, and other items mentioned in historic accounts have not survived. The historic documents themselves contain very few details specific enough to be useful.

The pieces we have chosen to illustrate in this volume are described with regard to their antiquity and cultural affinities. Except for the Clovis point on the first page of this book, we have not included any examples from the Paleoindian or Early Archaic periods, from approximately 9000 to 5000 B.C. Several specimens from the Middle and Late Archaic periods, from 4000 to 2000 B.C., are shown. A large increase in creative achievement began with the Ceramic period about 2000 B.C. and continued until the mid-sixteenth century. The artifacts are arranged in sections according to the materials used. Each section is preceded by a photograph of a natural environment in Florida—a habitat associated with the prehistoric sites where the artworks were created.

A great majority of the specimens featured here were collected in the late nineteenth and early twentieth centuries. Some of them have never been illustrated before, and information is sparse or missing for others. It has been very exciting for us to examine these objects and to learn something about their history, both recent and ancient. We hope that these pages convey our excitement and that you experience it also.

THIS PUBLICATION originated several years ago with a vision that materialized only with cooperation and support from many sources. We are grateful to the following institutions and private collectors: the University of Florida; the Florida Museum of Natural History, especially Elise LeCompte-Baer and Darcie A. MacMahon; the Florida Bureau of Archaeological Research, especially James J. Miller and David N. Dickel; the South Florida Museum and Bishop Planetarium, especially Laura Branstetter; the Jacksonville Museum of Science and History, especially Nadia McClure; the National Park Service at Fort Caroline National Memorial, especially Craig Morris; the Indian Temple Mound Museum at Fort Walton Beach, especially Gail Myer; the Graves Museum of Archaeology and Natural History, especially Gypsy Graves; the Silver River Museum, especially Guy Marwick; the Daytona Beach Museum of Arts and Sciences, especially Dana St. Claire; the Historical Society of Palm Beach, especially Susan Duncan and Ellen Donovan; the National Museum of the American Indian, especially W. Richard West, Jr., Mary Jane Lenz, Mark Clark, Kelton Bound, and Kevin De Vorsey; the Smithsonian Institution, especially Debra Hull-Walski; the University Museum in Philadelphia, especially Lucy Williams; several individuals who wish to remain anonymous; and many colleagues whose ideas we have consciously or unconsciously usurped. We acknowledge with much appreciation the assistance of others but we accept full responsibility for any errors of fact or interpretation in this book.

Publication of this volume has been financed in part through historic preservation grant assistance provided by the Division of Historical Resources of the Florida Department of State, Sandra B. Mortham, secretary of state.

Roy C. Craven, Jr., died on May 30 1996, after a lengthy illness. This book is largely a result of Roy's photographic and artistic talents. It was a pleasure and privilege to work with him, and I am distressed that he did not live to see the finished product.

BARBARA A. PURDY
June 1996

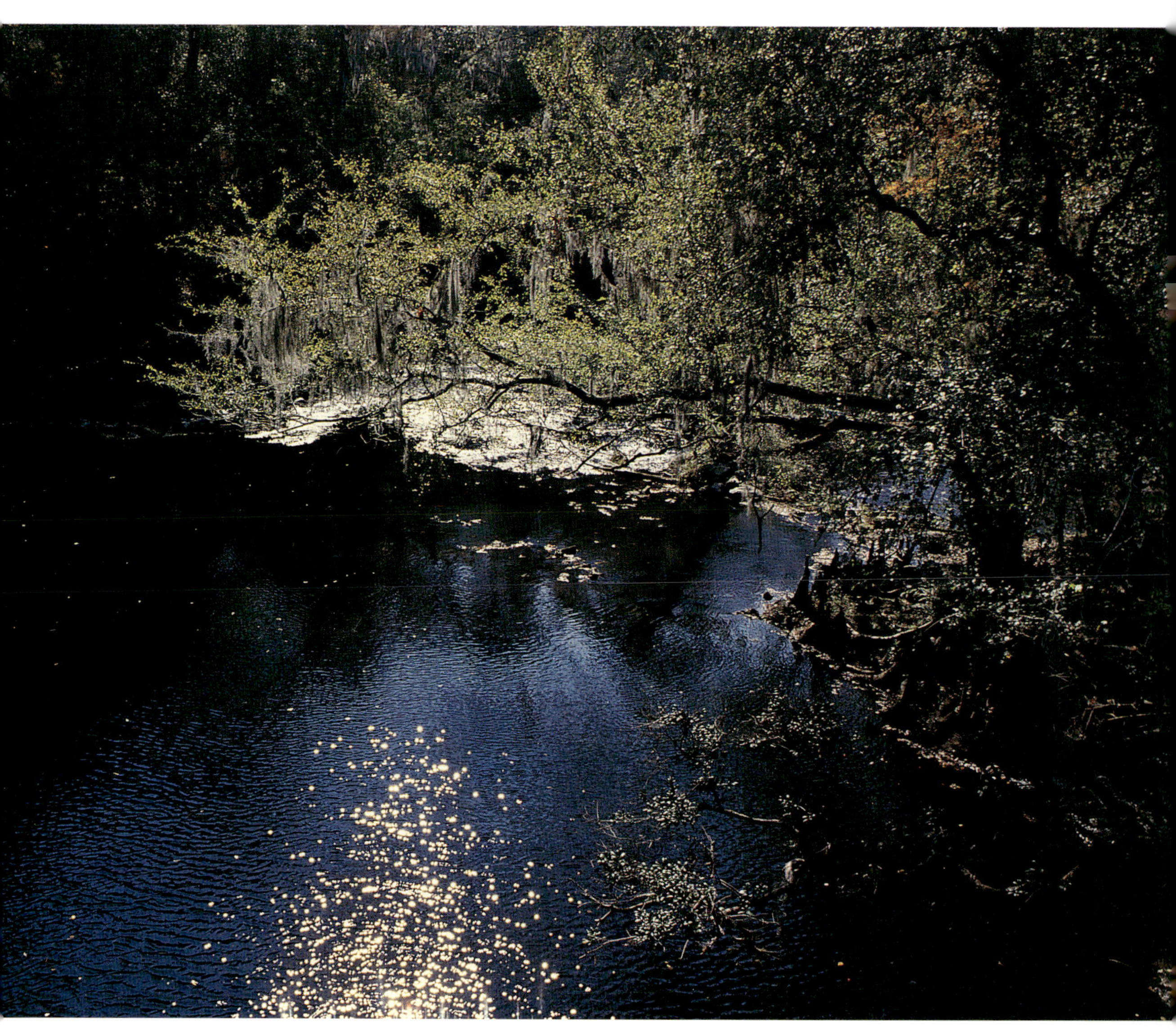

PROLOGUE

Art and Artifact

PEOPLE HAVE LONG HAD a profound desire to enhance and ornament themselves, their tools, and their surroundings. As we review these impressive creations from Florida's past, it is natural to ask ourselves why they were made. We intuitively understand that they were fashioned—as were perhaps most artifacts from early cultures—to honor and appease the gods, to pay homage to ancestors, to aid the dead in their journey into the next world, to indicate status, to adorn the body, and for utilitarian purposes to deal with everyday survival.

We are indebted to archaeologists for their tedious efforts in retrieving and describing these objects. Lamentably, barriers exist within our compartmentalized society between the disciplines of anthropology and art history. An object that is considered a scientific unit of data by an anthropologist is considered an aesthetic object—a work of art—by an art historian or museum curator. Obviously the object is both things, and this is the basic and happy purpose for assembling this book.

Every human creation, ultimately, is an anthropological specimen. The *Mona Lisa,* the lapis-and-gold mummy mask of Tutankhamen, and a Weeden Island animal-effigy incense urn are all records of past human activities and involvements upon this earth. The objects that we show here consistently exhibit a startlingly high quality of craftsmanship and aesthetic excellence—evidence of someone's desire to transcend the mundane and create something beautiful. The very earliest "art" images, made on the walls of caves, had a magical purpose; they emerged from the same mysterious sense of being that we modern people still possess. That idea is the key to comprehending all of human creation.

Notwithstanding the twentieth-century phenomenon of Cubism, which drew on African mask carvings as a source of inspiration, and the evolution of abstraction as a dominant art aesthetic, Westerners still tend to perceive the Precolumbian arts of America as "primitive" or "savage" because they do not conform to the European "classical" bias that originated in the Greek tradition of realism. We sometimes have to struggle to comprehend the arts of unfamiliar cultures. Much of Asia, for example, remains for many Americans an exotic aesthetic wasteland. Many of us are conditioned to think of art only in terms of stereotypical Western categories—painting, sculpture, drawing, printmaking—and of the "artist" as an exotic, free-willed, and colorful person who creates "art" under the control of an enigmatic and maybe even uncontrollable inspiration—such a person is a "fine artist." Anyone else who might fashion made-to-order images or objects for pay is relegated to a lower, "commercial" status and is certainly not an "artist." We in the West have come to accept the idea of the inspired, free-spirited individual as the sole legitimate creator of art, and "art for art's sake" has become an accepted motto of our times.

This is a comparatively recent concept and one that definitely has not been valid throughout the span of world history. Art historians agree that the art of the past was not created by what we call artists but by individuals we would call craftspeople—Leonardo da Vinci and Michelangelo, the anonymous sculptors of the Chartres cathedral and medieval Hindu temples, and the potters and architects of Precolumbian America, including ancient Florida.

Without exception, these people produced products for paying patrons—perhaps a religious organization or system or a person of high status. Rather than lessening the artistic achievement however, the values of craftsmanship enhanced art objects, making them functional parts of the community. Craftspeople created highly aesthetic ritual and utilitarian objects that were necessary and even central to their societies' needs. That is what confers weight and substance to their work. It is unfortunate that the context of the craftsperson bewilders modern viewers, who have been indoctrinated to understand art as something that is produced in a vacuum, beyond the values of society, by a singular individual creative agent.

It is our belief that the artworks assembled here—items fashioned by the Precolumbian peoples of Florida—will speak for themselves. They were wrought with a passion that, though dimmed by the passage of time, still excites us with its inventive beauty.

Roy C. Craven, Jr.

INDIAN ART OF ANCIENT FLORIDA

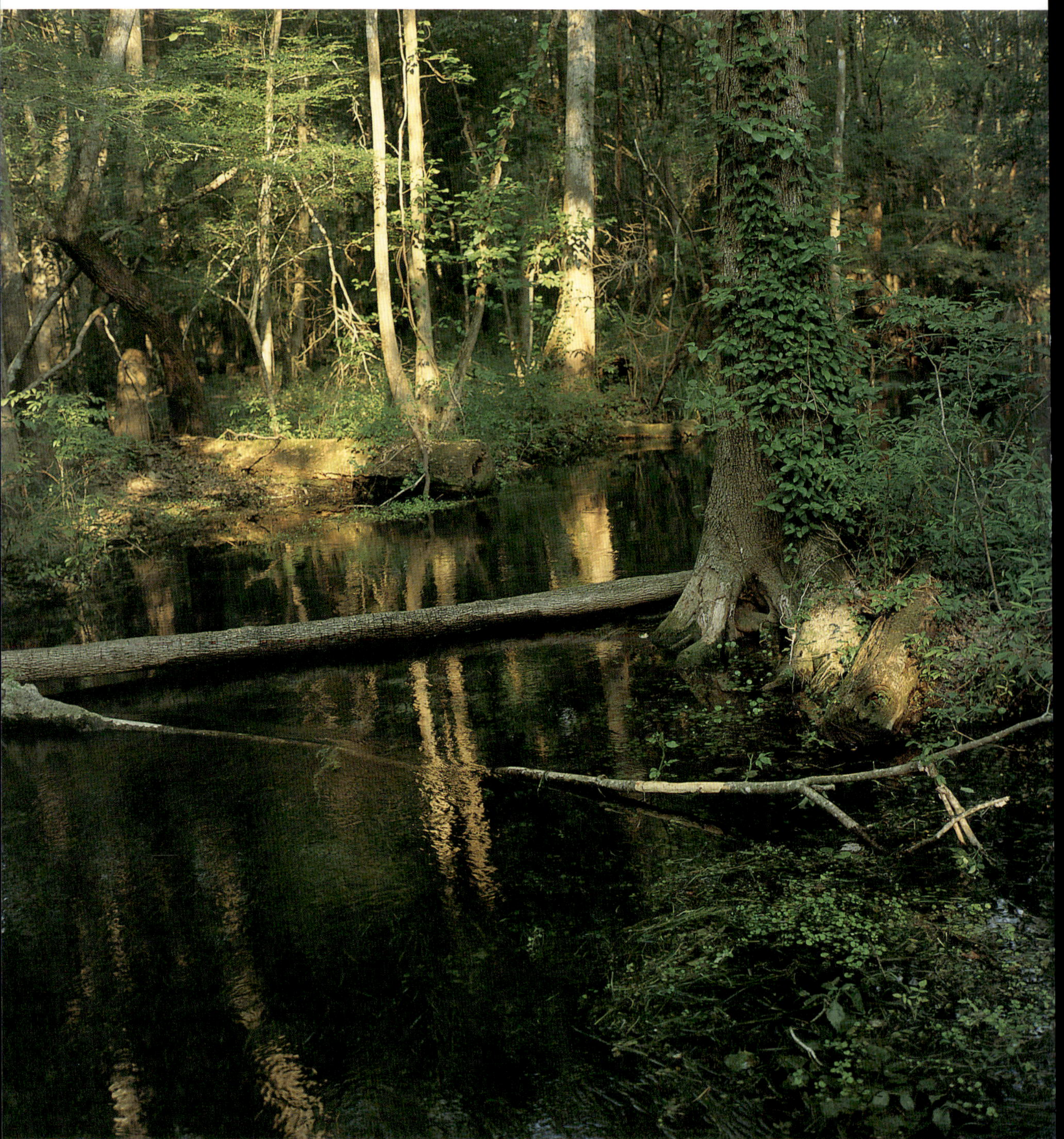

Ichetucknee Springs

ART STYLES AND LIFE STYLES

A PRINCIPAL INCENTIVE for bringing together the pieces illustrated in this volume was the realization that few people know that the Florida Indians created objects of beauty and distinctiveness comparable to those fashioned anywhere else in the world. Many of these artifacts have been described and pictured in archaeological publications or site reports since the mid-nineteenth century. Some have been included in books about North American Indian art. Until now, however, no attempt has been made to focus exclusively on the Indian art of Florida.

Every schoolchild can identify King Tut, but not a single one of them recognizes the images shown here. Nor do their parents. There are a number of reasons for this unfortunate situation. Florida was the first land explored in what is now the United States. The Europeans who did the exploring were concerned with their own survival and with finding gold and silver. They took little notice of the personal and community adornment of the natives except to label it paganistic. It is not likely that any Florida Indian artifacts were taken to Europe following the earliest voyages; if they were, they probably were manufactured of perishable materials and have not survived.

The Florida Indians themselves did not survive, and that is another problem. There is no continuity with the past. In contrast, for example, the Southwest and Northwest Coast Indians still reside in essentially the same geographic region they occupied in prehistoric times, and their artistic traditions endure.

In studying material culture, anthropologists find, in general, that stone, bone, and wooden artifacts are older than artifacts made of shell, ceramic, and metal. Specimens made of all of those materials are found in Florida, but it is crucial to examine each material separately to determine its importance and availability.

Chipped-stone implements of flint (chert) are known to be more than 11,000 years old in Florida. They underwent a number of stylistic changes over the years, but they were still being made when the earliest Europeans arrived. While spearheads are sometimes beautifully fashioned, they do not fit our definition of art. Florida does not have a type of stone suitable for producing small carvings or statuary. A few items of polished stone have been recovered in Florida, some at least 6,000 years old, but they have all been brought in from other places.

Bone and antler were used for weapons, tools, and ornaments from the very beginning of human occupation in Florida. Styles remained unchanged for thousands of years. Several dozen artifacts made from the ivory of elephant tusk have also been found, indicating that hunters killed those large animals before they became extinct 10,000 years ago. Two of the ivory objects (not illustrated in this book) bear zigzag incising, suggesting that their owners were decorating utilitarian specimens, perhaps creating the oldest designs ever discovered in the Western Hemisphere. By 6,000 to 8,000 years ago, the decorations on bone and antler objects had become quite elaborate. Some of those impressive artifacts survived in good condition in Florida because they became entombed in oxygen-free, water-saturated organic deposits with a neutral-alkaline pH. Bone will not survive in the acid, humid environment typical of most of Florida. Also, at typical terrestrial shell-midden sites, designs became eroded as the bone was trampled and crushed.

Archaeological evidence for the use of wood in Florida is more than 12,000 years old, and wooden artifacts with geometric designs were made beginning about 7,000 to 8,000 years ago. Botanical materials, including wood, are least likely to survive in Florida's climate. Even under the best of conditions, such as at sites that have remained continuously waterlogged, wood preservation is not excellent. In other words, the wood effigies that are lifted from bogs, hundreds and even thousands of years after they were made, do not resemble the magnificent, freshly worked and vividly painted specimens. Wood was the only natural material available to create large statues. It was also used for smaller figures, similar to those made of stone in other regions. All of the large carvings in Florida were made of pine, as were the nearly 300 canoes for which records now exist. Wood was probably used more extensively than any other medium, but evidence for its use depends upon its survival.

The widespread use of marine shell for containers, implements, and ornaments began around 6,000 years ago. The technology to produce these objects became more sophisticated over time, but the Indians seem to have concentrated on producing utilitarian items. Objects of personal adornment such as pendants are fairly common but were not usually fashioned into effigies or animal forms, although there are exceptions. As with bone, the size of the finished product was limited by the dimensions of the material.

The production of cooking pots from fired clay began about 2000 B.C. Throughout most of Florida during that time, pottery was utilitarian and plain or stamped with simple designs. For a brief time, in a fairly limited geographic region, elaborate effigy vessels were made to accompany burials.

There are no metals native to Florida, but beginning around the first century A.D., copper was brought into the state from the north in small quantities and in finished form. (It was probably traded from the area of the Great Lakes.) The earliest copper artifacts are usually utilitarian items and plummets that are similar to those made of marine shell. A few elaborate objects of copper appear in Late Prehistoric or Early Historic archaeological contexts. Unfortunately, they are poorly preserved. After European contact, gold, silver, iron, and glass beads were obtained by the Florida Indians from shipwrecks. Sometimes they reworked those materials. Historic accounts do not indicate that the Indians received objects of gold or silver from the Spanish or French. Certain "baubles"—scissors, knives, clothes, mirrors—were given to the Indians by the explorers and colonizers in exchange for the gold and silver the Indians possessed. The Europeans had gold fever!

All of these materials, whether native to Florida or imported, were found in local cultural contexts and form part of the heritage of the state.

From the expeditions of Juan Ponce de León in 1513 and 1521, Lucas Vasquez de Ayllón in 1526, Pánfilo de Narváez in 1528, and Fernando de Soto in 1539 come the first written records of Indian life in southeastern North America. The native peoples were hostile to the Spanish because the latter confiscated the Indians' food supplies, violated the women among them, took hostages, and killed anyone who tried to oppose them. Accounts of those confrontations mention the weapons, strategies, and tactics utilized by the Indians but give very few detailed or reliable descriptions of native culture. The early Europeans took little notice of rituals or of ceremonial objects.

Following the disastrous expedition of 1559 by Tristán de Luna y Arellano, the Spanish abandoned the idea of settling Florida because they found that other places in the New World had more potential for profit. They felt threatened, however, when the French established Fort Caroline in 1564. Within fifteen months of its construction, the Spanish attacked the fort and killed most of the French. From that brief period of French occupancy comes one of the most complete early chronicles written about the Indians of northeast Florida as well as the very first visual depictions of their way of life.

Events relating to the years of French occupancy, including French encounters with the Timucua Indians, are recorded in books by or about Jean Ribault, René Laudonnière, Jacques le Moyne, and Pedro Menéndez de Avilés. Le Moyne was a mapmaker who was with Laudonnière at Fort Caroline. He made forty-two watercolors on vellum showing Florida scenery and Indian activities. All of the original paintings were lost after they were engraved by Theodore De Bry around 1590. One should view the De Bry engravings with caution. The Indians' physical qualities were depicted in a style that resembles most European art of the time. The artifacts are equally stylized, and some decorative items look suspiciously like items from Mexico, South America, and even Europe. Nevertheless, the De Bry engravings furnish the only visual documentation of the Timucua Indians before their culture was destroyed following historic contact (below).

Many Spanish and French men and women were held captive by Indians. It is too bad that more of them did not record their experiences. The narratives of Juan Ortiz and Escalente Fontaneda include descrip-

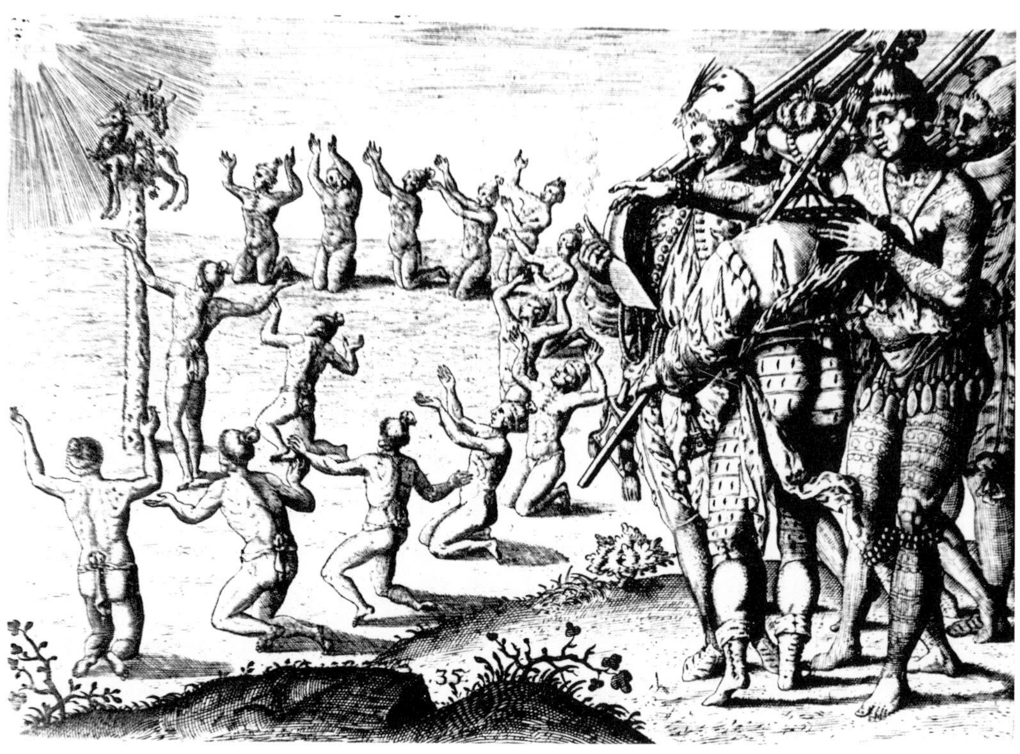

LeMoyne painting engraved by De Bry showing the Florida Timucua Indians in the mid-sixteenth century.

tions of day-by-day routines as well as some insights into native belief systems. Ortiz was among the Indians around Tampa Bay (probably the Tocobaga) for eleven years. He was rescued by de Soto in 1539. Fontaneda had been among the Calusa and other groups for seventeen years when he was rescued by Menéndez. Both men became fluent in Indian languages. Fontaneda claimed to speak four Indian languages.

More information about Indian life comes from the writings of missionaries who also learned the languages and who attempted to convert the Indians to Christianity. The most valuable of these documents is Francisco Pareja's *Confessionario* of 1613. From it we learn about the superstitions and cultural practices of the Timucua Indians—practices that the Spanish were attempting to abolish—including first harvest or first fish rites, bigamy, abortion, food taboos, lighting new fires, mortuary practices, the humanization of certain animals, shamanism, and more. The shaman was a powerful tribal influence, and the friar preached many sermons against him.

Other accounts furnish information about masks, temples, and souls. Father Rogel has the following to say about souls:

> They claimed that each man has three souls; one is the pupil of the eye, another one the shadow that each one makes, and the other one is the image one sees in a mirror or in clear water, and when a man dies, they say that two of the souls leave the body, and the third one, which is the pupil of the eye, always remains in the body (Milanich and Proctor 1978, 35).

The Spanish occupied Florida for nearly three hundred years, except for a twenty-year British period in the eighteenth century. During that time little notice was taken of the huge shell middens and sand mounds left by the Indians along the rivers and coastal areas. During the British period, in 1765, John Bartram and his son William explored the St. Johns River. An account of the journey by John Bartram mentions the shell mounds, which he and William frequently camped upon (John Bartram 1875). William Bartram returned to Florida in 1774 and published an interesting volume relating to his travels (William Bartram 1791; Wyman 1875, 14). Since there is no record to the contrary, we assume that most of the Indian habitation and burial areas remained intact when Florida was ceded to the United States in 1819. Following a series of wars between U.S. military forces and the Seminole Indians, which resulted in the Indians' removal to the Oklahoma Territory or their fleeing to the Everglades, Florida was opened to settlers, tourists, invalids, and developers. Beginning in the 1830s, a few written records describe "archaeological" activities in the state, but the most thorough early observations and excavations were carried out by Jeffries Wyman in the 1860s and C. B. Moore from around 1890 to 1907. In a steam-powered houseboat named the *Gopher,* Moore traveled to sites along the rivers and around the entire peninsula. He demolished (his word) burial mounds and shell middens. Archaeologists lament that Moore did not use modern excavation techniques but, to his credit, he published extensively on his findings, and the whereabouts of most of the objects he recovered are still known.

Despite Moore's unscientific approach to archaeological sites, his methods are preferable to those later used by road builders, construction groups, and agriculturalists who, unrestrained, used the contents of shell middens for road beds, septic tanks, and fertilizer. Although some sites, such as temple mounds, are now on the National Register of Historic Places or are located on state or federal lands, truckloads of shell are still being carted off, and wetlands are still being drained, dredged, and filled. The American presence in Florida accounts for only 2 percent of Florida's human history, but Americans are responsible for nearly 100 percent of the modifications of the landscape. Most of the artificial structures created by the Indians, depicted in nineteenth- and early-twentieth-century illustrations (below and pp. 7 and 8), have disappeared forever.

Without precise details, how can we describe and interpret ancient cultural objects? Techniques include examination of documents and artifacts, the direct historic approach, and studies of comparable cul-

Man on horse on mound in St. Petersburg (from a 1908 postcard). By permission of the St. Petersburg Museum of History.

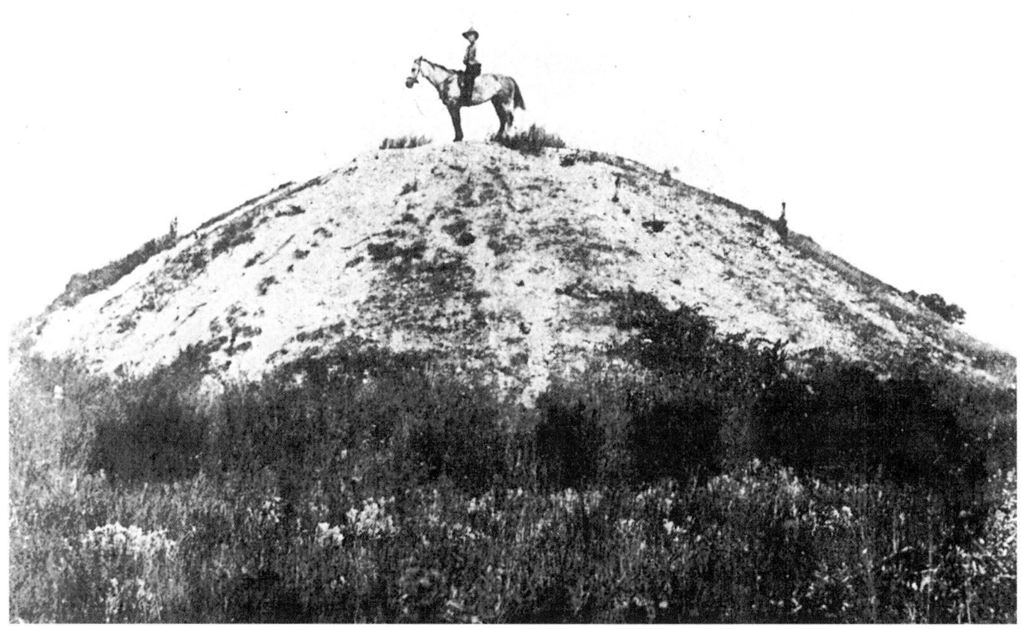

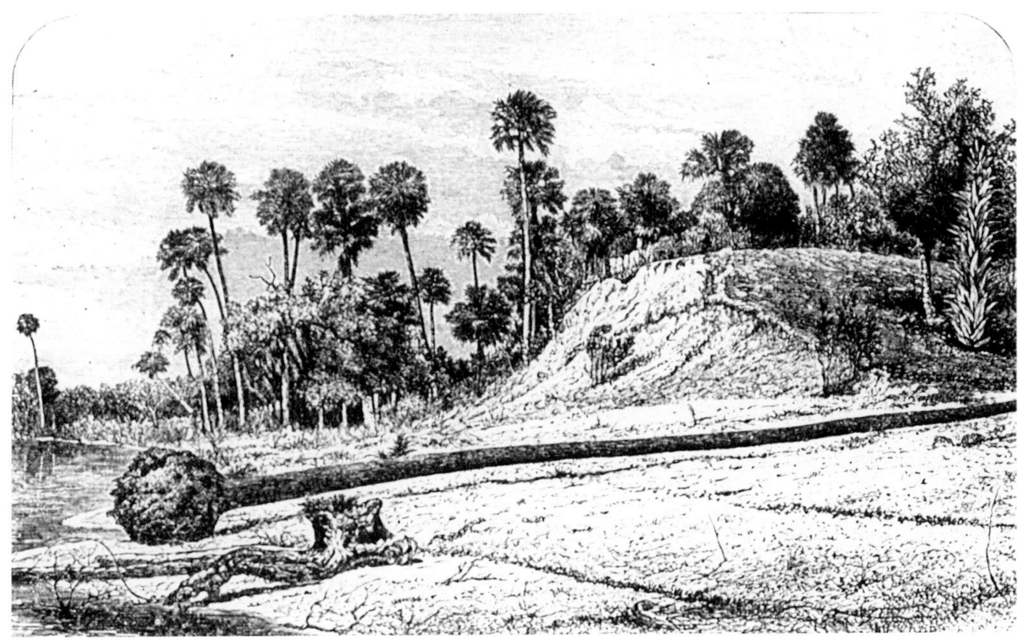

The Old Enterprise Midden at Lake Monroe in 1874.

tures, oral histories, and archaeological site reports. There is always a certain amount of speculation involved in interpretation, especially when the objects are thousands of years old. From the first century A.D. onward, evidence improves primarily because, by that time, cultures had become more complex. At those more recent sites people left more "trash" to be found by archaeologists, and materials are better preserved. Therefore, extensive descriptions and accurate interpretations of art forms are possible for Woodland, Mississippian, and Early Historic sites. Similar eye motifs, for example, have been noted that may be related to Father Rogel's story about the soul.

While it is true that all material objects represent ideas that have been objectified, it is not possible to identify precisely what the maker had in mind when a item was produced. Residues of past cultures are seldom found in detailed context. The anthropological concept of emic and etic is worthy of some discussion here. Taken from the linguistic terms *phonemic* and *phonetic,* they can be defined as the difference between what is understood by a member of society about a particular event or object (emic) and what is merely described by an outsider (etic). Just as there are a range of distinctive speech elements for a language that are recognized by its native speakers (the phonemes), there are also nuances of meaning understood only by those socialized into a particular culture. The observer (etic) may bias his interpretation because of the social system into which his thoughts have been internal-

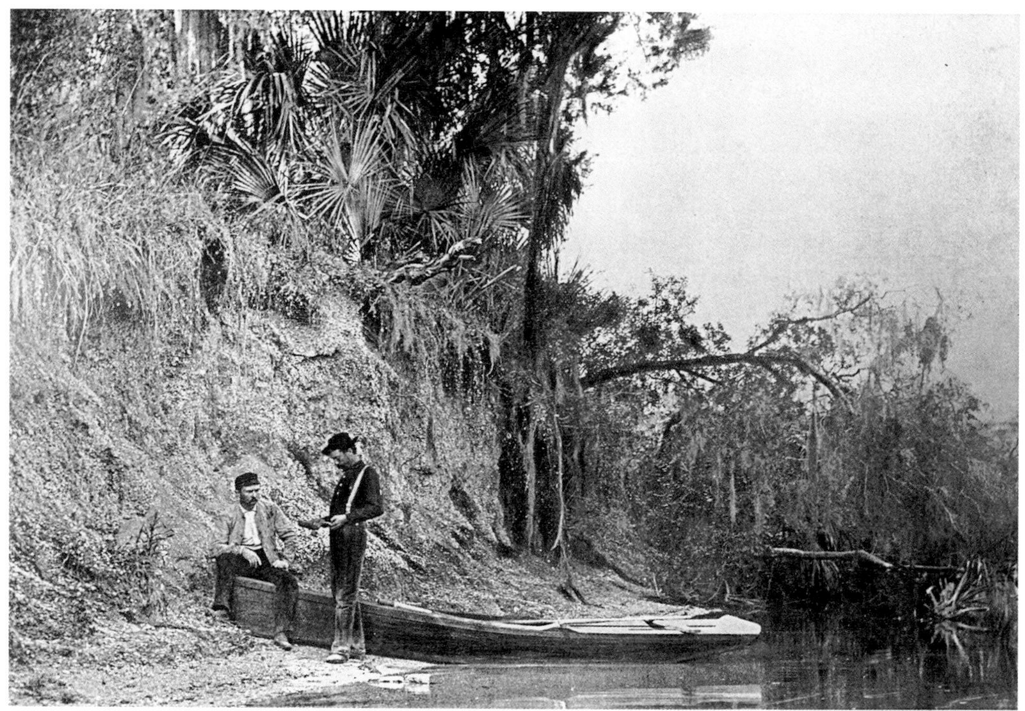

Hontoon Island in an early-twentieth-century picture taken by C. B. Moore.

ized. There is also the danger that some historic accounts described native activities after Christianity had already modified their patterns to a certain extent.

Despite these misgivings, there are recurring themes in the motifs and art forms of the southeast that provide clues to the belief systems of the native peoples. Important among these are the sun and moon, the cardinal points, gods of the underworld (fish, frogs), gods of the sky (eagles, falcons), the forked eye, the long-nosed god mask, the hand-and-eye symbol, and more.

AS THE CHRONOLOGICAL CHART on the next page indicates, it is not certain when people first entered Florida; nor is it clear whether they became permanent residents immediately. The major cultural periods in Florida are called Paleoindian, Archaic, Ceramic, and Historic. Each period is further divided into units based on analyses of materials from archaeological sites and on radiocarbon dating. Deptford, Swift Creek, and Weeden Island are names applied to Florida cultures that date from approximately 500 B.C. to A.D. 800. Those cultures correspond in time and complexity to the Woodland cultures of the midwestern and eastern United States. Safety Harbor and Fort Walton are Florida names for Mississippian cultures that were still extant in the Southeast when Europeans arrived in the sixteenth century.

Early cultures of Florida

Date	*Name*	*Major Identifying Features*	*Location*
A.D. 1492+	**Historic**	European artifacts; decreased populations; written documents	Statewide, especially coastal areas
	Ceramic		
500 B.C.–A.D. 1492	Late	Regionalism in ceramic styles; burial and temple mounds; ceremonial pottery;	Nearly statewide
1000–500 B.C.	Middle	Transitional with changes in ceramic technology; increasing social complexity; efficient exploitation of aquatic resources; influences from distant cultures	Statewide, especially Gulf Coast
2000–1000 B.C.	Early	First ceramic pots (Orange, fiber-tempered); efficient exploitation of aquatic resources; changes in stone point styles; shell technology diversifies	Mostly Atlantic coast and St. Johns River
	Archaic		
4000–2000 B.C.	Late	Shell middens appear along coasts and rivers; small stemmed stone bifaces; marine shell technology becomes major addition to culture; steatite and other imported materials	Statewide, but most evident along rivers and coasts
5000–4000 B.C.	Middle	A variety of stemmed stone bifaces; wetsites with preserved human remains, plants, and wood and bone technology; intense use of chert quarries	Statewide; wet sites mostly in South Florida
7000–5000 B.C.	Early	Distinctive stemmed stone bifaces (Arredondo and Kirk Serrated)	Nearly statewide, but evidence not abundant
	Paleoindian		
8,000–7000 B.C.	Late and Middle	Bolen (Late); Suwannee and Simpson (Middle) most common stone bifaces; period is poorly dated	Nearly statewide, especially rivers and springs
9,500–8000 B.C.	Early	Butchered bones of Pleistocene animals; Clovis biface; distinctive tools of stone and elephant ivory	Nearly statewide in springs and rivers
BEFORE 9,500 B.C.	Pre-paleoindian	Largely unkown; absence of stone bifaces; crude stone tools; butchered bones of Pleistocene animals; wood, bone, and antler tools	Rivers, springs, and stone quarries

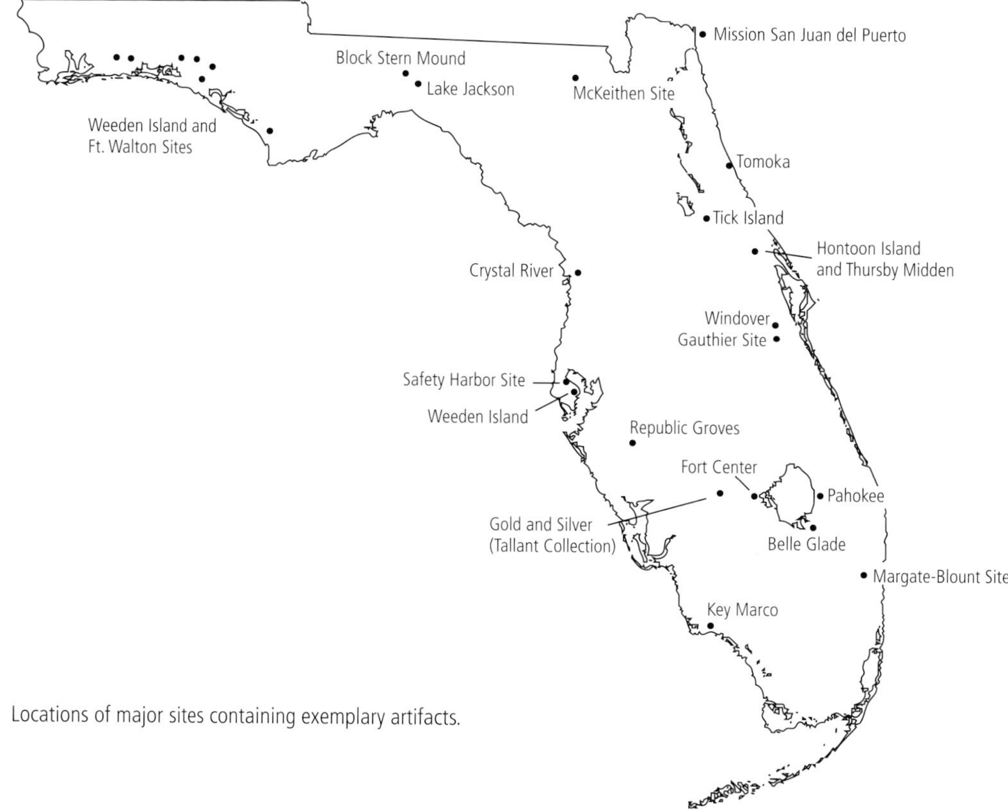

Locations of major sites containing exemplary artifacts.

A zigzag design on an implement made from a mammoth ivory tusk found in the Aucilla River may be the oldest decorated object yet discovered in the Western Hemisphere. We will never know what prompted the maker to incise the piece, but it is tempting to believe that he had an urge, as do we, to make his handiwork more attractive. Or perhaps the design records some event that is unidentifiable to us. In any event, there is little other indication of artistic expression in Florida prior to 6000 B.C. Many incised bone and antler artifacts from about 5000 to 6000 B.C. were recovered from submerged deposits at the Windover cemetery near Titusville (Doran and Dickel 1988; Purdy 1991). These objects were fragmentary when found, but they demonstrate that even at this early time people were interested in beautifying their products and sending them with the deceased to the hereafter. One can only wonder what may still lie beneath our feet that was made by the native peoples of Florida more than 7,000 years ago.

Around 4000 B.C. people began a way of life that remained in place until European contact in the early sixteenth century. They exploited

Florida's extensive aquatic resources so successfully that they were able to live a nearly sedentary existence compared to the nomadic pattern that had prevailed previously. Non-Florida materials such as steatite have been found at many sites dating from the Middle Archaic to more recent times. These materials as well as design motifs suggest a connection between the peoples of Florida and the southern Piedmont areas of Alabama and Georgia. Our pictorial story begins with antler and bone from this time period, because specimens made of these materials are the oldest surviving decorated objects that are well preserved. See the map on the facing page for locations of the major areas in Florida from which outstanding specimens have been recovered.

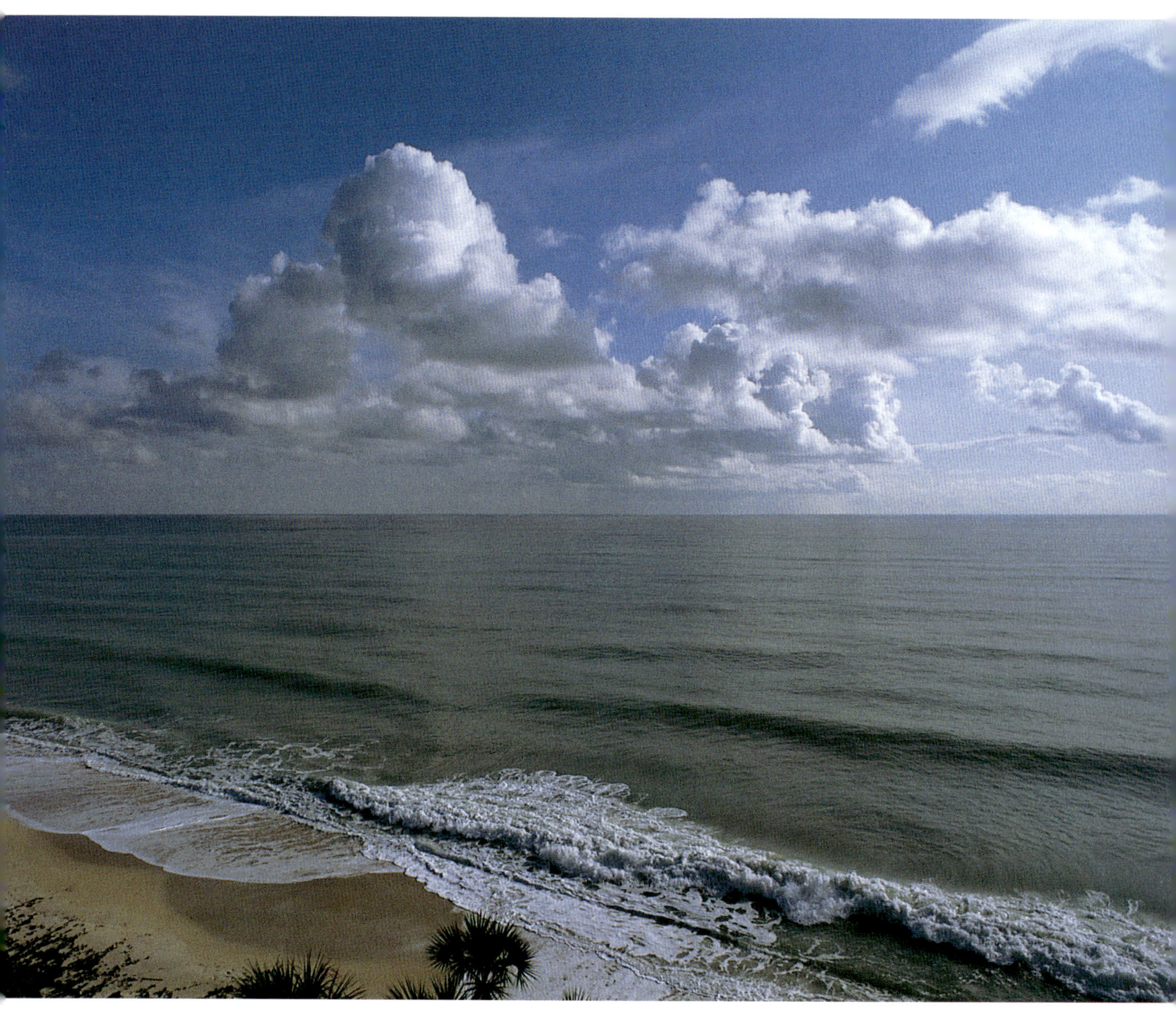

Beach and ocean, Cocoa Beach

ANTLER AND BONE

A MOST UNIQUE artifact is illustrated in plate 1. It is made from the tibia (?) of a large deer (*Odocoileus virginianus;* S. David Webb, pers. comm. 1995). It is an excellent specimen with a waterbird incised on one face and branches and leaves (?) on the opposite face. The upper part of the bird's body is eroded, suggesting that the less-eroded portion of the object had been partially buried in a riverbed while the rest of it was exposed. This type of wear is typical of fossilized bones preserved in Florida's waterways. The specimen could be very ancient, but no method has yet been developed to date it.

It has been said that development projects are archaeologists' best friends and also their worse enemies. In addition to Windover, there are four Archaic period burial sites in Florida that were "discovered" by earth-moving equipment. Hundreds of human skeletons with accompanying gravegoods were preserved in near-perfect condition at three of these sites, because they had become entombed in water-saturated deposits that hindered their deterioration. At the other site, preservation occurred because interment took place in a wet sand deposit, and the bones became mineralized. All of these sites date from around 4000 B.C. Decorated antler objects from Republic Groves (Wharton et al. 1981) (plate 2) and Gauthier (Jones 1981) (plates 3 and 4) contain complex design motifs that resemble some of those dredged from the Tick Island site (Jahn and Bullen 1978) (plates 5 through 9). Similar designs are found on pottery sherds and shell ornaments from Tick Island and from other sites. Jones has this to say about the objects shown in plates 3 and 4:

> What appears to be a headdress is made up of several different kinds of bones. It consists of two pieces of antler, one piece worn on each side of the head. Both of these pieces have a single small diameter . . . hole through their central portions which apparently permitted a lock of hair to be drawn through, and then a raccoon penis bone was stuck through the lock of hair acting something like a beret. . . . This head wear was associated with one individual who had a total of fifty-two artifacts. (Jones 1981, 86)

Most of the items in plate 10 are also from Tick Island, but it is difficult to assign a date to them because of the way the material was recovered. One of the specimens in plate 10 is almost identical to one from the Key Marco site, which has a probable date of around A.D. 600–800.

Plates 11 through 19 underscore the great creative diversity applied to bone and antler, which were plentiful raw materials. Decorative hair or clothing ornaments, weapons, and utilitarian objects were the most common objects produced, usually from deer bone. After what appears to be a decline in embellishment on bone following the Archaic and Early Ceramic periods, different and extremely elaborated styles returned just prior to and during the Early Historic period. Nearly all of the bone objects that have survived unbroken with their designs intact have come from water-saturated deposits.

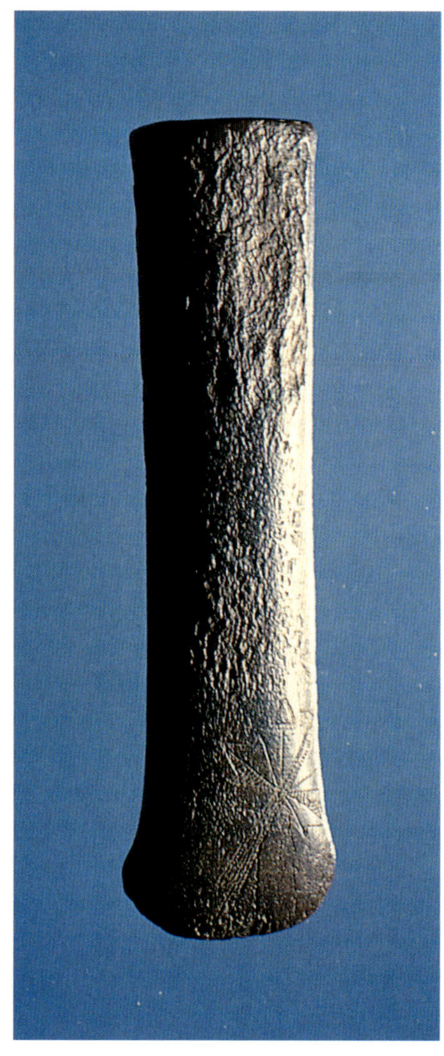

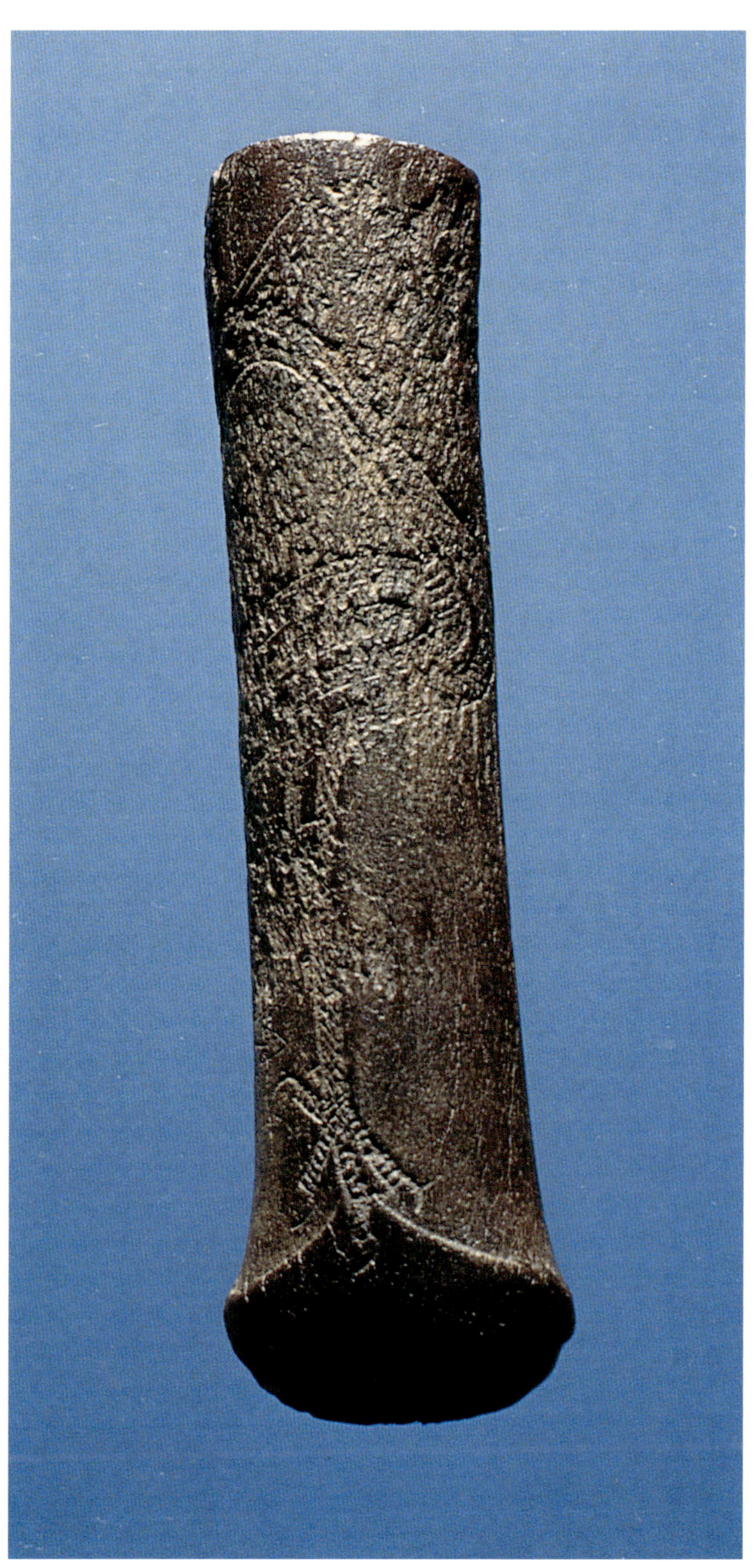

1. Tool handle (?), incised. Lower Withlacoochee River, Citrus County. Date unknown but probably very old. Fossilized bone (deer tibia?), 15.0 cm long x 3.0 cm wide x 1.2 cm thick. Silver River Museum, Ocala. On loan from private collection.

2. (right) Pendant or hair ornament. Republic Groves site, Hardee County (8-Hr-4). Middle to Late Archaic, ca. 4000–3000 B.C. Antler, 6.0 cm long x 2.5 cm diameter. Florida Museum of Natural History, Gainesville, no. 93-18-26.

3. (below) Hair ornament. Gauthier site, Brevard County (8-Br-193). Middle to Late Archaic, ca. 4000–3000 B.C. Antler (?), 15.0 cm long x 1.5–2.0 cm wide. Bureau of Archaeological Research, Tallahassee, no. 88-166-1013.

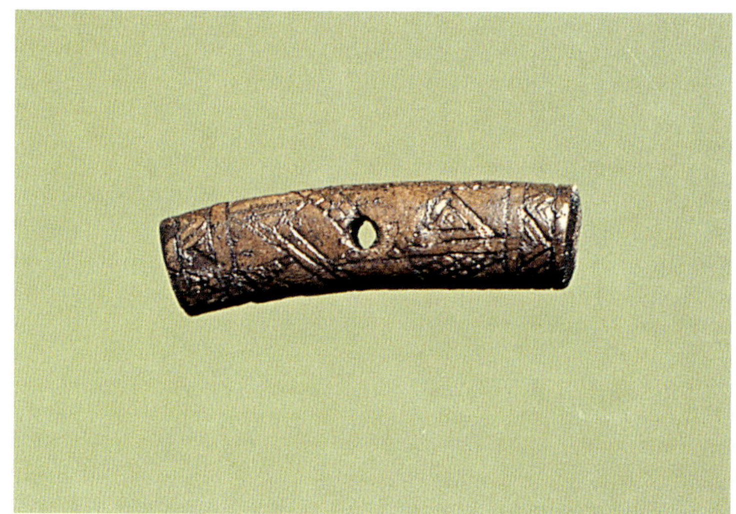

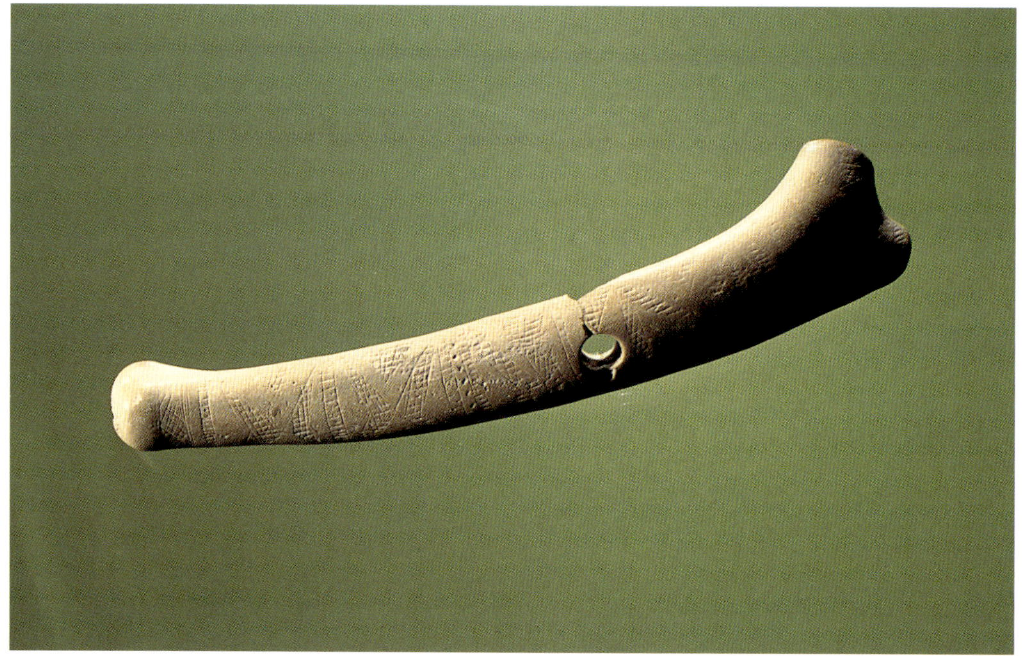

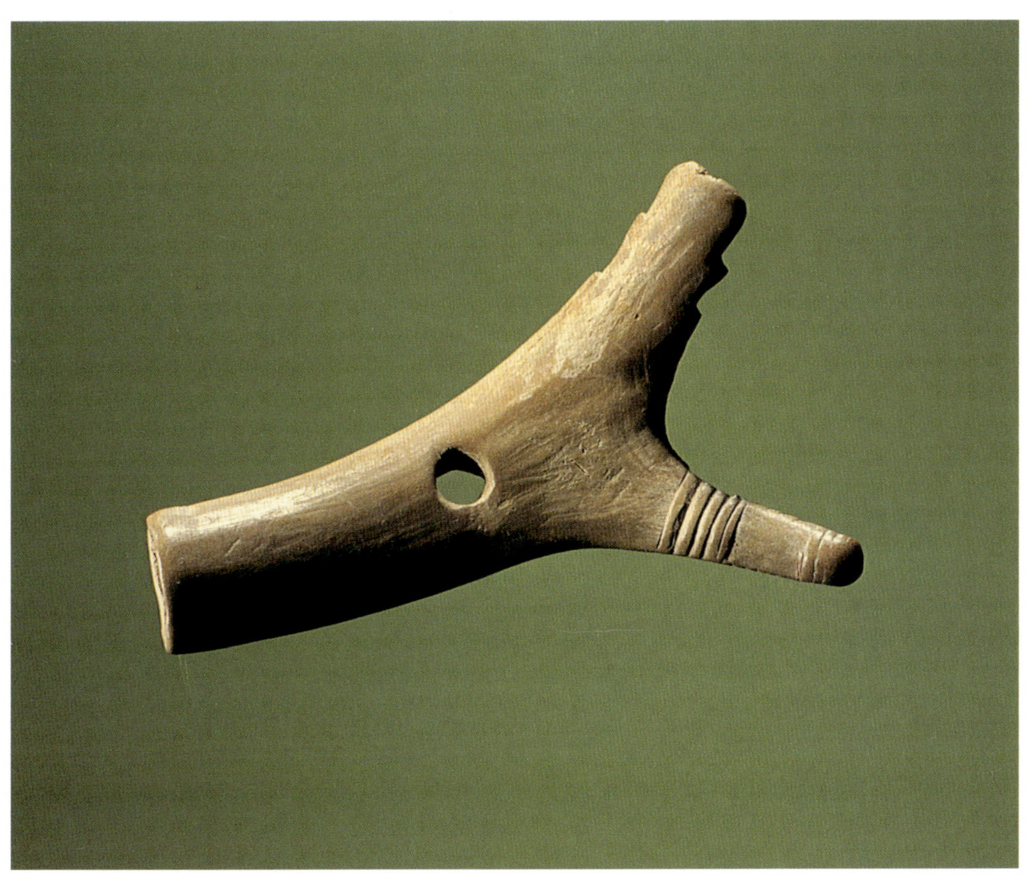

4. Hair ornament. Gauthier site, Brevard County (8-Br-193). Middle to Late Archaic, ca. 4000–3000 B.C. Antler, 9.5 cm long x 1.0–5.5 cm span between tines. Bureau of Archaeological Research, Tallahassee, no. 88-166-1013.

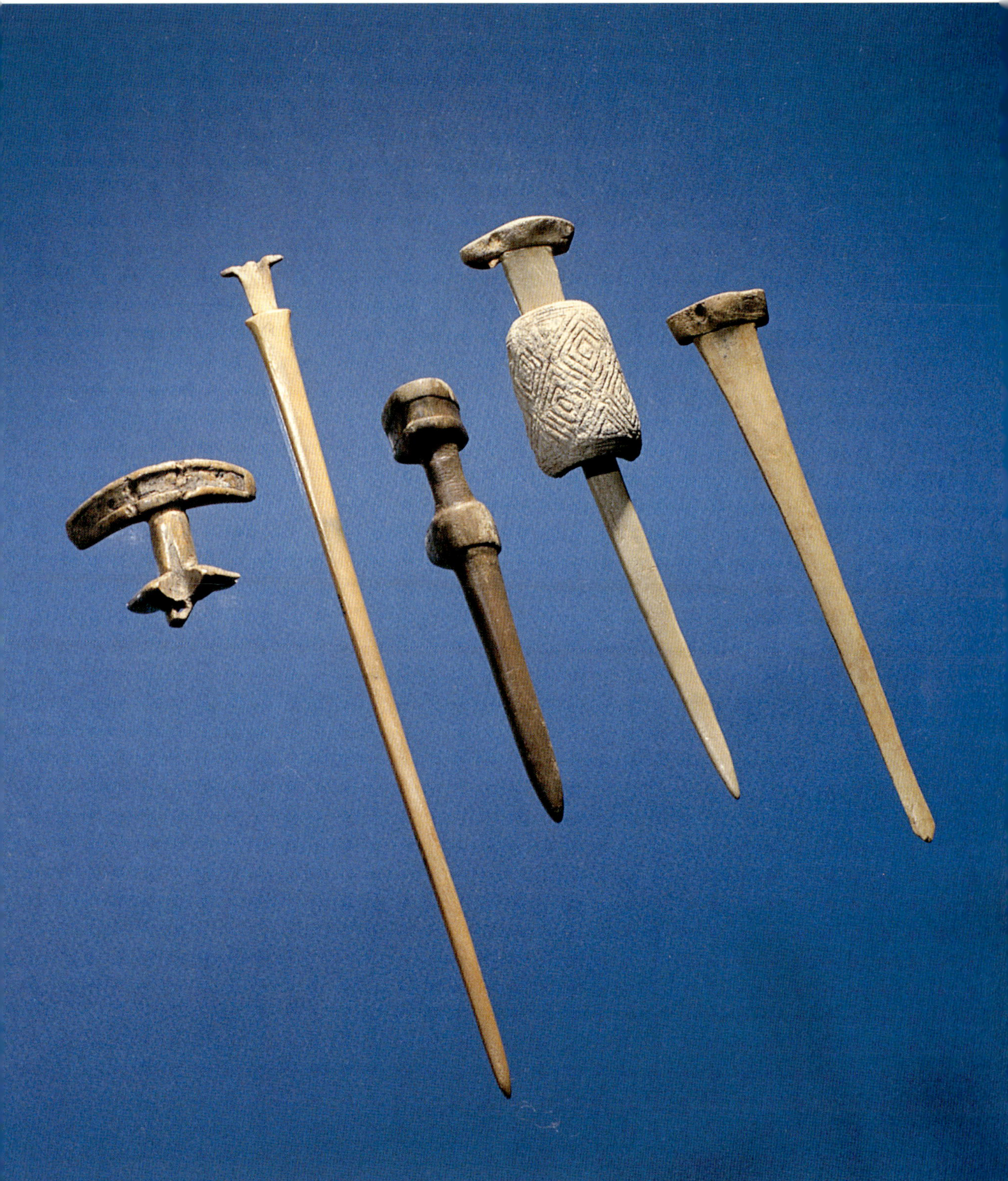

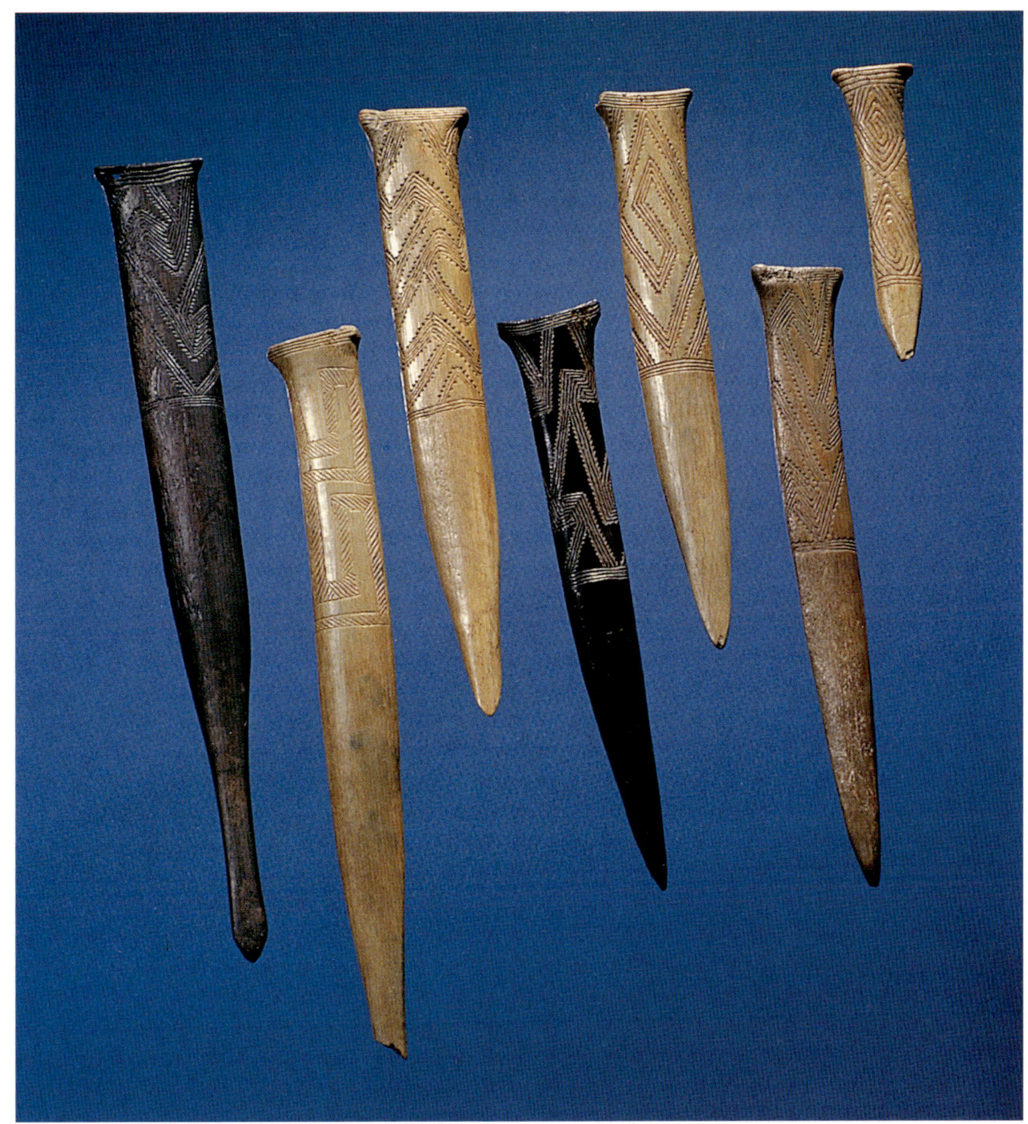

5. (facing page) Five hairpins used as feather attachers. Tick Island site, Volusia County (8-Vo-24), except middle specimen from Orange City. Middle Archaic to St. Johns II, ca. 4500 B.C.–A.D. 800. Bone, 19.5 cm long x 2.0 cm wide (longest). Private collection.

6. (above) Hairpins with incised geometric motifs. Tick Island site, Volusia County (8-Vo-24), except specimen on left from the Withlacoochee River. Middle Archaic to St. Johns II, ca. 4500 B.C.–A.D. 800. Bone, 12.0 cm long x 3.0 cm wide x 0.2 cm thick (specimen on left). Private collection.

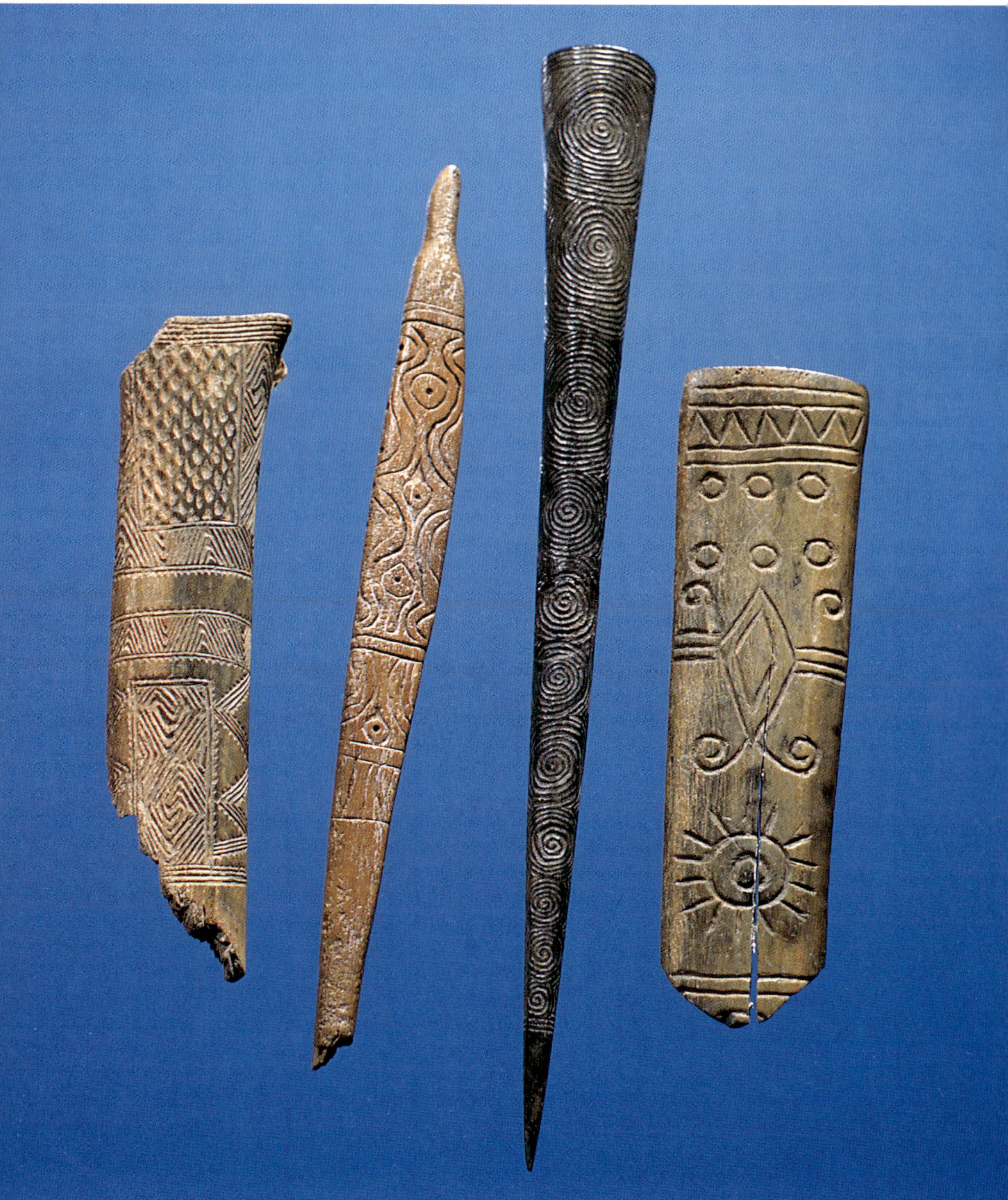

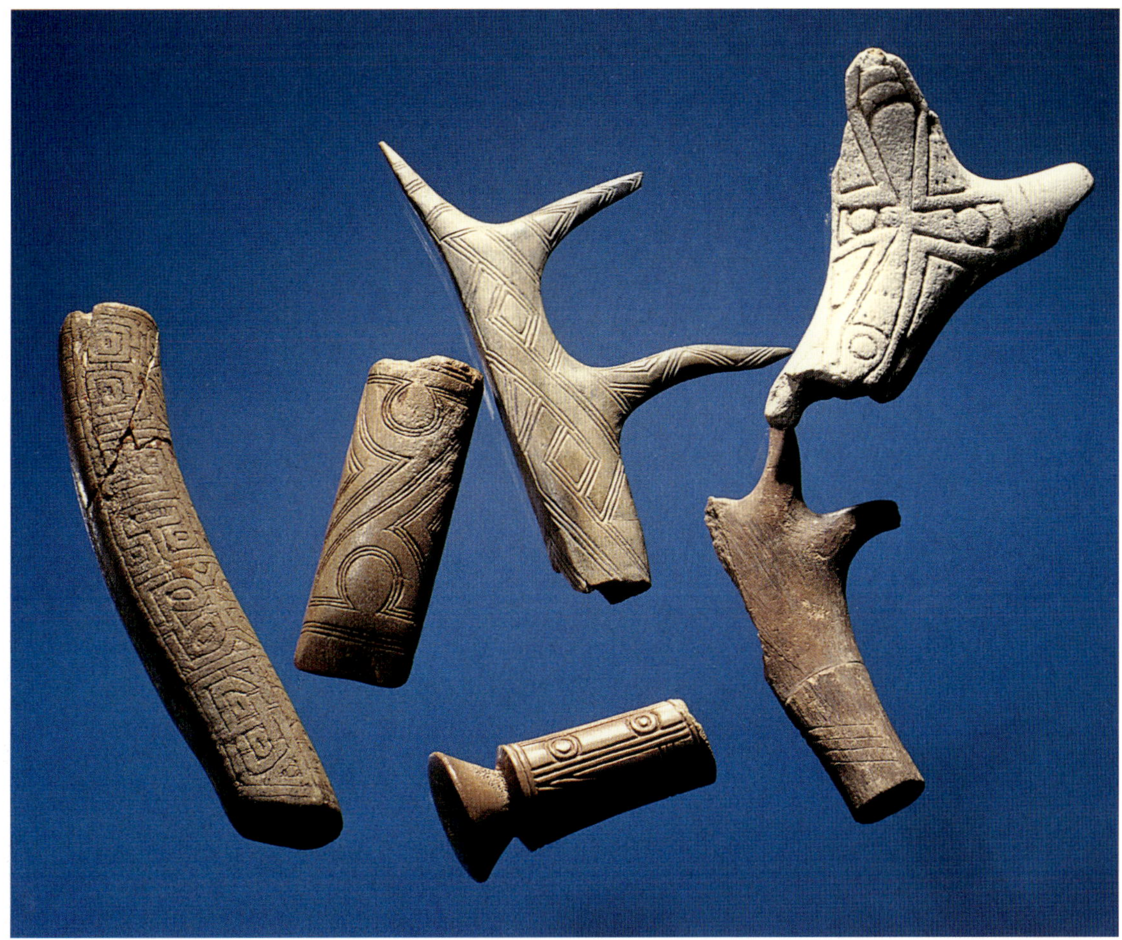

8. Incised antler. Tick Island Site, Volusia County (8-Vo-24). Middle Archaic to St. Johns II, ca. 4500 B.C.–A.D. 800. Antler, 15.0 cm long x 3.0 cm wide x 10 cm circumference (object on left). Private collection.

7. Four hairpins. Tick Island Site, Volusia County (8-Vo-24). Middle Archaic to St. Johns II, ca. 4500 B.C.–A.D. 800. Bone, 17.0 cm long x 2.0 cm wide (complete specimen). Private collection.

9. Carved animal jaws and a shell replica of a jaw. Tick Island Site, Volusia County (8-Vo-24). Middle Archaic to St. Johns II, ca. 4500 B.C.–A.D. 800. Bone and shell, 7.5 cm long x 3.0 cm at ascending ramus and about 0.2 cm thick (shell jaw). Private collection.

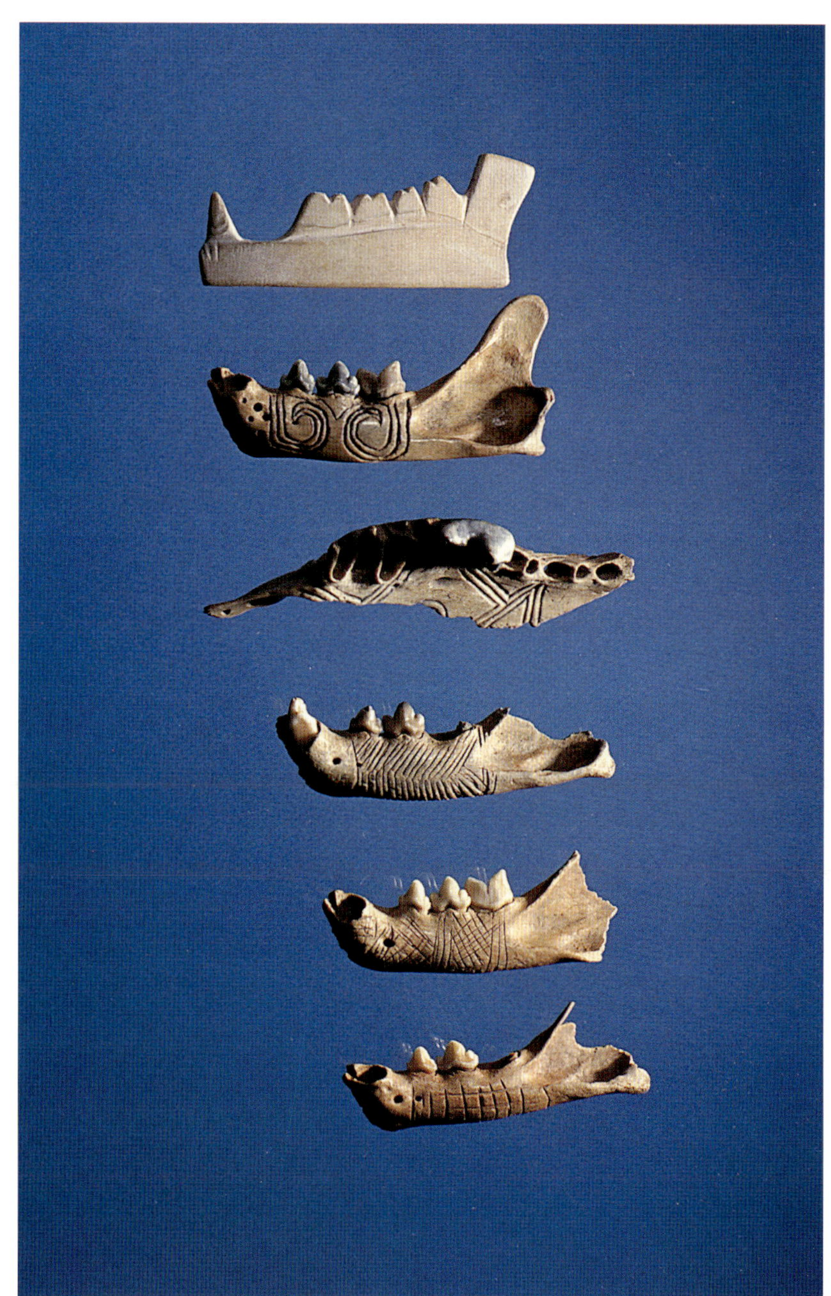

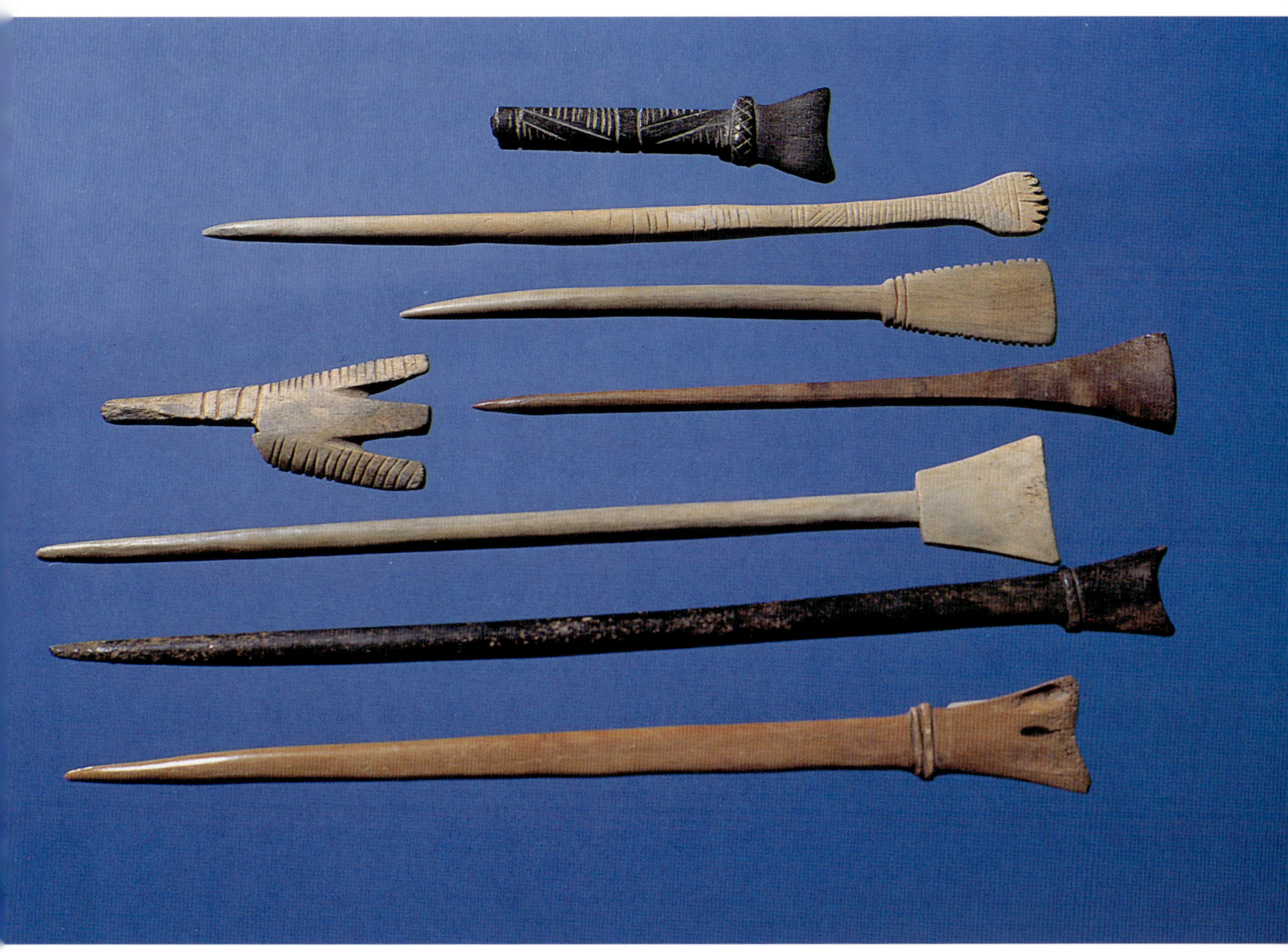

10. Feather holders. Tick Island site, Volusia County (8-Vo-24), except middle specimen from Orange City, Volusia County. Date unknown. Bone, 10.6 cm long x 2.0 cm wide x 1.8 cm thick (middle specimen). Private collection.

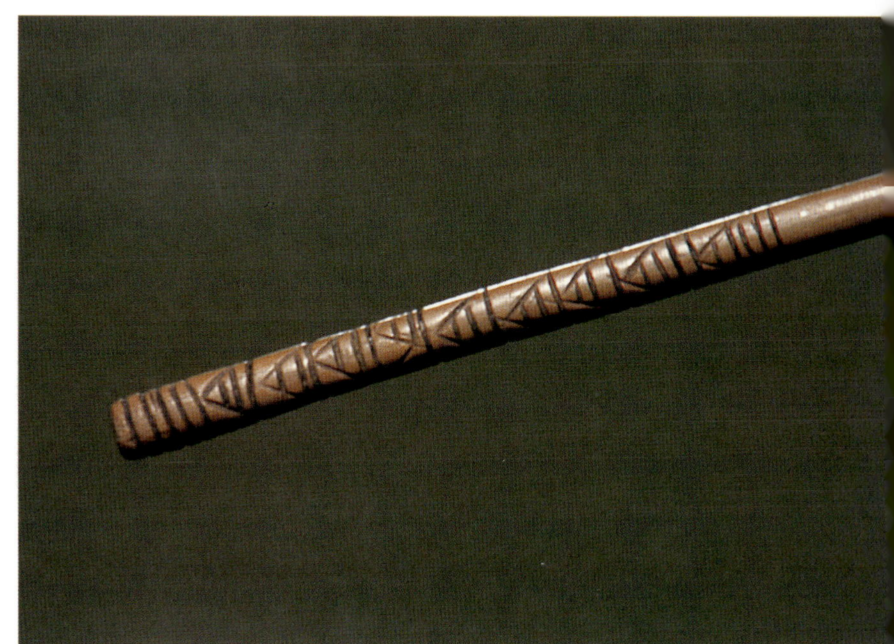

11. Decorated hairpin. Hontoon Island, Volusia County (8-Vo-202). St. Johns II, A.D. 1200–1300 (level 2, zone IV). Bone, 20.0 cm long x 0.6 cm wide. Florida Bureau of Archaeological Research, Tallahassee, no. 90-58.

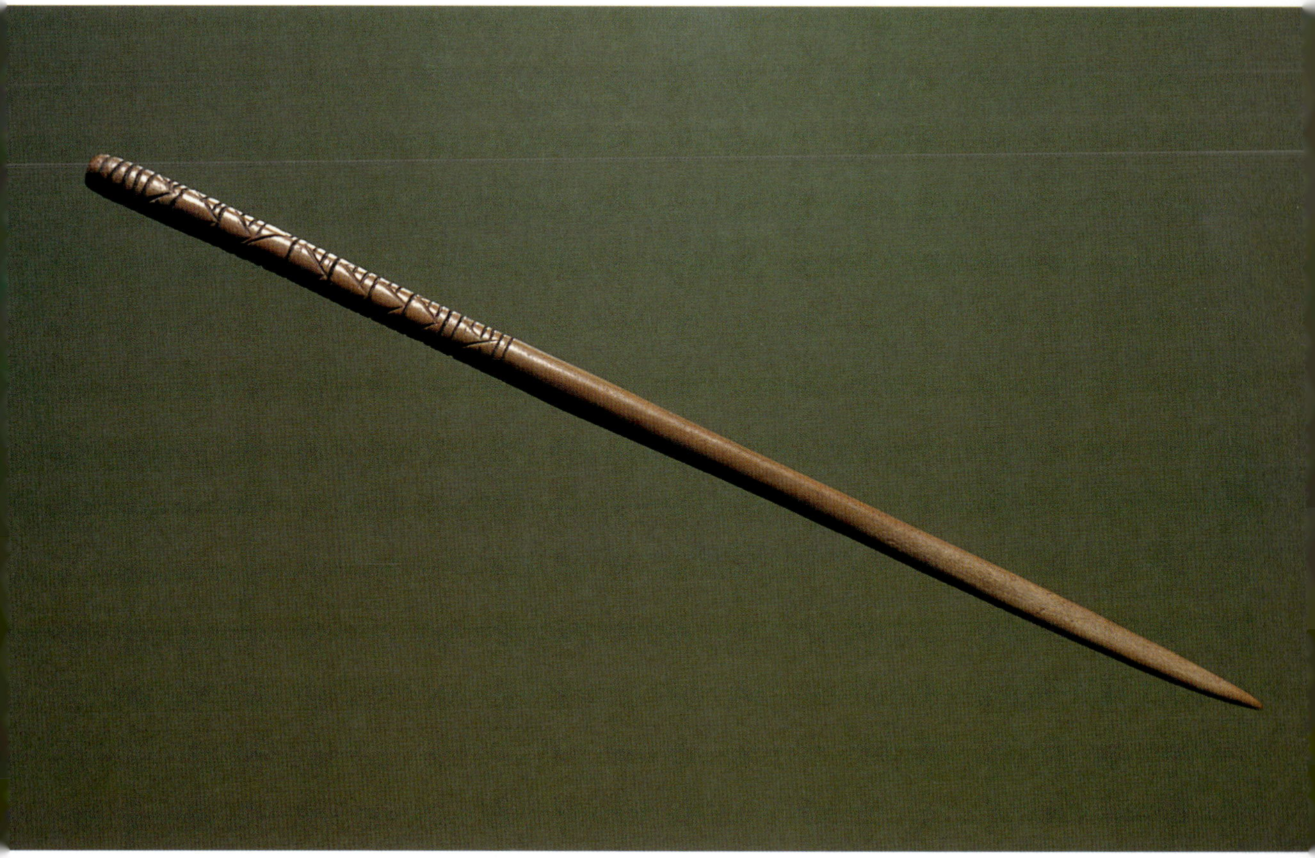

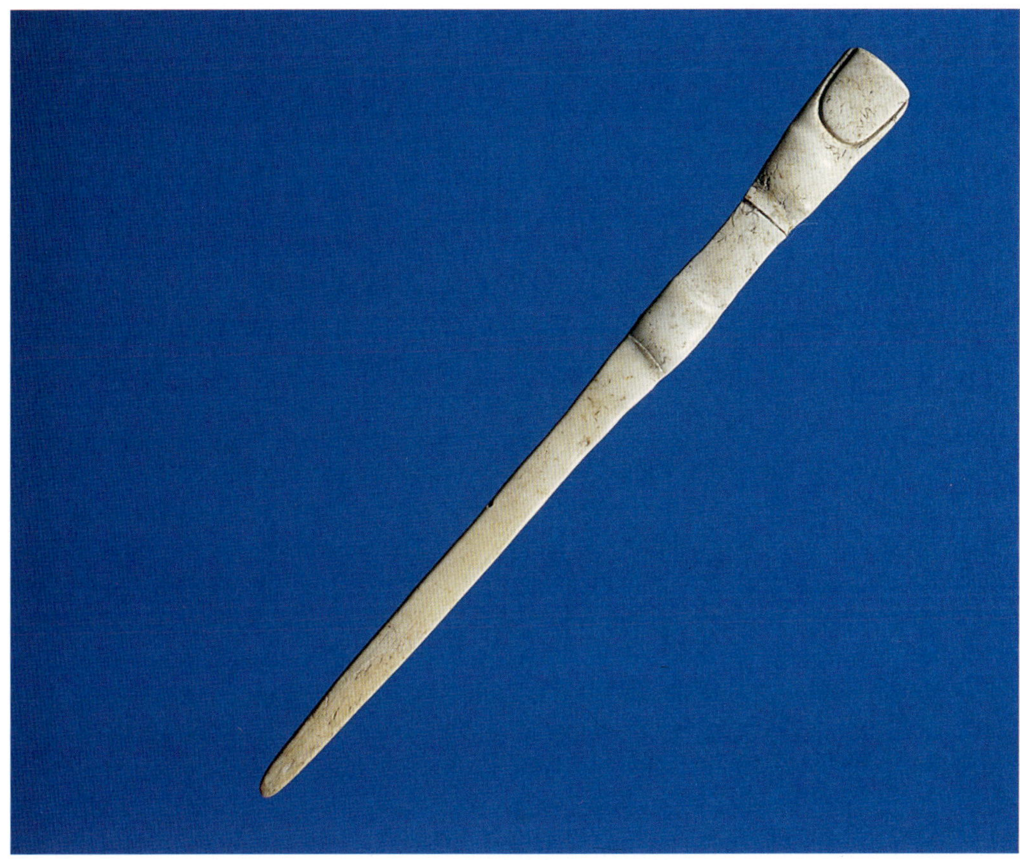

12. (above) Artifact with fingernail design. Surface collection, Bell site, Okaloosa County (8-Ok-19). Thought to be Weeden Island based on associated materials. Bone, 17.5 cm long x 1.7 cm wide x 1.3 cm thick. Temple Mound Museum, Fort Walton Beach, Florida, no. B38.

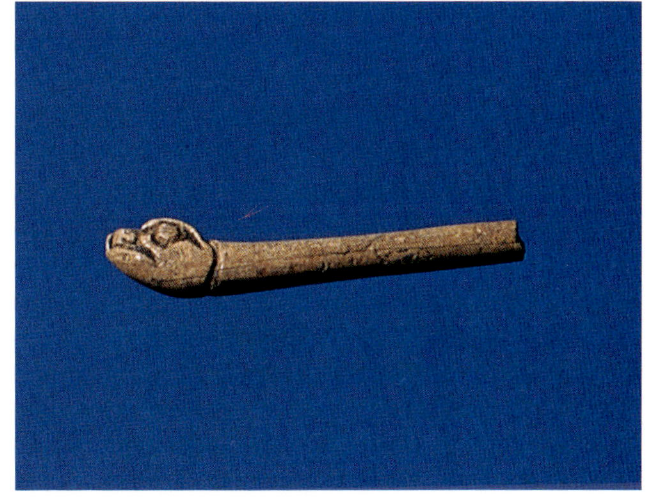

13. (right) Carving of turtle or snake head. Jupiter Inlet I Site (8-PB-34), Palm Beach County. About A.D. 800. Bone, 3.5 cm long (broken) x 0.5 cm wide. Department of Anthropology, Florida Atlantic University, Boca Raton, no. A2672.

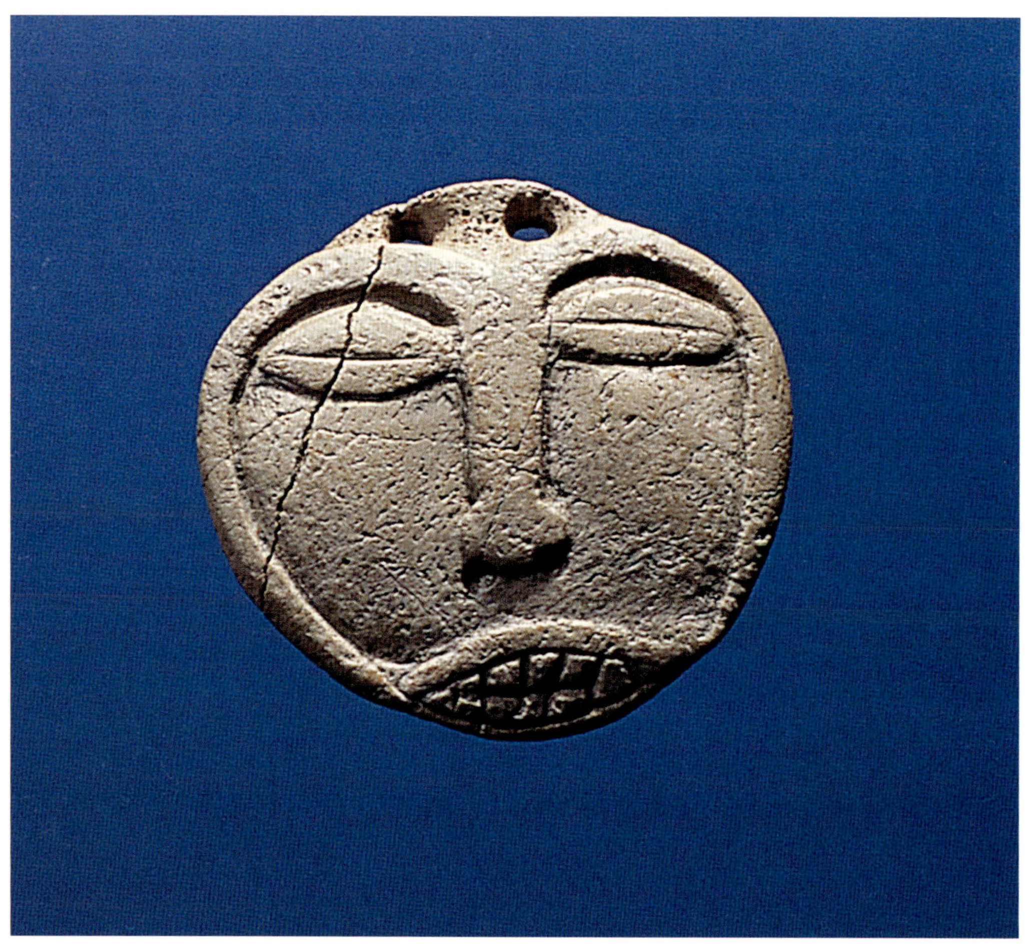

14. Trophy head mask (?). Creek bed near Orange City, Volusia County. Date unknown. Human bone, 4.2 cm diameter x about 0.3 cm thick. Private collection.

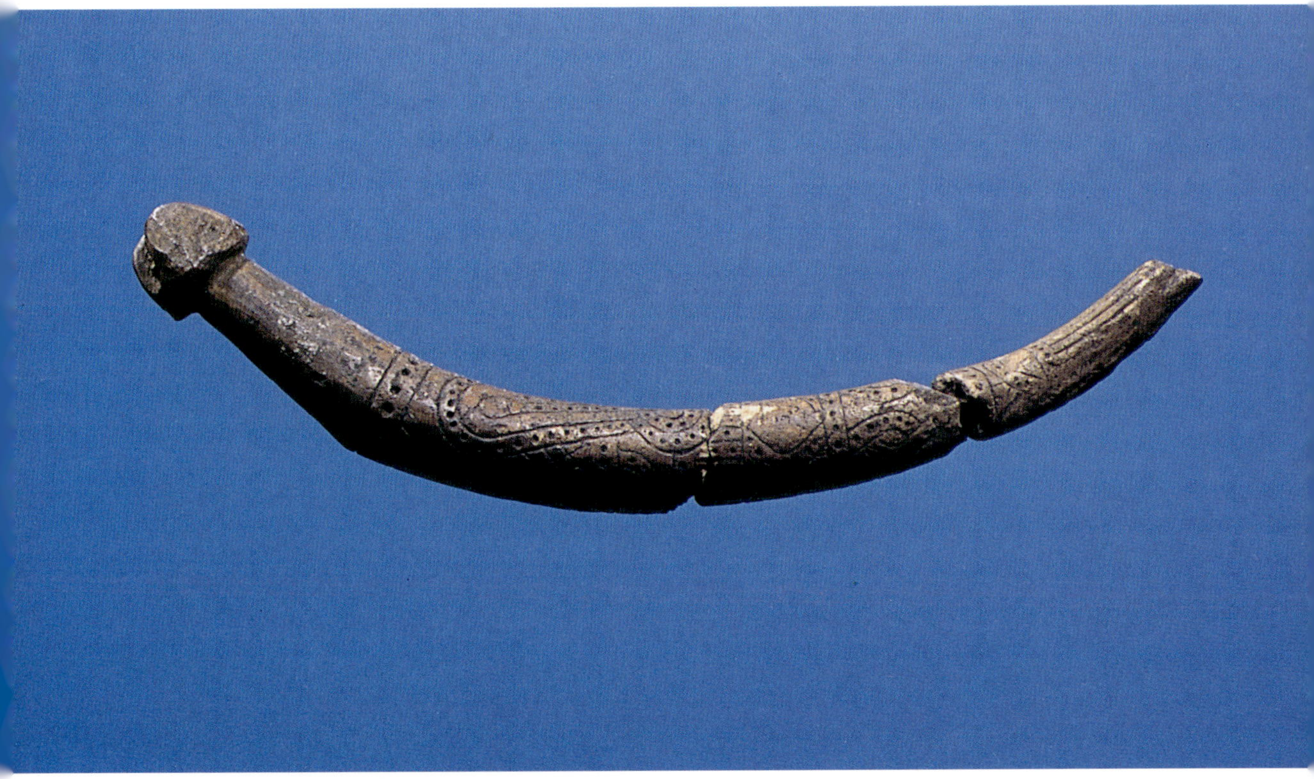

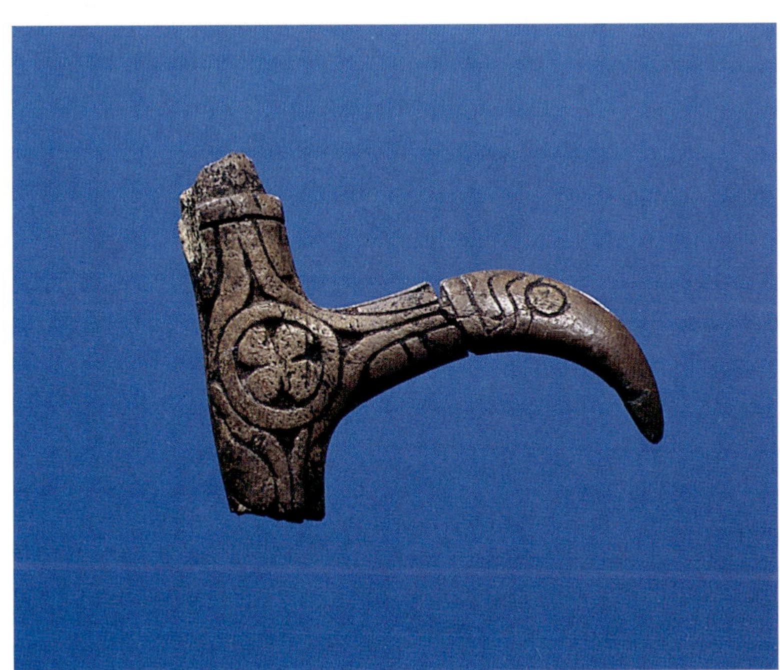

15. (above) Decorated bone object. Margate-Blount site, Broward County (8-Bd-41). Probably Late Prehistoric or Early Historic. Bone, 13.0 cm long x 4.8 cm circumference. Graves Museum of Archaeology and Natural History, Dania, Florida, no. MB-120.

16. (left) Decorated antler object. Margate-Blount site, Broward County (8-Bd-41). Probably Late Prehistoric or Early Historic. Antler, 7.0 cm long x 5.0 cm high x 1.5 cm thick. Graves Museum of Archaeology and Natural History, Dania, Florida, no. MB-100.

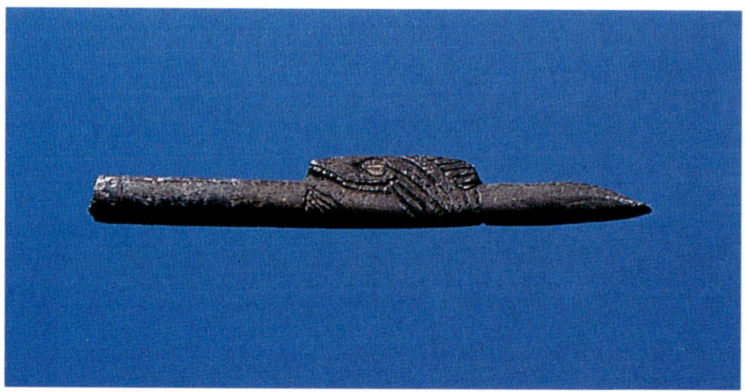

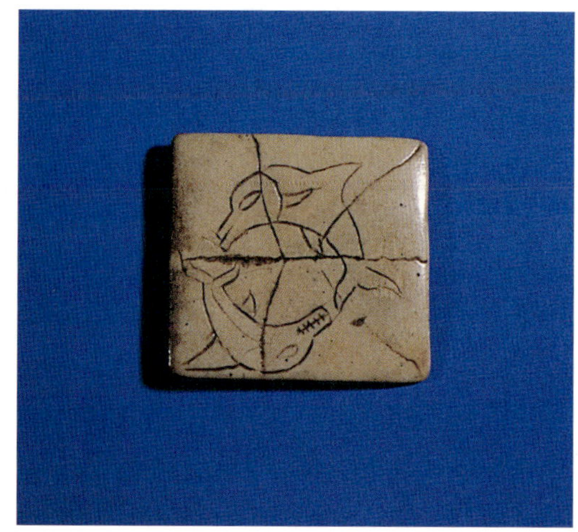

17. (above) Pin with "fish" carving. Margate Blount site, Broward County (8-Bd-41). Probably Late Prehistoric or Early Historic. Bone, 7.0 cm long x 1.0 cm wide x 2.8 cm circumference. Graves Museum of Archaeology and Natural History, Dania, Florida, no. MB-110.

18. (right) Turtle carapace engraved with dolphin motifs. Key Marco site, Collier County (8-Cr-49). Date unknown, possibly ca. A.D. 600–800. Turtle carapace, 5.0 cm long x 5.0 cm wide x 0.1–0.2 cm thick. University Museum, Philadelphia, no. 40801.

19. (facing page) Comb. Murphy Island, Putnam County. Probably Early Historic. Bone, 3.9 cm high x 16.3 cm long. National Museum of the American Indian, New York City, no. 17-24.

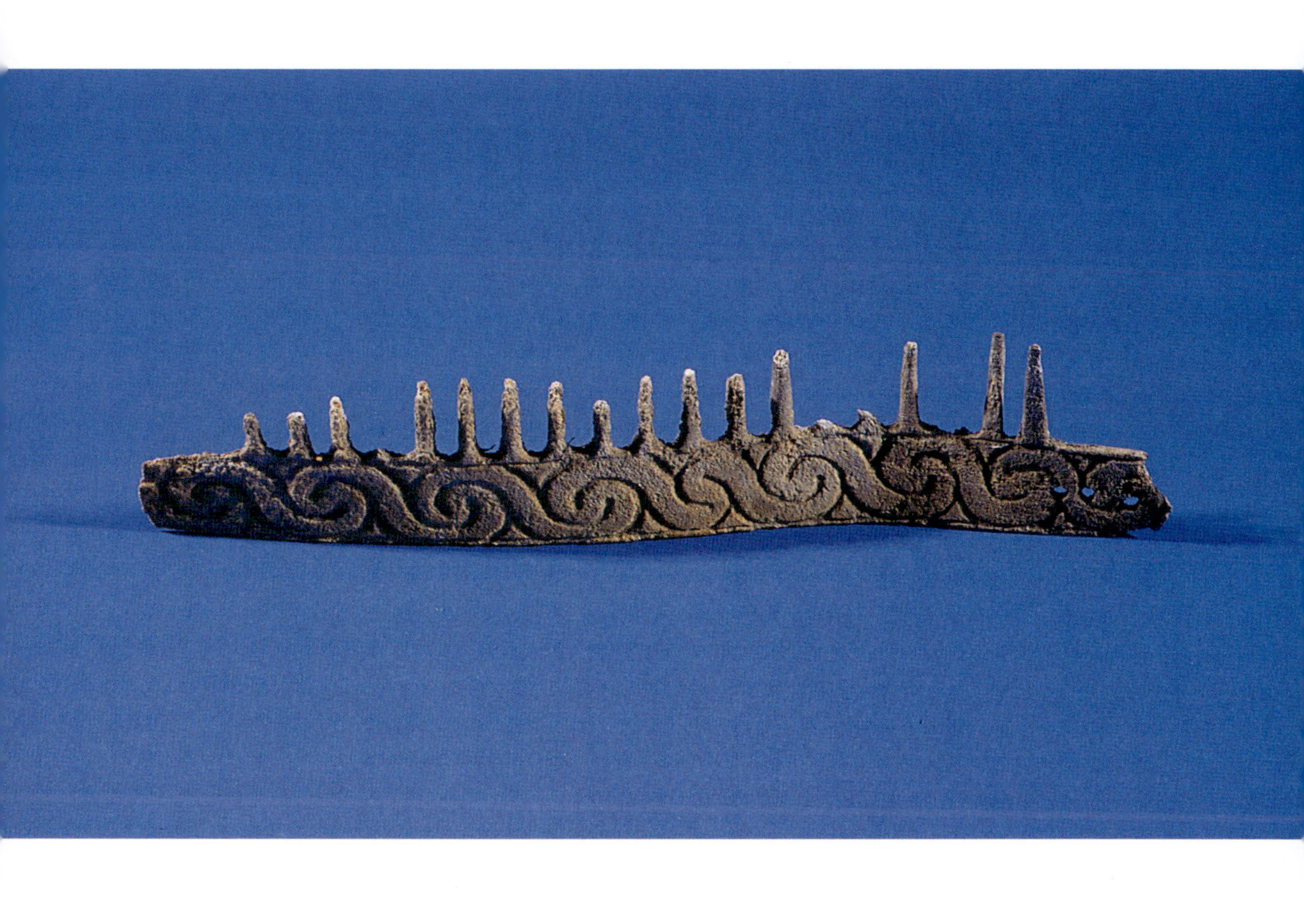

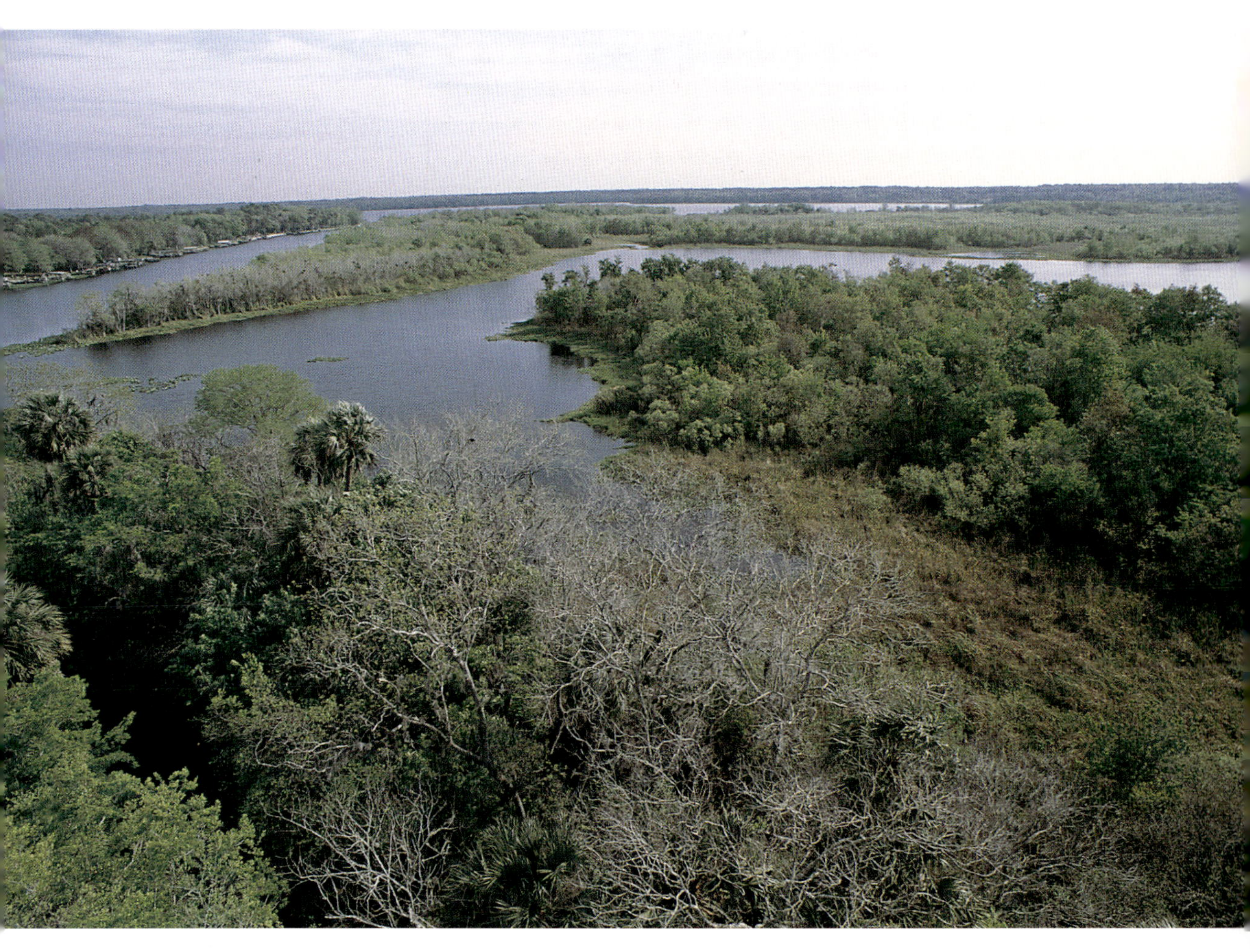

St. Johns River at Hontoon Island

WOOD

THE SURVIVAL OF botanical materials at a number of waterlogged sites in Florida is unparalled in North America. The oldest wooden artifact was recovered from a spring. It is a spear or stake made of red mulberry that was found in association with an extinct species of giant land tortoise. The specimen was dated by radiocarbon analysis at somewhat greater than 10,000 B.C.

The 5000–6000 B.C. Windover cemetery in Brevard County (8-Br-246) has yielded a number of wooden artifacts. At least one of those bore geometric incising, but it was too fragile to save. Another specimen, manufactured from pine, may be a whistle. It was found in excellent condition, but it contains no decoration. There were 163 burials at Windover. Many of the bodies were wrapped in textile materials. Seven twining/weaving variants have been identified. These fabrics are the most complex and diverse set of textile materials from this time period currently known in the Americas (Doran and Dickel 1988, 274) and the only clue we have to weaving patterns in the state until after the introduction of pottery around 2000+ B.C. While no other woven materials have been found except for bits of cordage, weaving patterns have been identified from pot bottoms. Evidently the potter set the unfired clay on a mat to shape it (next page). Historic records furnish clues of woven materials. Laudonnière (1975, 140) was given "two small mats which could not have been more artfully made," and Dickenson writes that the Ais Indians wore "a piece of Plaitwork of Straws, wrought of divers Colours" (True 1944, 53).

All of the Middle to Late Archaic mortuary sites mentioned above, except Gauthier (Jones 1981), contained wooden artifacts. They were either damaged when recovered or could not be preserved. There is little information from these sites about decorated wood or wood carvings.

The eagle carving shown from the fort center site in plate 20 is the symbol of the Florida Museum of Natural History. The Fort Center site (8-Gl-13) is located along Fisheating Creek west of Lake Okeechobee in Glades County. Between A.D. 200 and A.D. 600 the inhabitants set aside a portion of the site as a mortuary area, which included a platform built over an artificial pond where bundled burials were placed. Sometime around A.D. 500 the platform burned and collapsed into the pond, carrying with it approximately 300 bundled burials and between

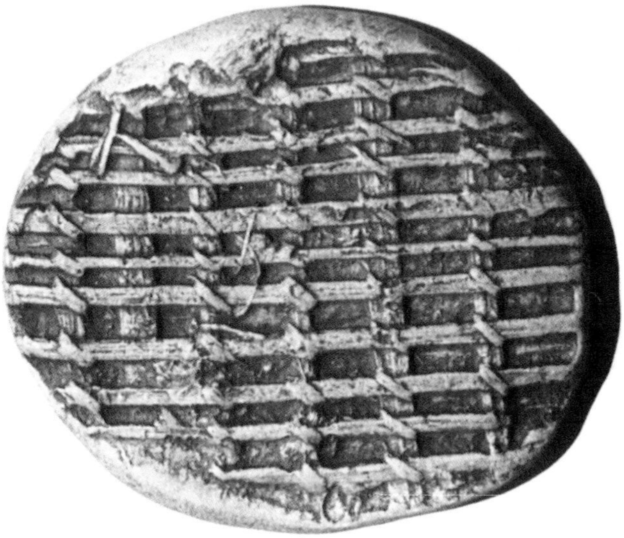

Mat design taken from a ceramic pot bottom.

100 and 150 wooden carvings or fragments of carvings thought to represent a total of 69 complete specimens.

The realistically carved turkey vulture head shown in plate 21 came from the Tick Island site. Its beak is opened in anguish because the talons of a large raptorial bird, possibly an eagle, are clutching it by the throat. The skin on the vulture's head is wrinkled, and its exposed tongue provides even more realism. The artifacts from Tick Island were found during and following a dredging operation that mixed materials as old as 4000 B.C. with some as recent as A.D.1000. The specimen in plate 21 is thought to have been made between 200 B.C. and A.D. 500, based on associated materials that emerged at the same time (Benson 1967).

The carved duck head in plate 22 is from the Belle Glade site, Palm Beach County (8-PB-40). No dates are available for the specimens from this site, but at least some of the objects recovered at the Belle Glade site are thought to be contemporaneous with Fort Center and Key Marco. The site was excavated under the Federal Emergency Relief Administration in 1933–34 and was described thoroughly by Willey (1949a).

The kneeling human figure pictured in plate 23 was found near Pahokee, Palm Beach County, in 1928 (Purdy 1991, 243). It is interesting because it is kneeling in a manner similar to the famous feline figure from Key Marco (plate 24) and may represent a shaman.

Key Marco is one of the most famous sites in the world from which well-preserved examples of Precolumbian wooden carvings have been recovered. The site was excavated by Frank Hamilton Cushing in 1896

(Cushing 1897; Gilliland 1975). There is some uncertainty about the age of Key Marco, but the materials recovered by Cushing probably range from around A.D. 200 until after A.D. 1300. Many of the specimens deteriorated almost immediately after they were removed from the muck. Fortunately a visual as well as a written record exists, because Cushing had Wells M. Sawyer, an artist and photographer, with him at the site. Gilliland (1975; 1989) furnishes a complete account of the field expedition, the events surrounding the dissemination of the artifacts, and the present condition of those that have survived. The specimens in plates 24 through 32 were photographed by us specifically for inclusion in this volume. Plates 33 through 35 are from the Photographic Archives of the University Museum in Philadelphia.

There is no locational or age information about the small feline effigy figure shown in plate 36. It is very eroded but retains what may be small patches of white pigment. It is possible that it is contemporaneous with the Key Marco feline carving that Cushing believed was "a man-like being in the guise of a panther" (1897, 59)—a shaman in transformation.

Several wooden plaques similar to the one in plate 37 have been recovered in the state. These wooden specimens are larger than, but otherwise almost identical to, metal ornaments from the Early Historic period. Many of these objects have no decoration, and a few have been found that are more than a meter long. They were also produced in stone. They are discussed more fully in the section illustrating metal artifacts (see plates 106 and 107).

The totem representing a horned owl is shown in plate 39. It is the largest prehistoric wooden carving found in the Western Hemisphere. Feathers are carefully and symmetrically depicted on its back. It was recovered in 1955 near the banks of the St. Johns River and the Thursby Midden, which was completely demolished by C. B. Moore in the late nineteenth century (Bullen 1955). The otter (?) in plate 38 was found in 1978 in essentially the same area as the owl. It is much smaller than the owl but shares many of the same design elements. These two carvings plus one of a fragmented pelican also recovered in 1978 could have been made by the same craftsman. The carving styles are different than those described for the Fort Center site, but they are all made of pine and portray animal totems.

Plates 40 through 42 are of specimens recovered from Early Historic period contexts as determined by radiocarbon analysis or by association with materials of European origin.

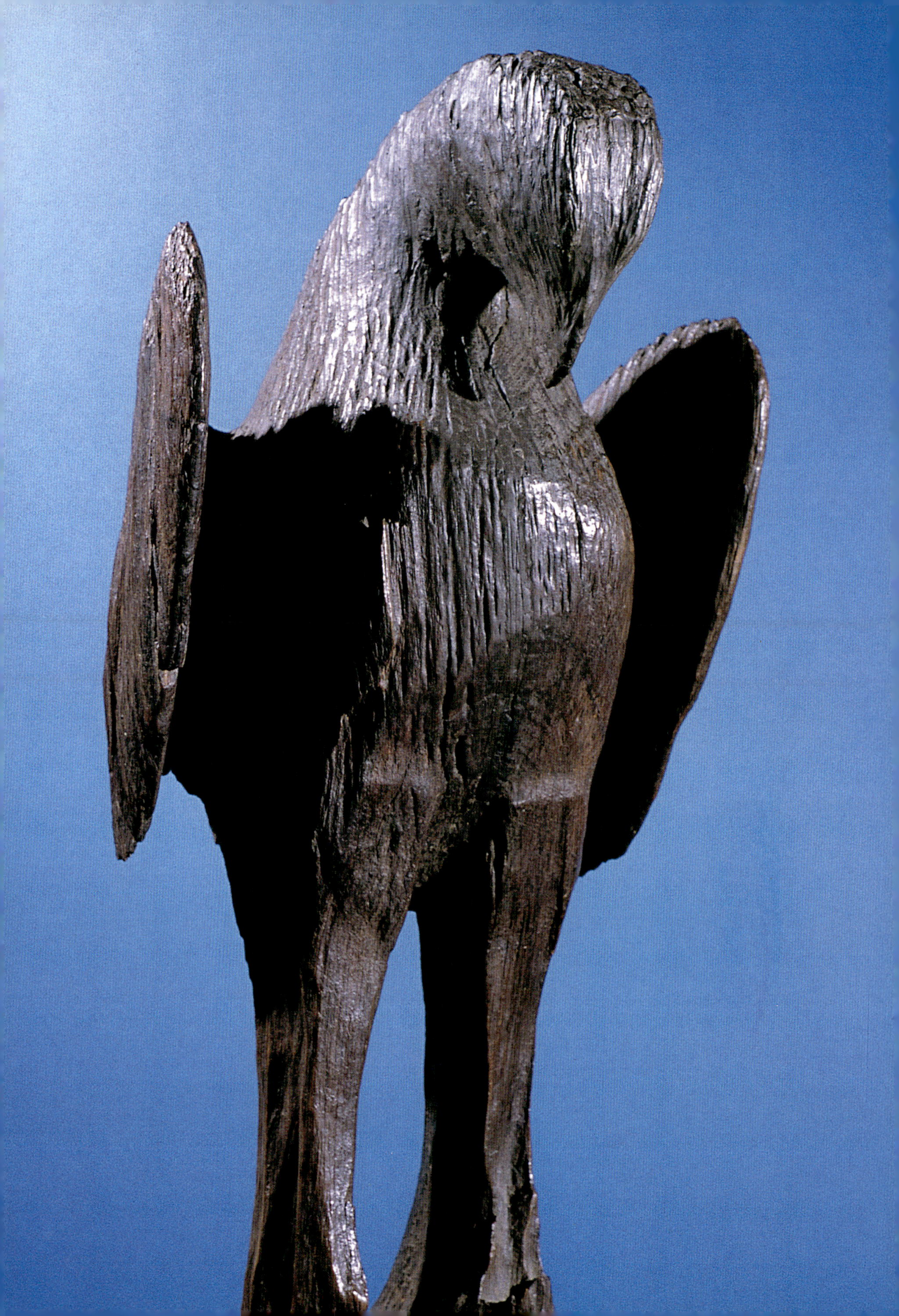

20. (facing page) Eagle totem. Fort Center site, Glades County (8-Gl-13). Ca. A.D. 200-600. Wood (pine), carved portion is 66.25 cm long; total figure is 155 cm long. Florida Museum of Natural History, Gainesville, no. A-3030.

21. Turkey vulture. Tick Island, Volusia County (8-Vo-24). Ca. 200 B.C.–A.D. 500. Wood (lighter knot), 12.5 cm high. Silver River Museum, Ocala. On loan from private collection.

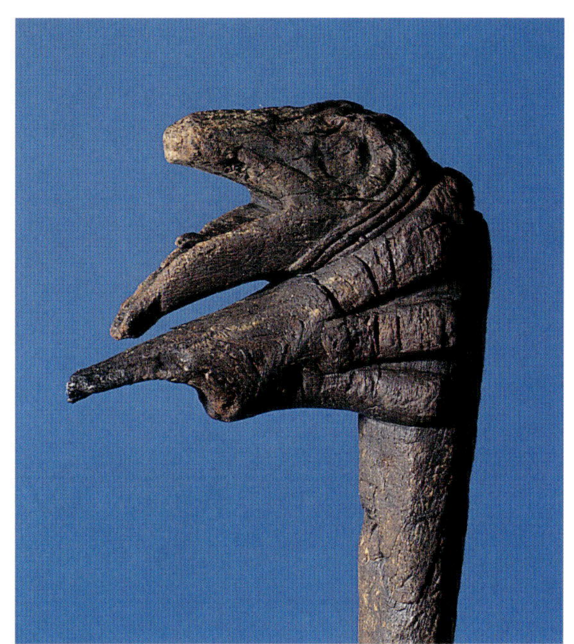

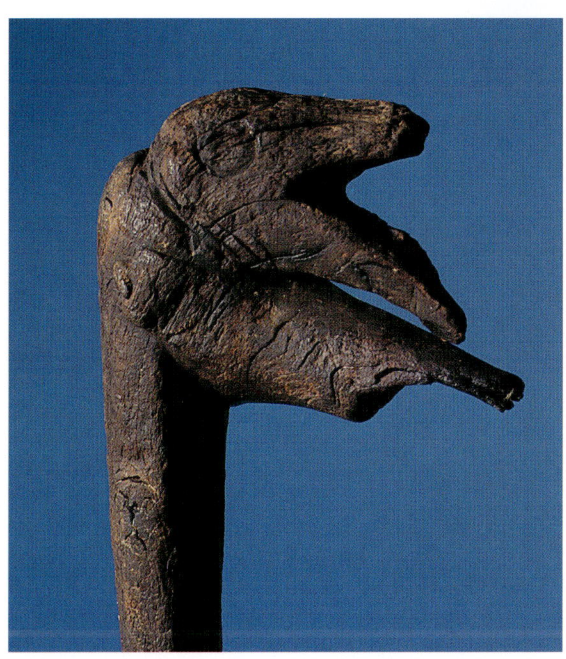

23. Kneeling human figure. Found near Pahokee, Palm Beach County in 1928. Date unknown, probably Late Prehistoric. Wood, 22.9 cm high x 9.0 cm wide at shoulders x 10.0 cm deep at knees. Historical Society of Palm Beach County, no. 85/12-26.

22. Bird head (duck?). Belle Glade site, Palm Beach County (8-PB-40). Date unknown, possibly ca. A.D. 200 to Historic. Wood, 19.5 cm high x 16.5 cm wide x 7.0 cm thick. Smithsonian Institution, Washington, D.C., no. A383868.

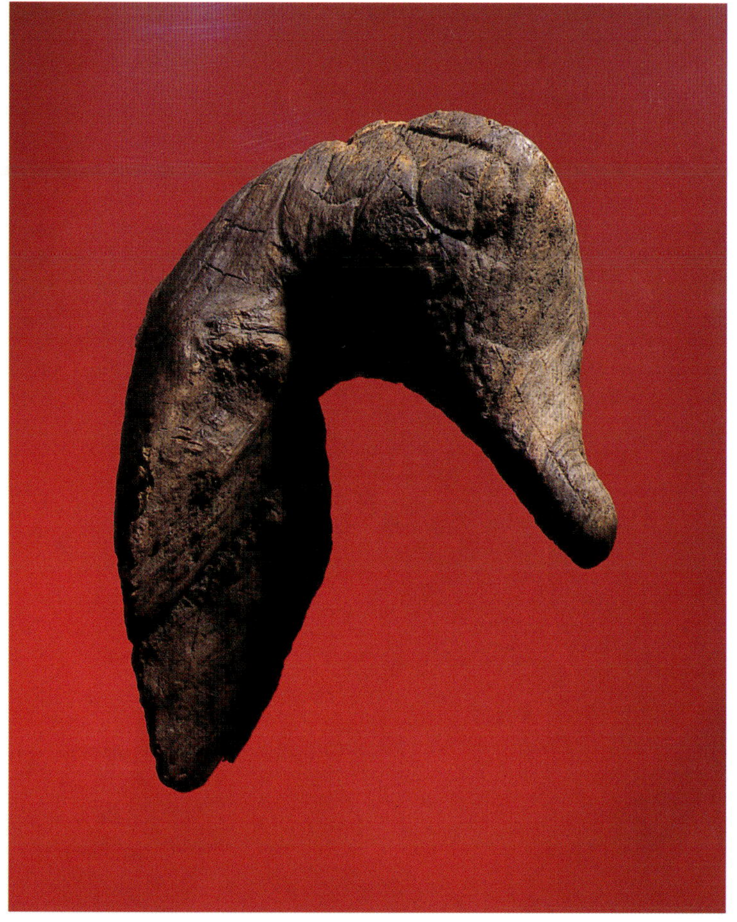

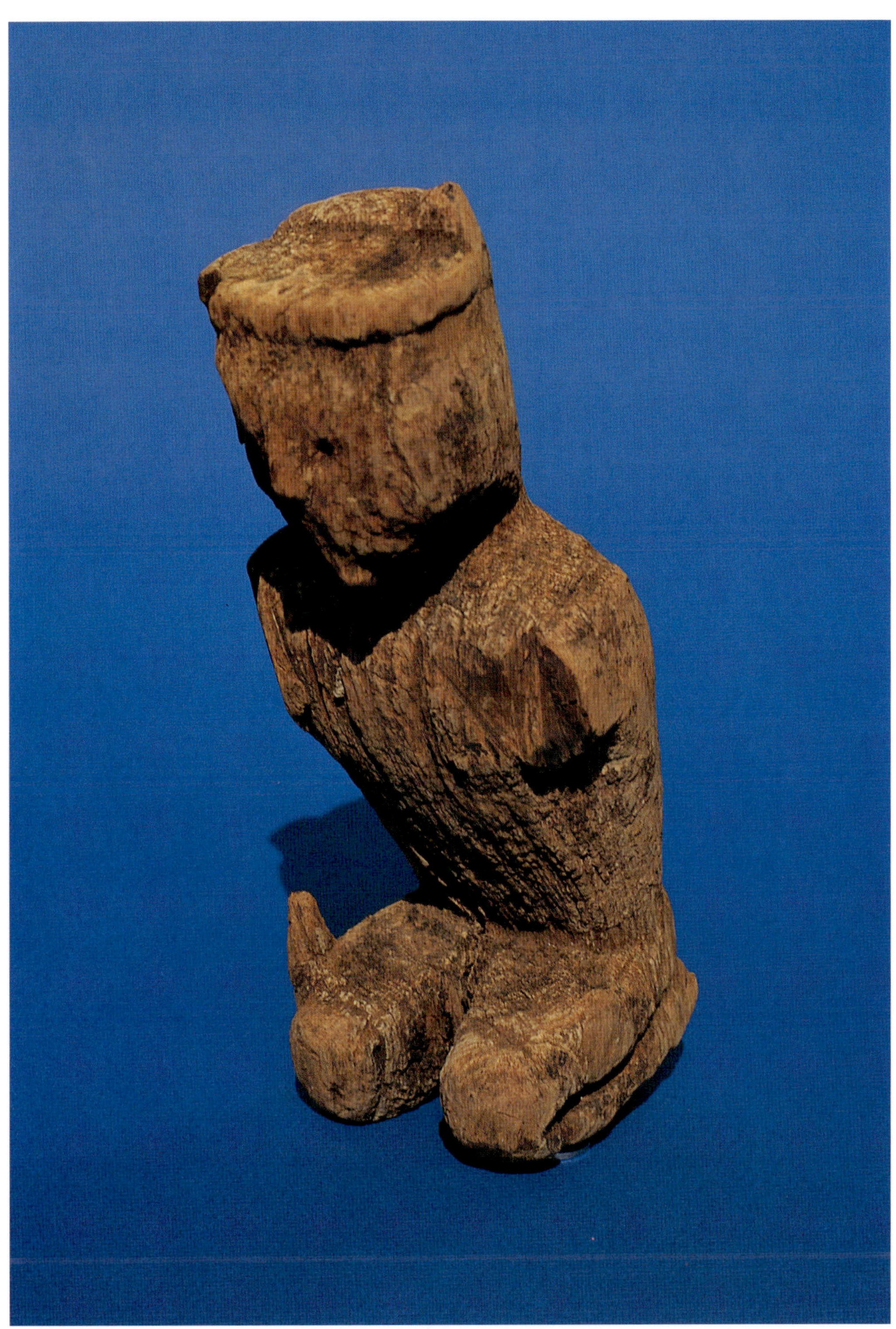

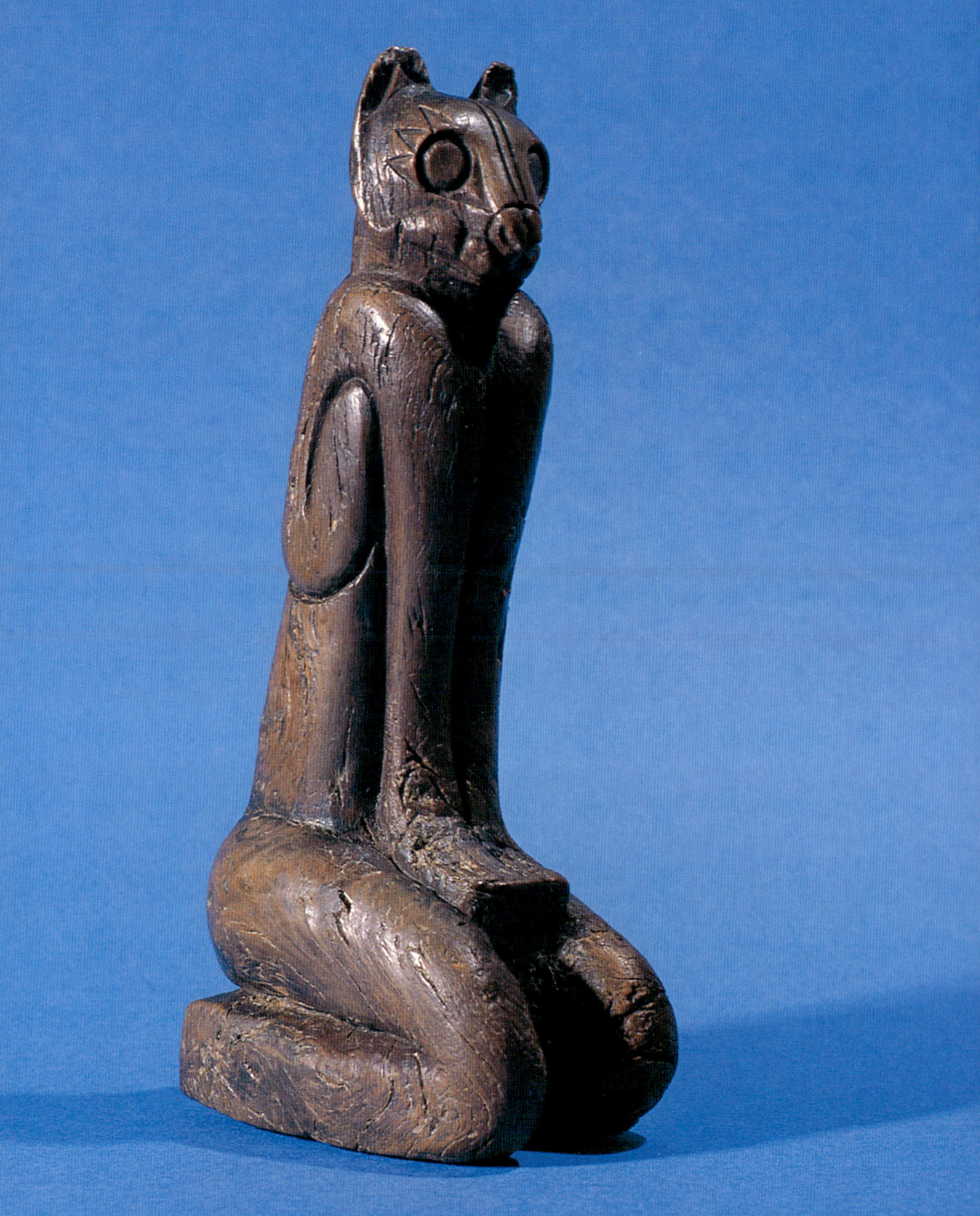

24. Feline figure. Key Marco site, Collier County (8-Cr-49). Date unknown, probably Late Prehistoric. Wood, 15.0 cm high x 3.5 cm wide at knees and 6.0 deep at knees. Smithsonian Institution, Washington, D.C., no. 240915.

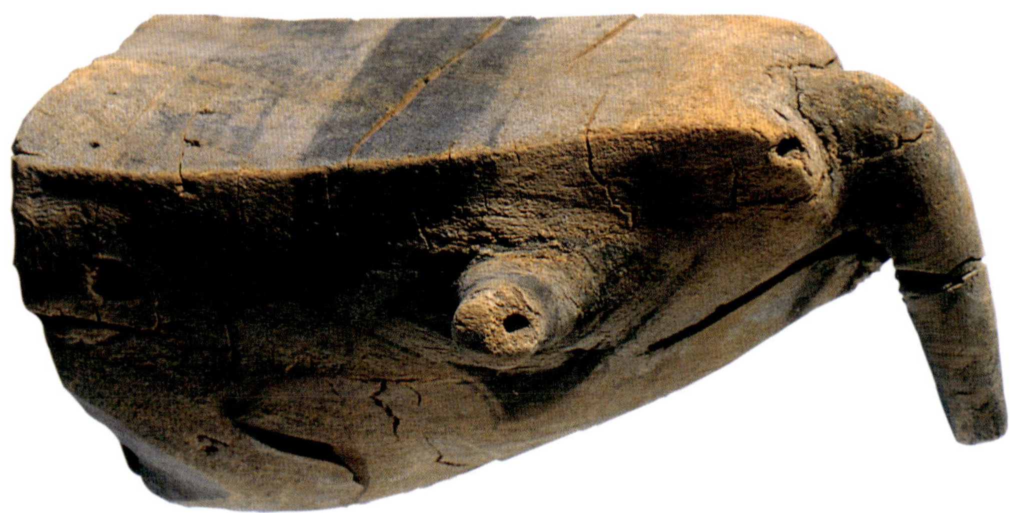

25. (above) Beaked sea turtle figurehead. Key Marco site, Collier County (8-Cr-49). Date unknown, possibly between A.D. 600–800. Wood, 16.8 cm long x 8.4 cm wide x 10.0 cm high; originally painted black, white, blue, and red (only black and white remain). University Museum, Philadelphia, no. 40715.

26. (facing page) Board with painted woodpecker design. Key Marco site, Collier County (8-Cr-49). A.D. 670 ± 60. Wood, 40.6 cm long x 21.6 wide x 3.5 cm thick; originally painted in black, white, and blue. Florida Museum of Natural History, Gainesville, no. A5537 (40697).

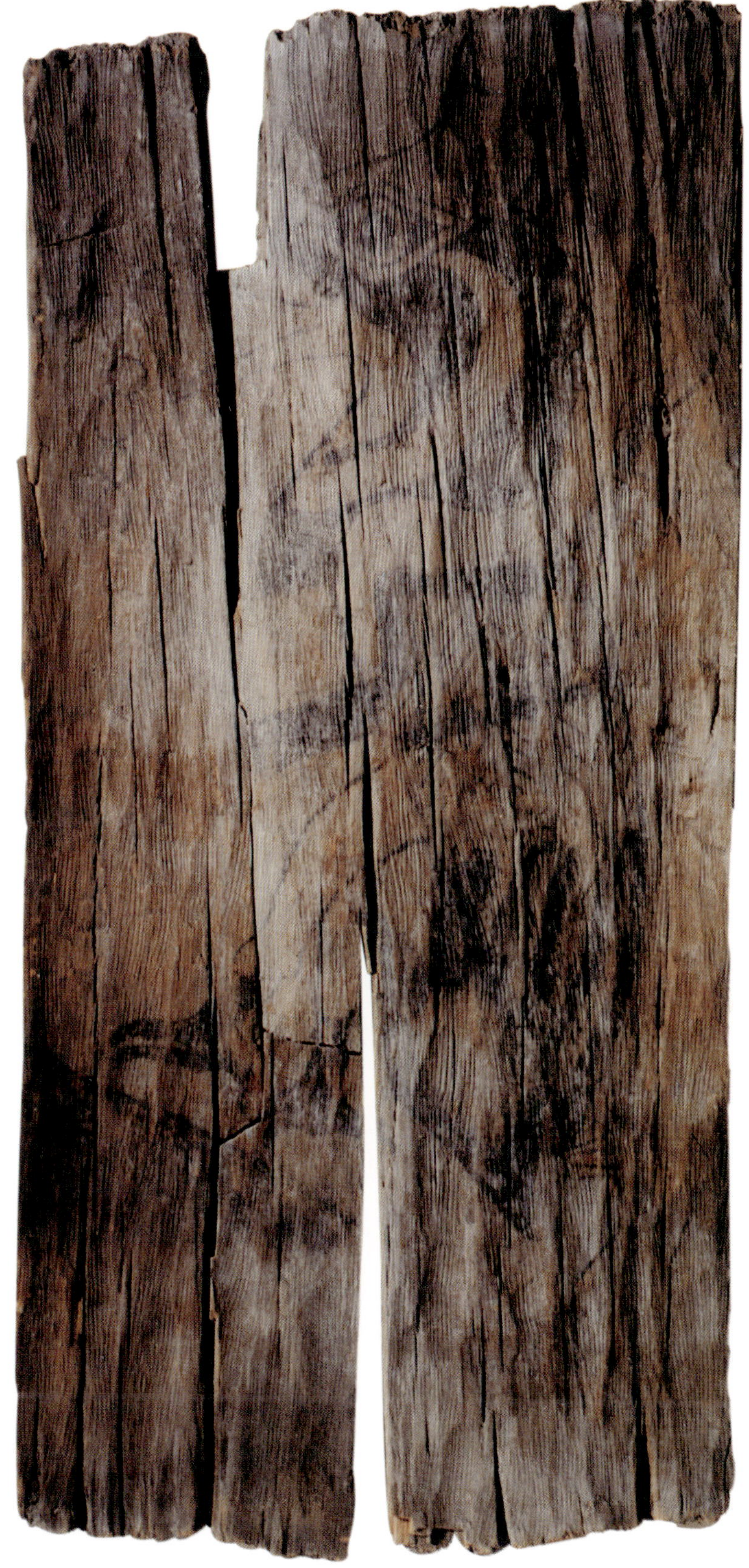

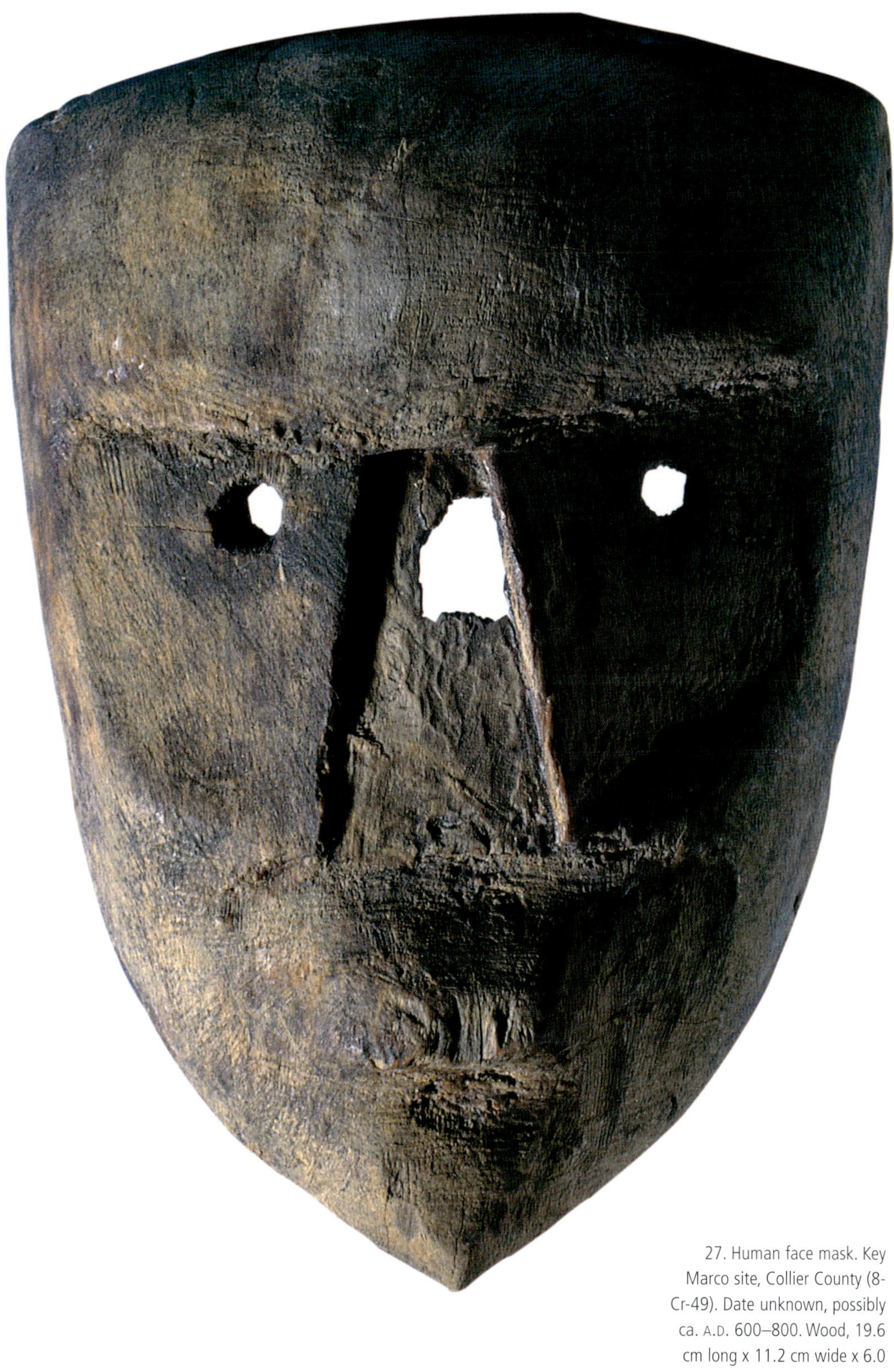

27. Human face mask. Key Marco site, Collier County (8-Cr-49). Date unknown, possibly ca. A.D. 600–800. Wood, 19.6 cm long x 11.2 cm wide x 6.0 cm thick. University Museum, Philadelphia, no. 40713.

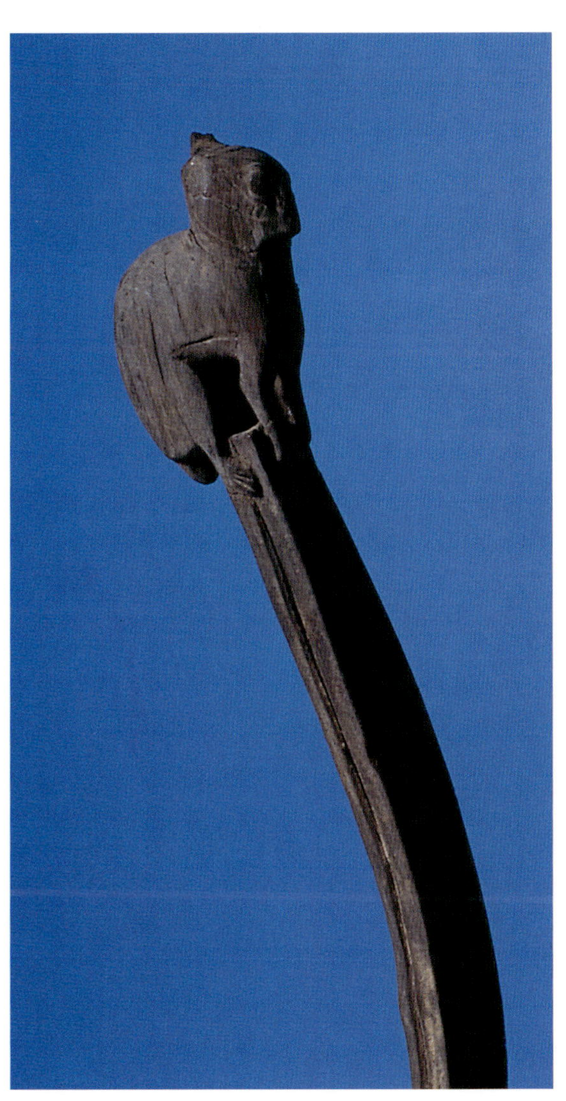

28. "Thumping rabbit" (?): the spur end of a single-holed atlatl. Key Marco site, Collier County (8-Cr-49). Date unknown, possibly ca. A.D. 600–800. Wood, entire specimen is 43.5 cm long; carving is 5.0 cm long. University Museum, Philadelphia, no. 40609.

29. Decorated bowl encircled by fire serpent symbol (?). Key Marco, Collier County (8-Cr-49). Date unknown, possibly ca. A.D. 600–800. Wood (buttonwood knot), 22.0 cm long x 17.0 cm wide x 7.5 cm high. Smithsonian Institution, Washington, D.C., no. 240189.

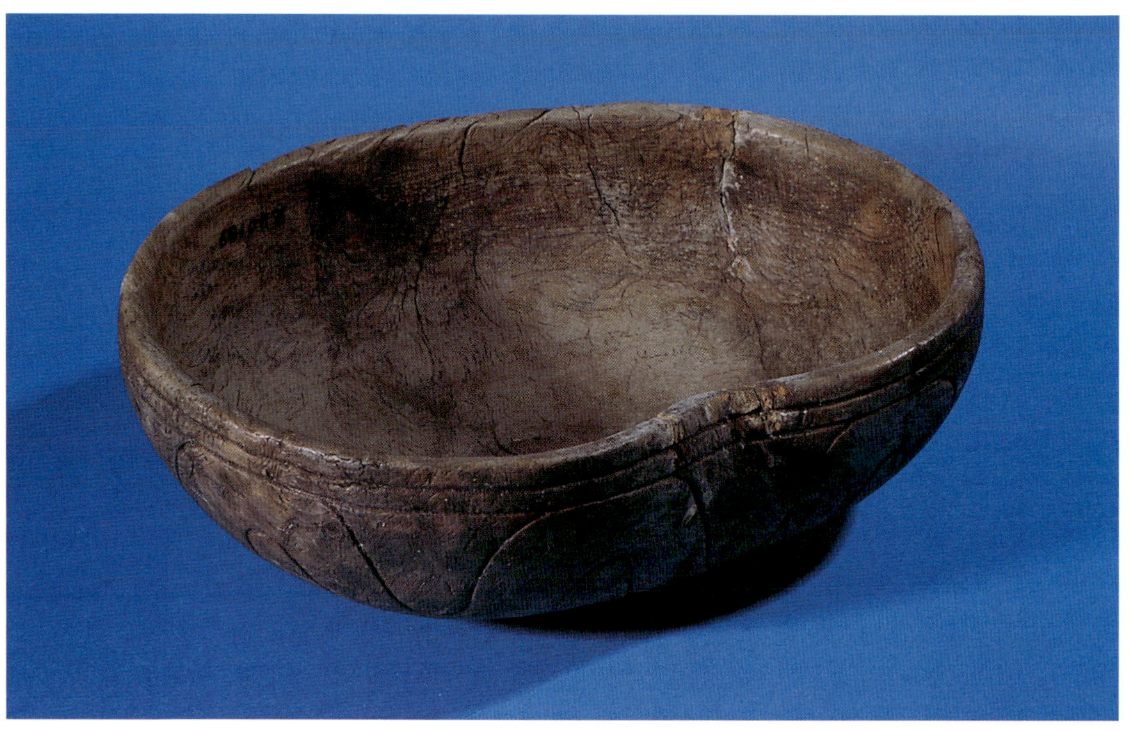

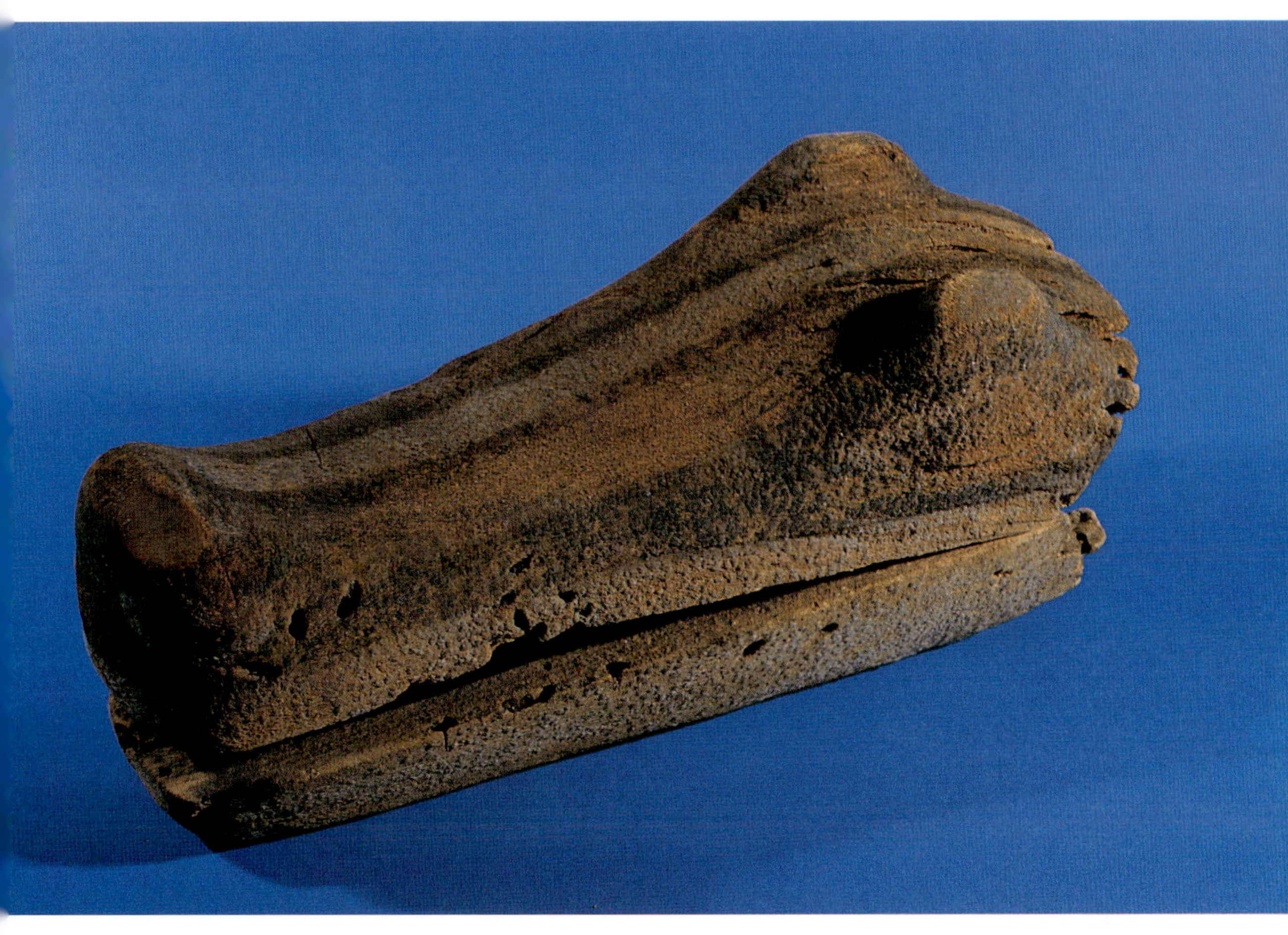

30. Alligator in two pieces (lower jaw separate). Key Marco, Collier County (8-Cr-49). Date unknown, possibly ca. A.D. 600–800. Wood, 14.5 cm high x 25.5 cm long x 9.0 cm wide. Originally painted white, black, and blue. University Museum, Philadelphia, no. 40718.

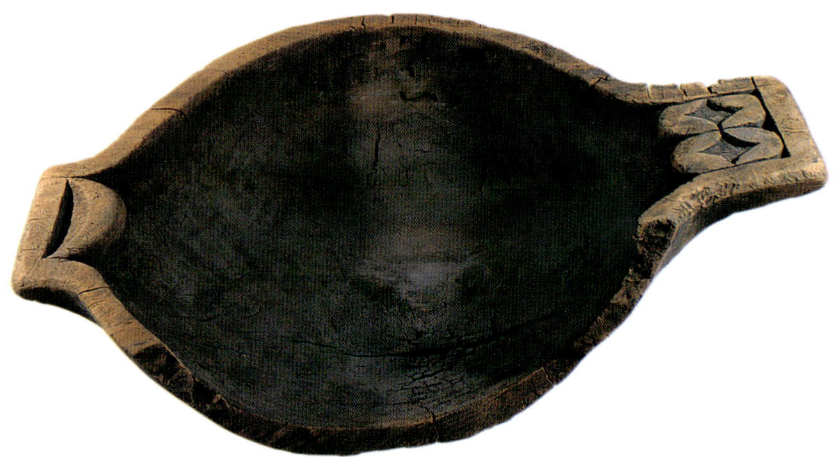

31. (above) Bowl. Key Marco (?), Collier County (8-Cr-49). Date unknown, possibly ca. A.D. 600–800. Wood, 9.0 cm high x 31.0 long x 20.5 cm wide. Smithsonian Institution, Washington, D.C., no. ATO5541 (probably Key Marco 240175).

32. (below) Feasting bowl. Key Marco, Collier County (8-Cr-49). Date unknown, possibly ca. A.D. 600–800. Wood, 15.8 cm high x 51.2 cm long x 32.5 cm wide. University Museum, Philadelphia, no. 40184.

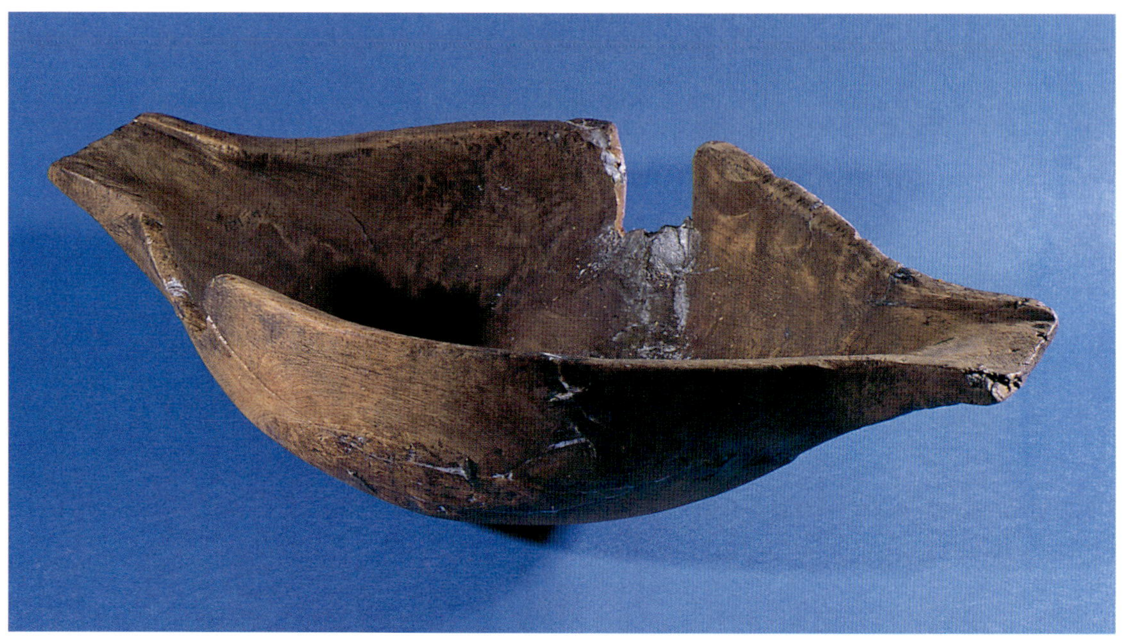

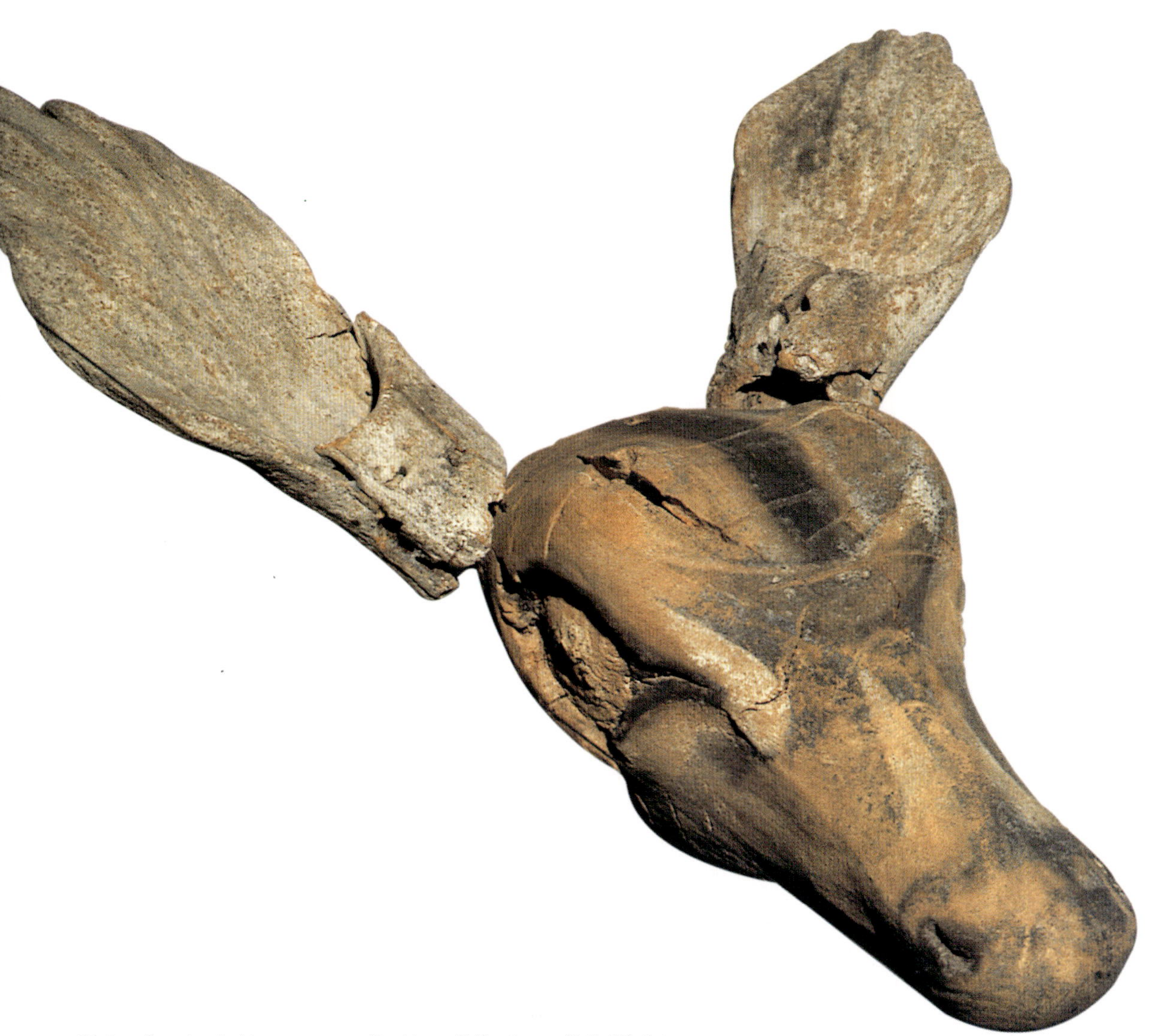

33. Deer figurehead with separate ears. Key Marco, Collier County (8-Cr-49). Date unknown, possibly ca. A.D. 600–800. Wood, head is 16.0 cm high x 8.0 cm wide x 8.5 cm deep; left ear is 12.0 cm x 6.0 cm; right ear is 12.4 cm x 6.0 cm; originally painted in blue, black, and white. University Museum, Philadelphia, no. 40707. Photo courtesy of the University Museum.

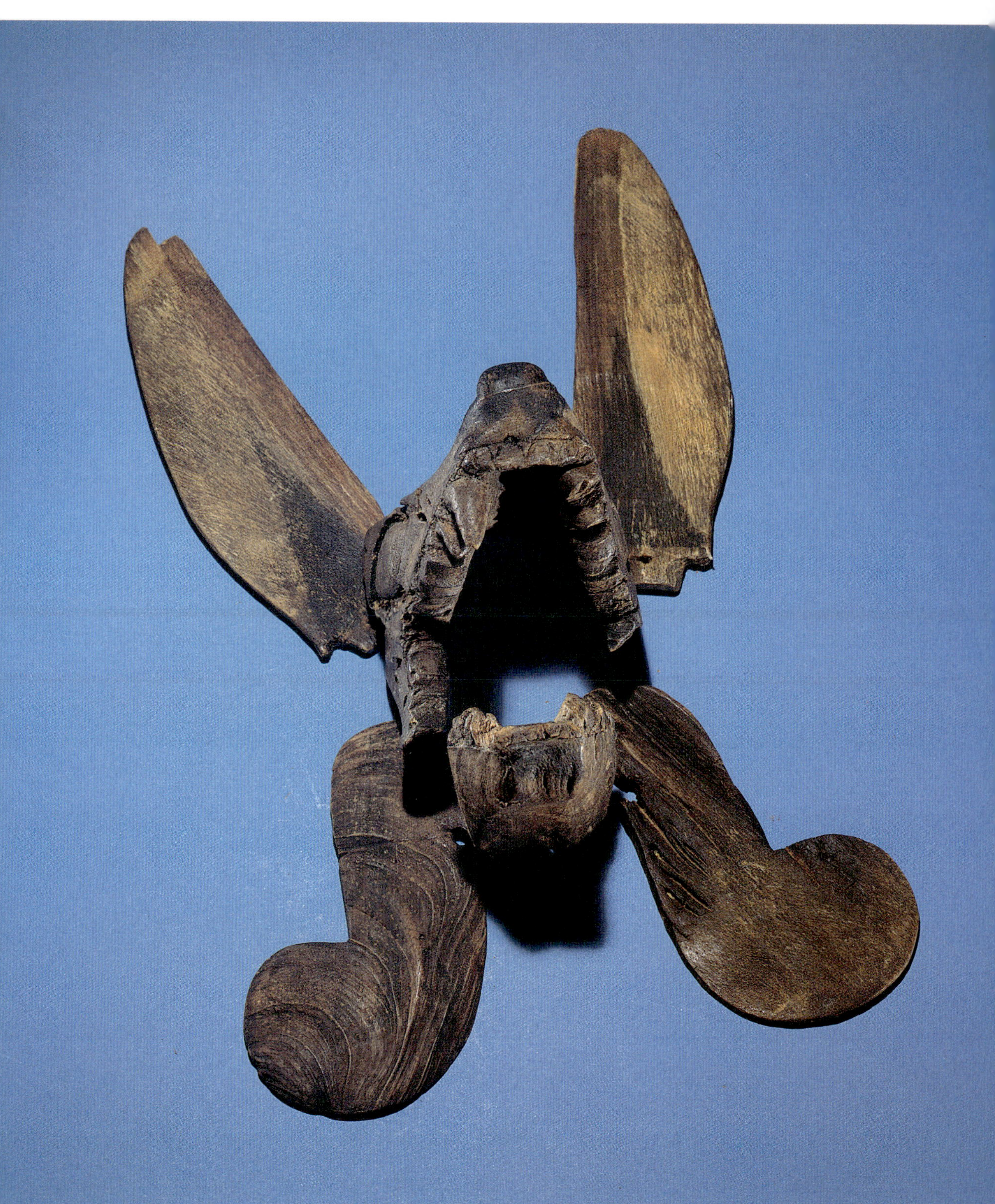

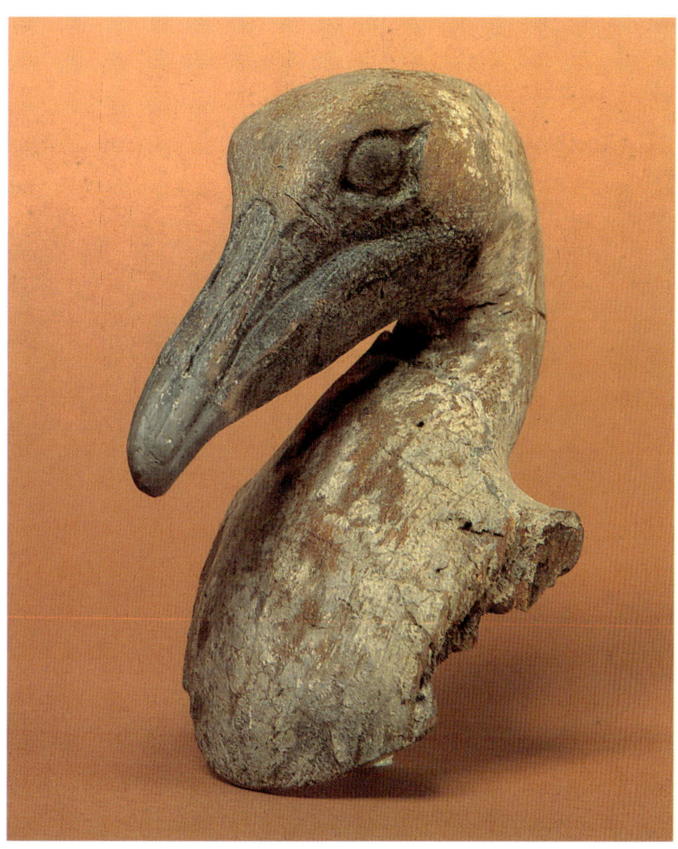

35. (above) Figurehead of a pelican found with fragments of wing pieces. Key Marco, Collier County (8-Cr-49). Date unknown, possibly ca. A.D. 600–800. Wood, 10.7 cm high x 6.1 cm x 6.7 cm. University Museum, Philadelphia, no. 40708. Photo courtesy of the University Museum.

34. (facing page) Wolf figurehead with separate ear and shoulder attachments. Key Marco, Collier County (8-Cr-49). Date unknown, possibly ca. A.D. 600–800. Wood, upper jaw is 15.6 cm long; lower jaw is 16.0 cm long x 8.6 cm wide; originally painted in white, black, and pink. University Museum, Philadelphia, no. 40700. Photo courtesy of the University Museum.

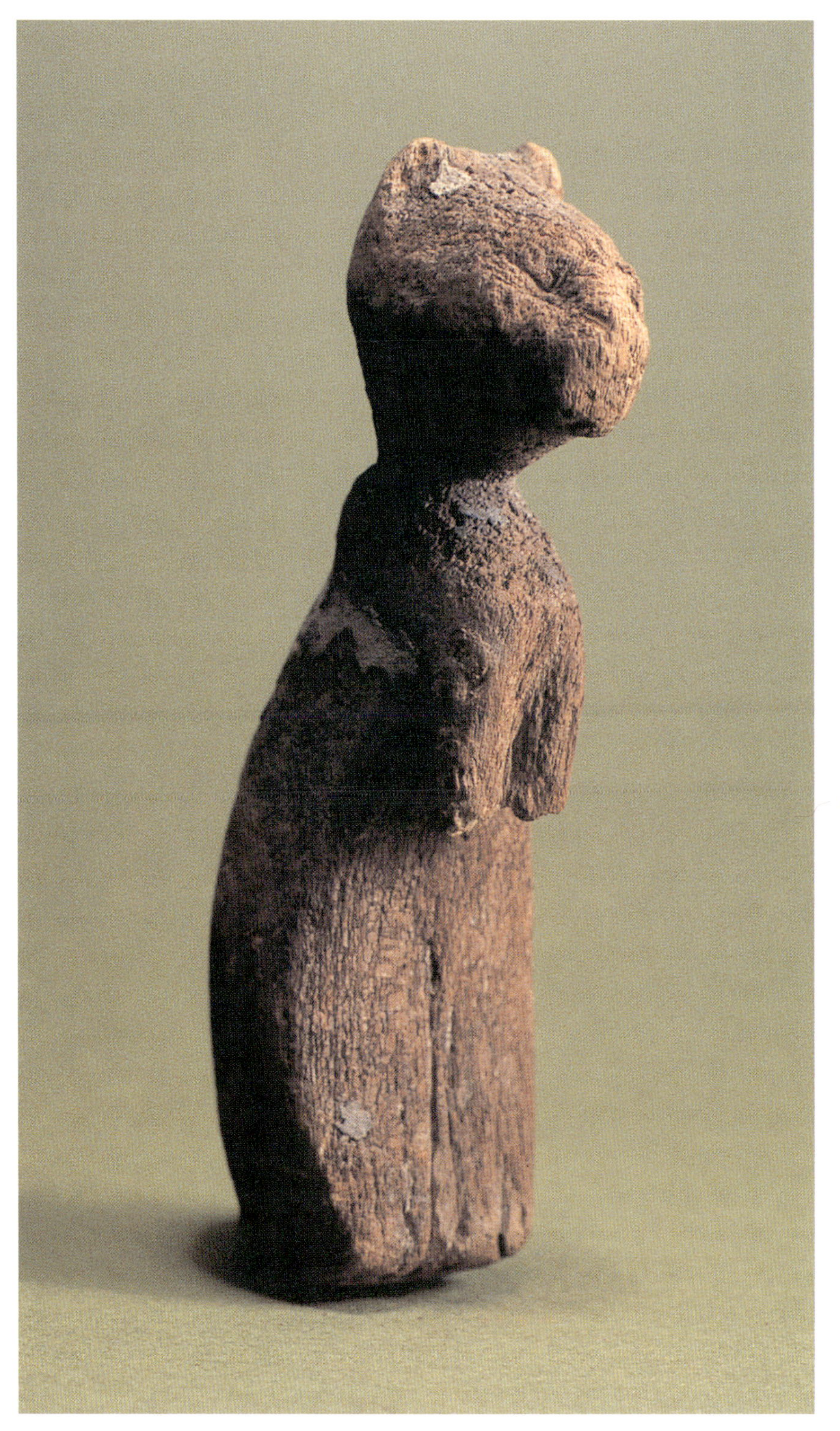

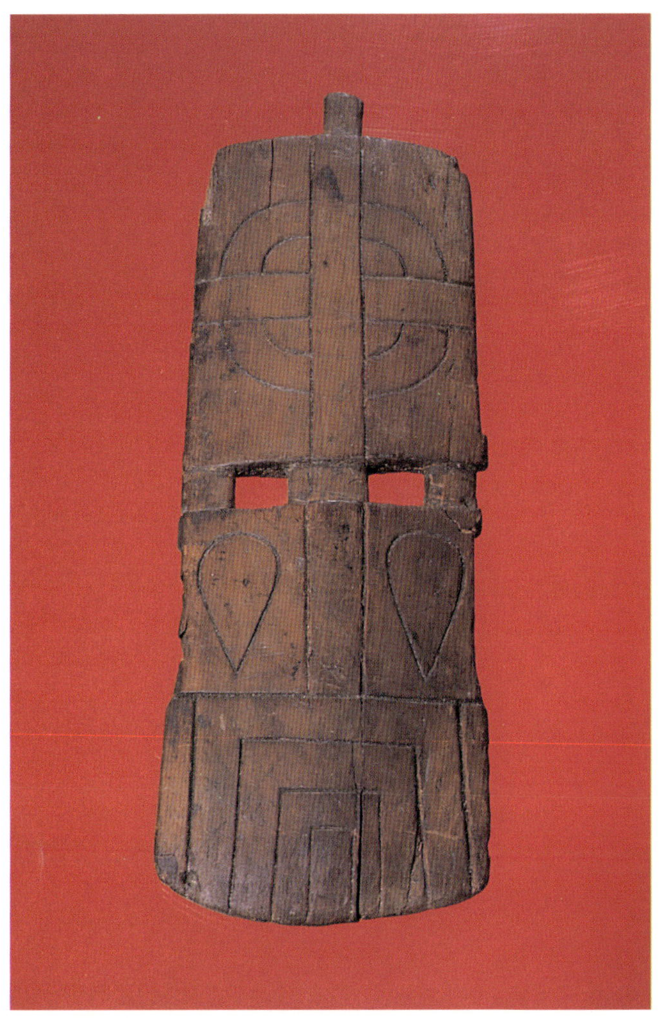

37. (above) Plaque incised on both faces. Caloosahatchee River area west of Fort Myers (8-L-17), Lee County. Date unknown, probably Late Prehistoric–Early Historic. Wood, 21.0 cm long x 7.5 cm wide x 0.5 cm thick. Smithsonian Institution, Washington, D.C., no. 329599.

36. (facing page) Feline effigy figure. Source unknown. Date unknown. Wood, 13.5 cm high x 3.6 cm wide. Rollins College, Winter Park, Florida (in a collection obtained sixty to seventy years ago that also includes some Fort Walton period pottery).

38. Otter (?) holding a fish. Thursby Midden, Volusia County (8-Vo-35). Ca. A.D. 1200 (dated by association with owl). Wood (pine), 70.0 cm high. Bureau of Archaeological Research, Tallahassee, no. 81-37-02.

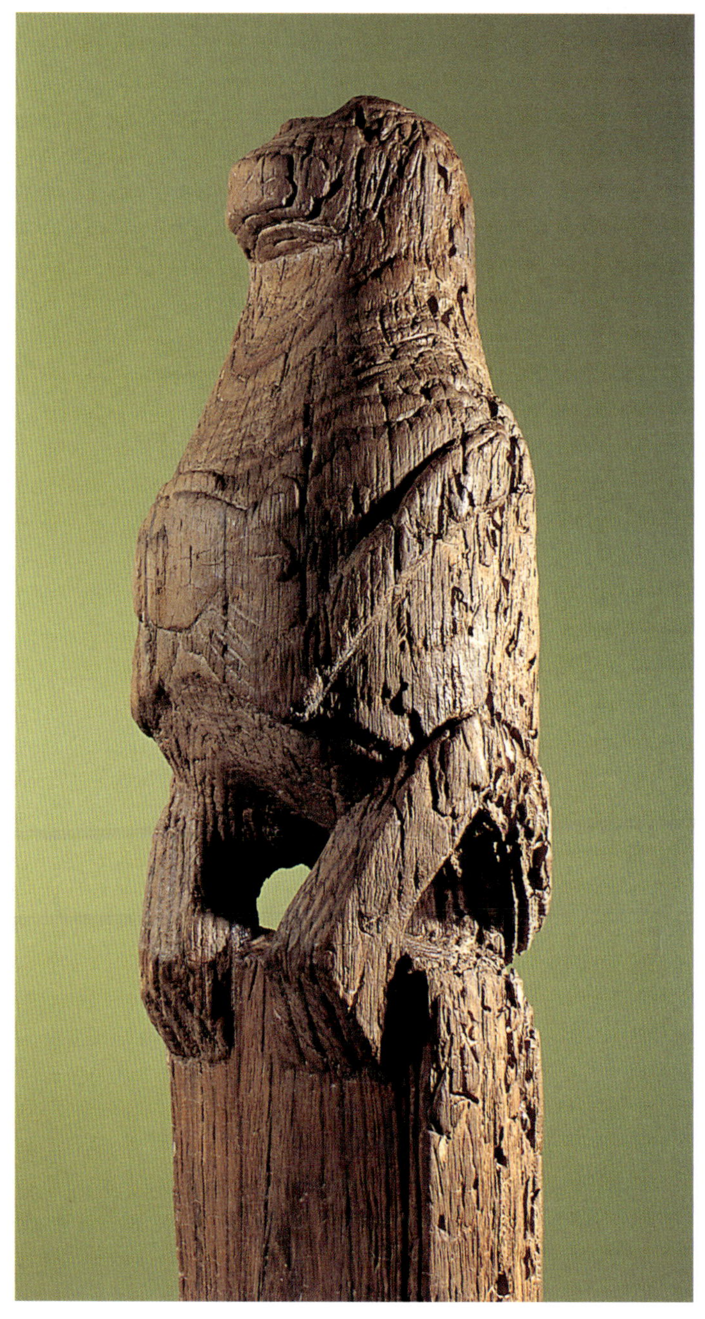

39. Owl effigy totem. Thursby Midden, Volusia County (8-Vo-35). ca. A.D. 1200. Wood (heart pine), carved portion 1.87 m high x 42.5 cm wide x 27.5 deep. Fort Caroline National Memorial, Jacksonville, no. FOCA-00252.

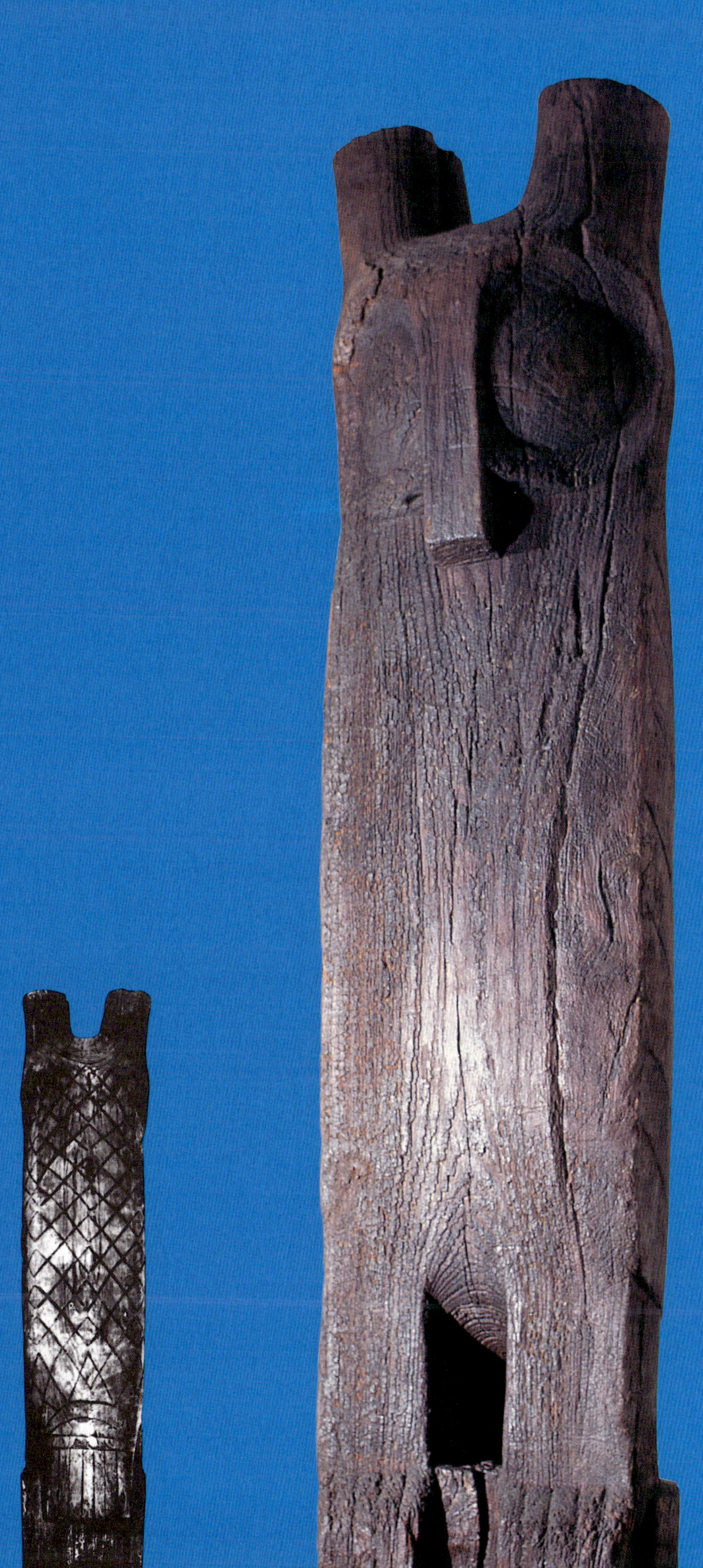

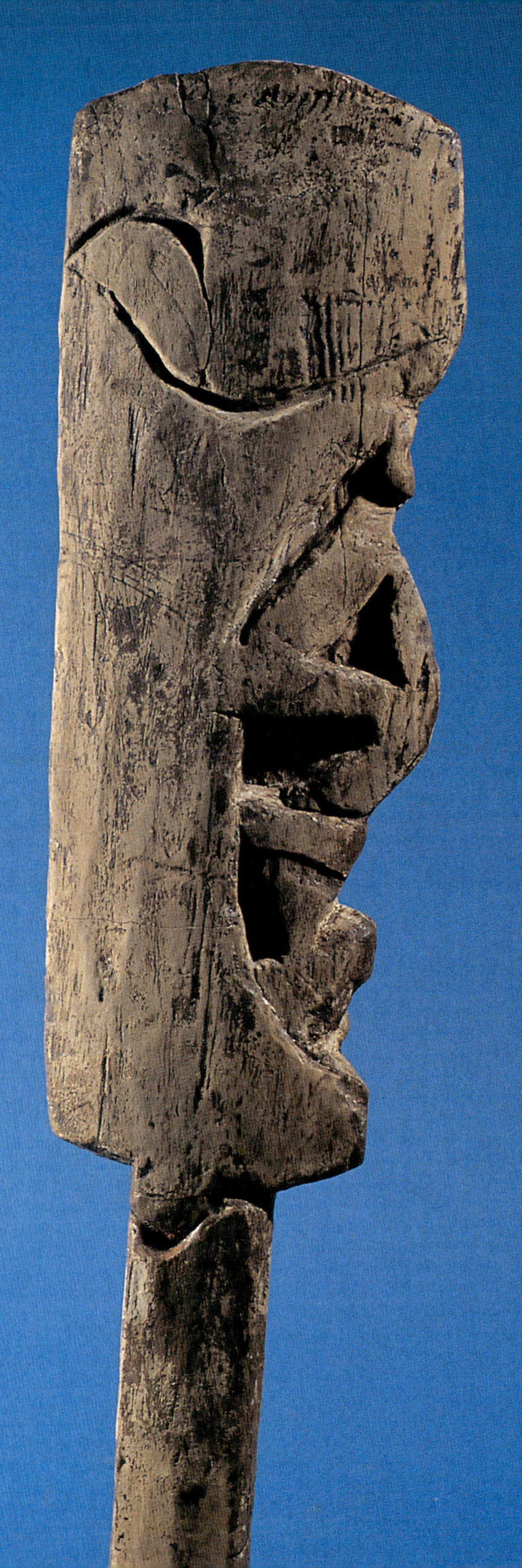

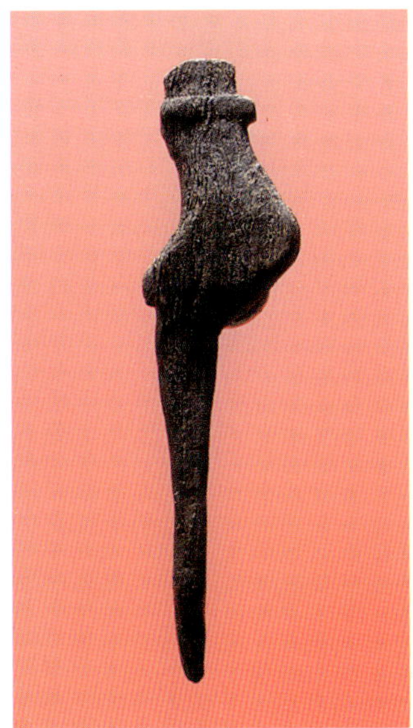

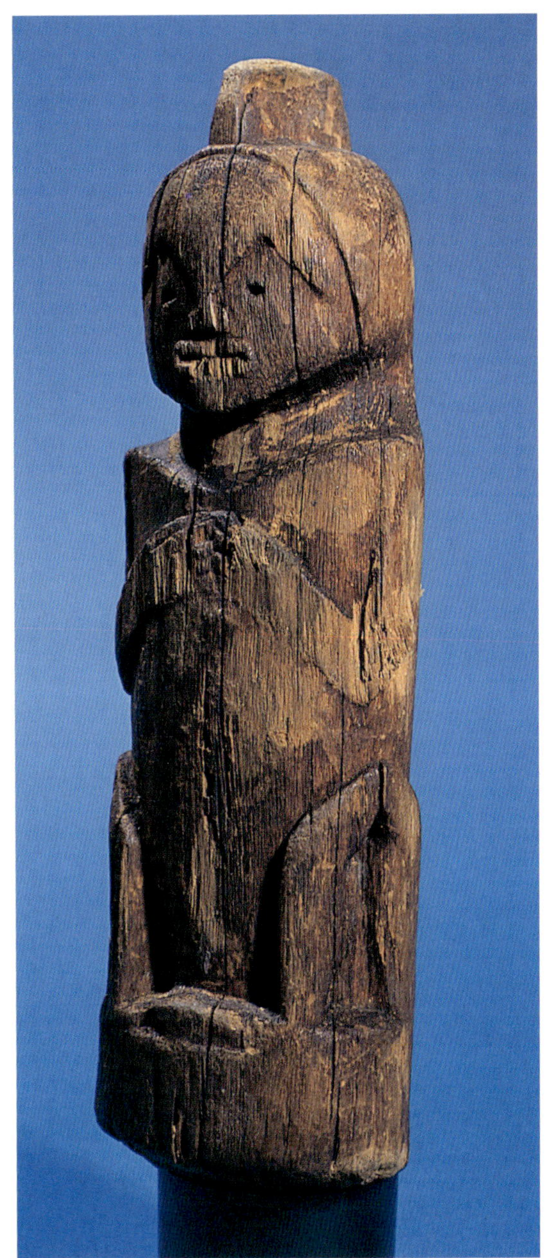

40. (above) Bird hair ornament. Hontoon Island, Volusia County (8-Vo-202). Historic, Zone II, ca. A.D. 1500. Wood (red cedar), 14.7 cm high x 3.5 cm wide x 1.0 cm thick. Florida Bureau of Archaeological Research, Tallahassee, no. 90-58.

41. (right) Small seated human figure. Tomoka River, Flagler County. A.D. 1480 ± 60. Wood (Brazilwood), 21.8 cm high x 6.0 cm wide x 6.0 cm thick. Tomoka State Park, Ormond Beach, Florida, no. 11.

42. (facing page) Carved club with human face. Mission San Juan del Puerto, Fort George Island, Duval Co. (8-Du-53). Mission period (?); radiocarbon date of associated materials was A.D. 1480. Believed to have been made with iron tools by Guale Indians. Wood (hickory), 57.5 cm long x 12.5 cm wide x 2.0 cm thick. Florida Museum of Natural History, Gainesville, no. 4513.

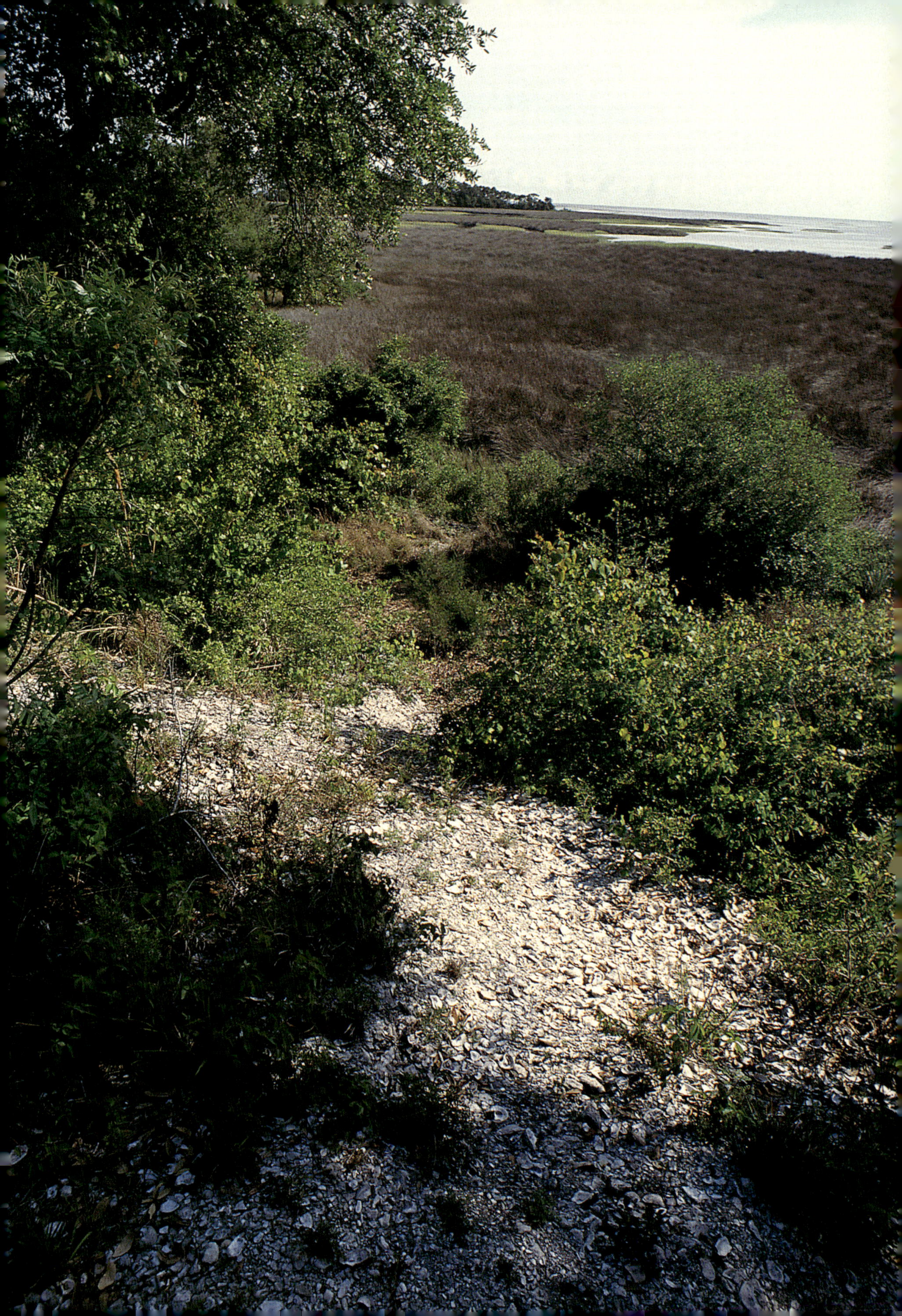

SHELL

IT IS INTERESTING to contemplate the place of marine shell technology in southeastern prehistory and iconography. Marine shell was not available as a raw material to people north of Florida except through trade. Copper and stone suitable for fashioning into art objects were not available in Florida except through trade. Many artifacts and decorative motifs produced in shell are identical to items produced in stone and copper, such as celts, pendants, and certain designs. It is therefore possible to conclude that in the absence of critical raw materials the Indians in Florida developed methods to work shell in order to keep pace with technologies occurring elsewhere. Or, the reverse reasoning can be applied.

Freshwater and marine shellfish species had become significant food items in Florida by 4000 B.C. Marine shell, in addition, furnished an important source of raw material for all manner of tools, utensils, and ornaments. Many shell pendants made from the columella of marine gastropods have been recovered. Their shapes are almost identical to those made of stone and copper that are reported from states to the north. Moore (1903, 401, 407) pictures stone and copper pendants recovered near Crystal River in Florida. The fact that these kinds of specimens were produced in several media and that they are so plentiful suggests that they must have had special individual or group relevance. Most of these objects were not decorated, although occasionally they were fashioned into effigies.

The exact age of the decorative shell artifacts we are illustrating is not known. Some of them can be tentatively assigned a date because of similarities in style to examples from other locations. Those shown in plates 43 through 46 are from Tick Island. As mentioned previously, a dragline removed the shell midden and its contents at Tick Island, making it impossible to determine associations reliably (Jahn and Bullen 1978). Objects similar to the small owl (?) carvings in plate 43, the stylized animal with pointed nose, the rattlesnake tail, and the bi-halved triangular pendant in plate 44 are not known elsewhere in the state. The eye pattern executed in shell on the left-hand specimen in plate 44 is similar to motifs on antler and bone from the same site as are the complex geometric designs on the gorgets in plate 45. A central, stylized human figure is present on the left object in plate 45. Two of the three shell gorgets in plate 46 are similar to specimens recovered at

Shell midden, Cedar Key

Key Marco (see Gilliland 1975, 176, plate 112) and at other sites in Florida.

No information other than that in the caption is available about the interesting shell carving in plate 47.

The turkey vulture (?) design on the shell pendant shown in plate 48 suggests a Caribbean influence. Coleman et al. (1983, 140) show that "pendants of remarkable similarity in style have been found on the island of Vieques near Puerto Rico."

The shell gorget in plate 49 was found in a burial mound associated with a male in his late forties. It has twenty-five scallops around the outside rim. There are two circular lines around the inner edge of the outer rim. Two perforations are at the top. An eight-pointed star with a cross is carved in the center of the piece and is surrounded by an inscribed circular line. The cross represents the four directions, and the swastika-like design on the cross might symbolize the moving wind. The swastika is a fairly typical motif of the Late Mississippian period. Plate 50 is a similar but less elaborate specimen.

The spider motif on the object in plate 51 is common during the Late Mississippian period. It was used on different media, including wood, and may have become popular because the spider has a natural cross on the underside of the body. (Many specimens illustrated in the literature have a cross design in the center. The cross is one of the most repeated of all symbols in Mississippian iconography.)

The shell gorget in plate 52 has a pattern of incised lines and contains sixteen pearl seats, probably sunken with a flint drill. One of the seats contained a pearl when the specimen was received by the Florida Museum of Natural History. There are two holes at each upper corner for a cord to suspend the piece.

Nothing is known about the shell "fish" in plate 53 other than the information given in the caption.

The specimen in plate 54 is painted with a masked dance figure. It has an elaborate headdress and plaited wristlets and leg bands done in black pigment. See Gilliland (1975, 179) for a description of the prolonged and serious controversy which took place over this shell. It was claimed that Frank Hamilton Cushing manufactured the painting and passed it off as a genuine example of aboriginal art from Key Marco. Most authorities of the time, including John Wesley Powell, believed that the piece was authentic, but there has been general doubt about it expressed over the years. Gilliland (1975, 183) concluded that the majority of evidence favors its genuineness.

43. Owl (?) figures. Tick Island, Volusia County (8-Vo-24). Date unknown. Marine shell, 8.0 cm long x 4.0 cm wide x 0.2–0.5 cm thick at base (object on left). Private collection.

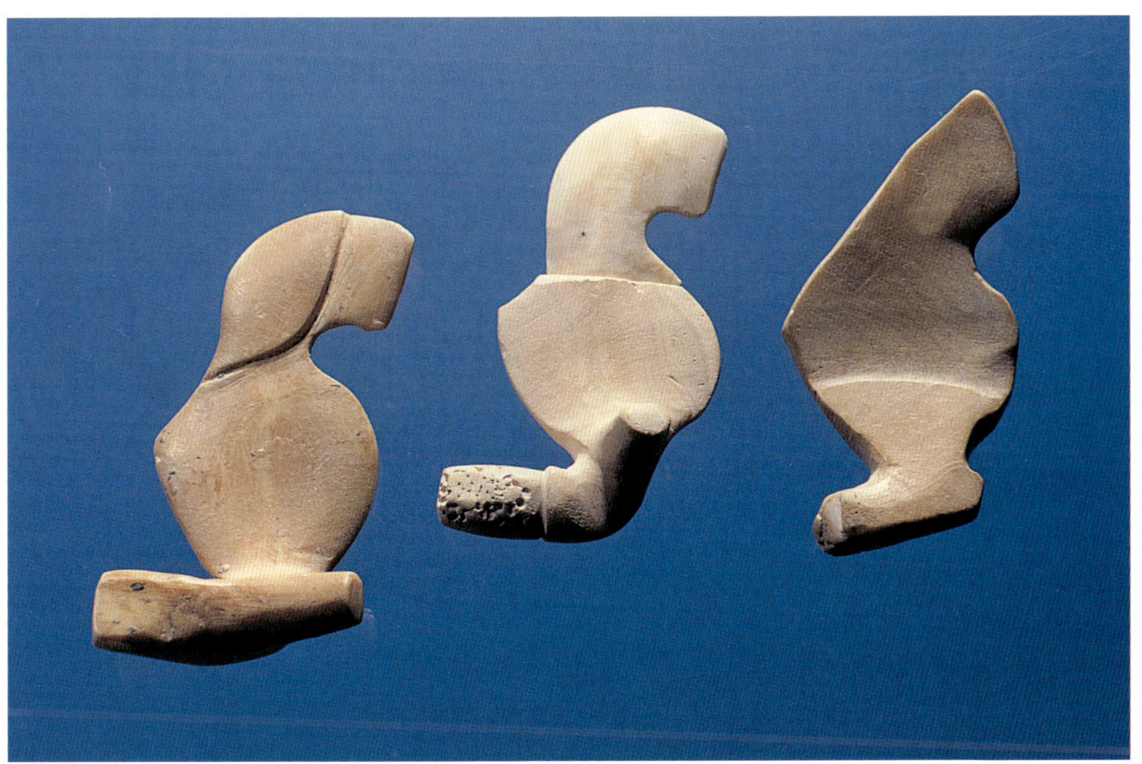

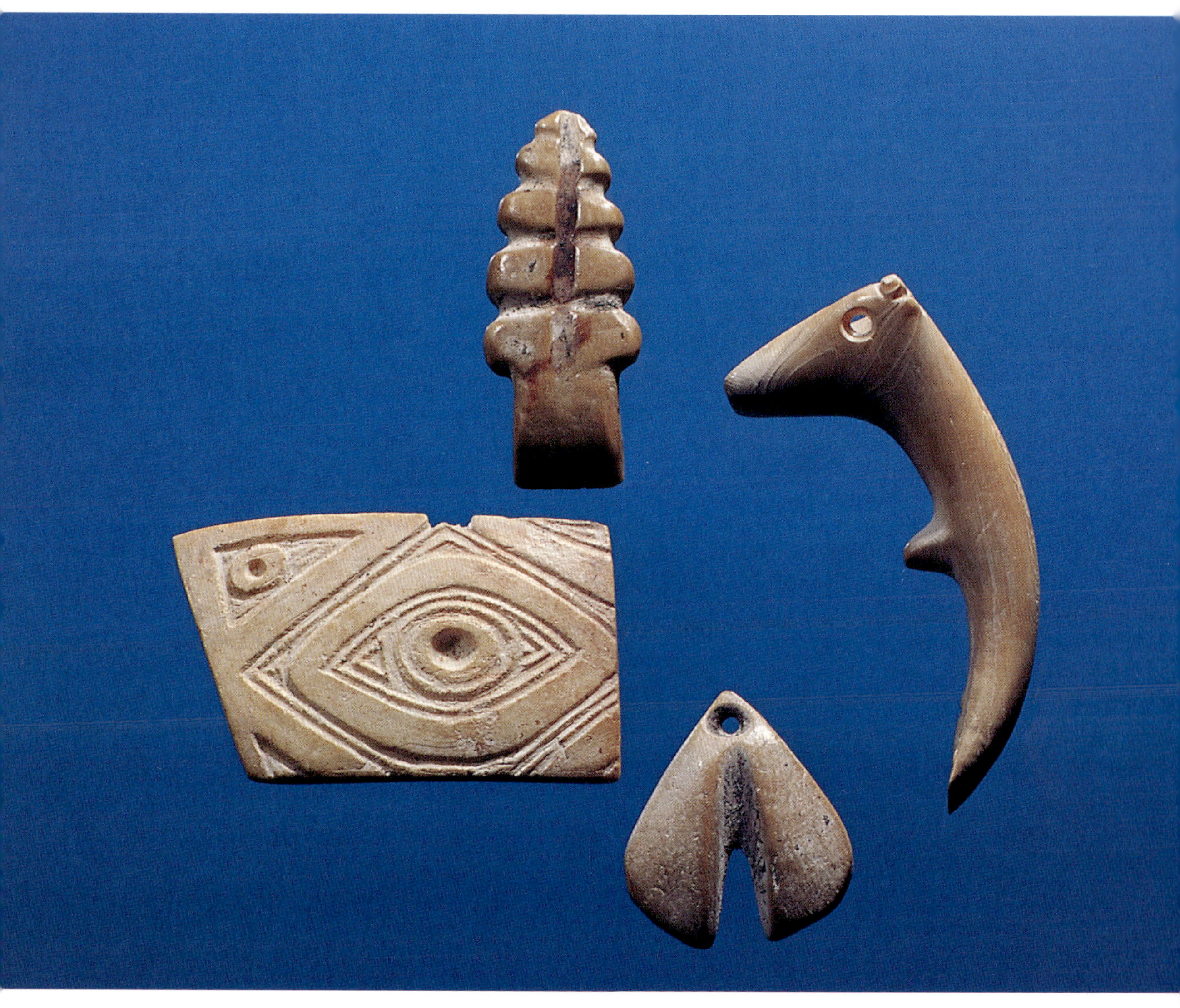

44. Group of four objects. Tick Island, Volusia County (8-Vo-24). Date unknown. Marine shell, 3.8 cm long x 6.0 cm wide x 0.5 cm thick (object on left). Private collection.

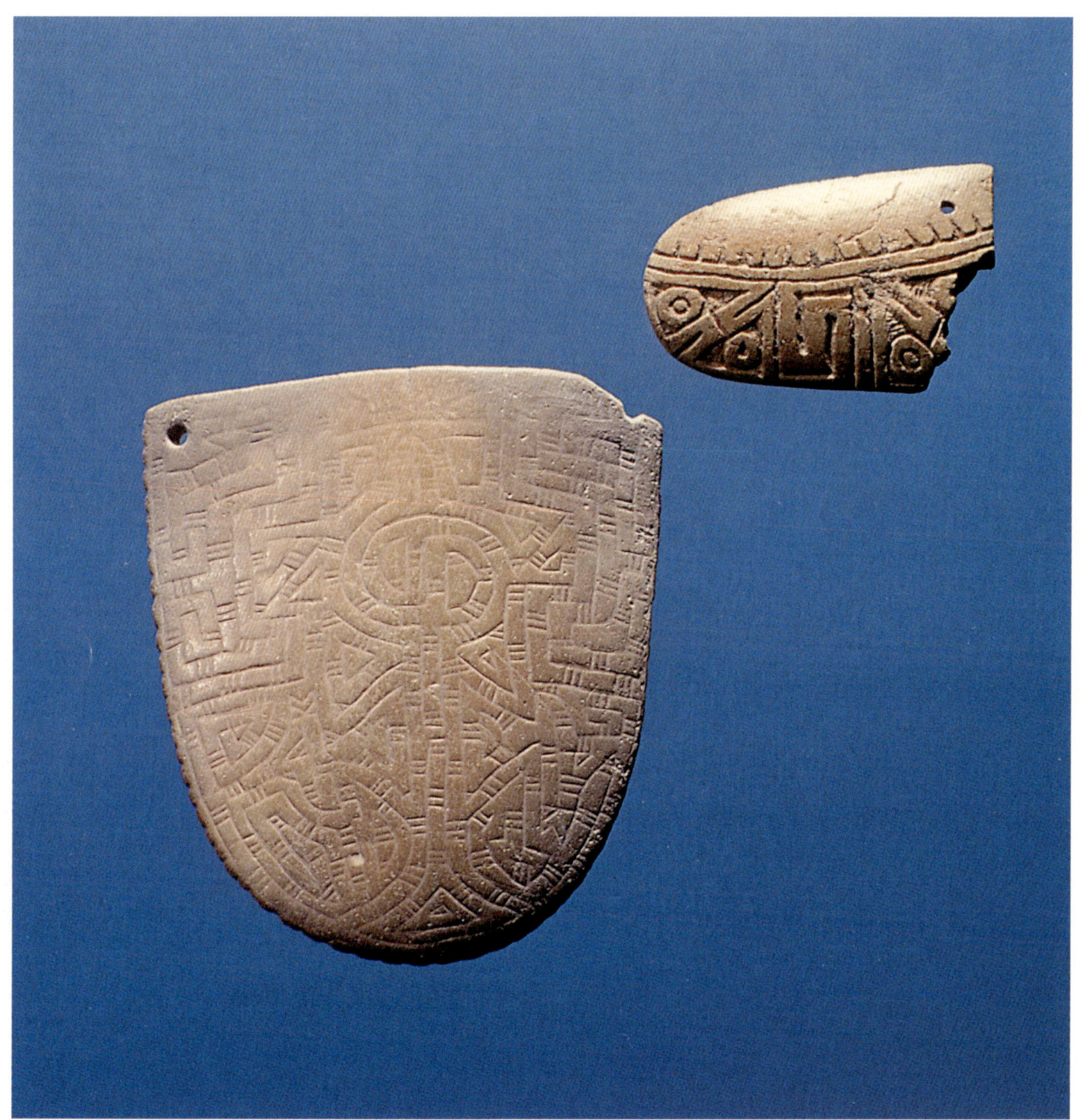

45. Two decorated gorgets. Tick Island, Volusia County (8-Vo-24). Date unknown. Marine shell, 7.5 cm long x 6.4 cm wide x 0.5 cm thick (object on left). Private collection.

47. (right) Shell carving of a bird eating a dead fish (?). Citrus County. Date unknown. Marine shell, 3.9 cm high x 12.9 cm long x 1.9 cm wide. National Museum of the American Indian, New York City, no. 17/6300. Object was purchased by the museum in the 1920s.

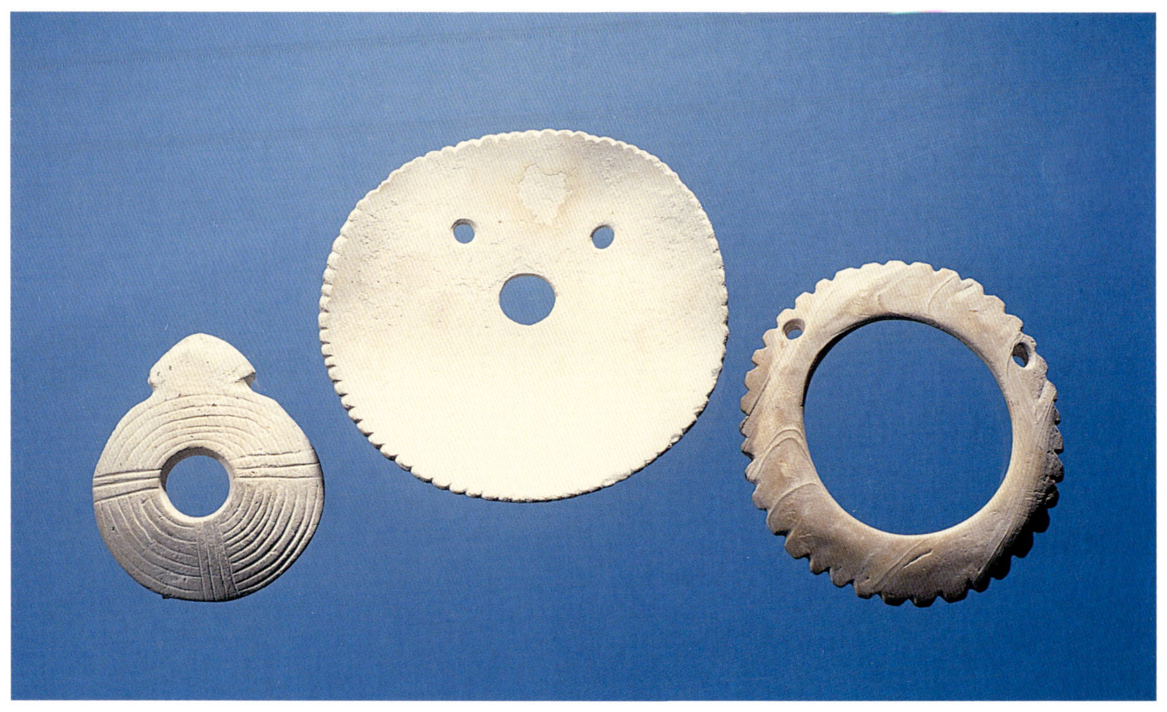

46. Three gorgets. Tick Island, Volusia County (8-Vo-24). Date unknown, possibly ca. A.D. 600–800. Marine shell, 9.1 cm diameter (middle object). Private collection.

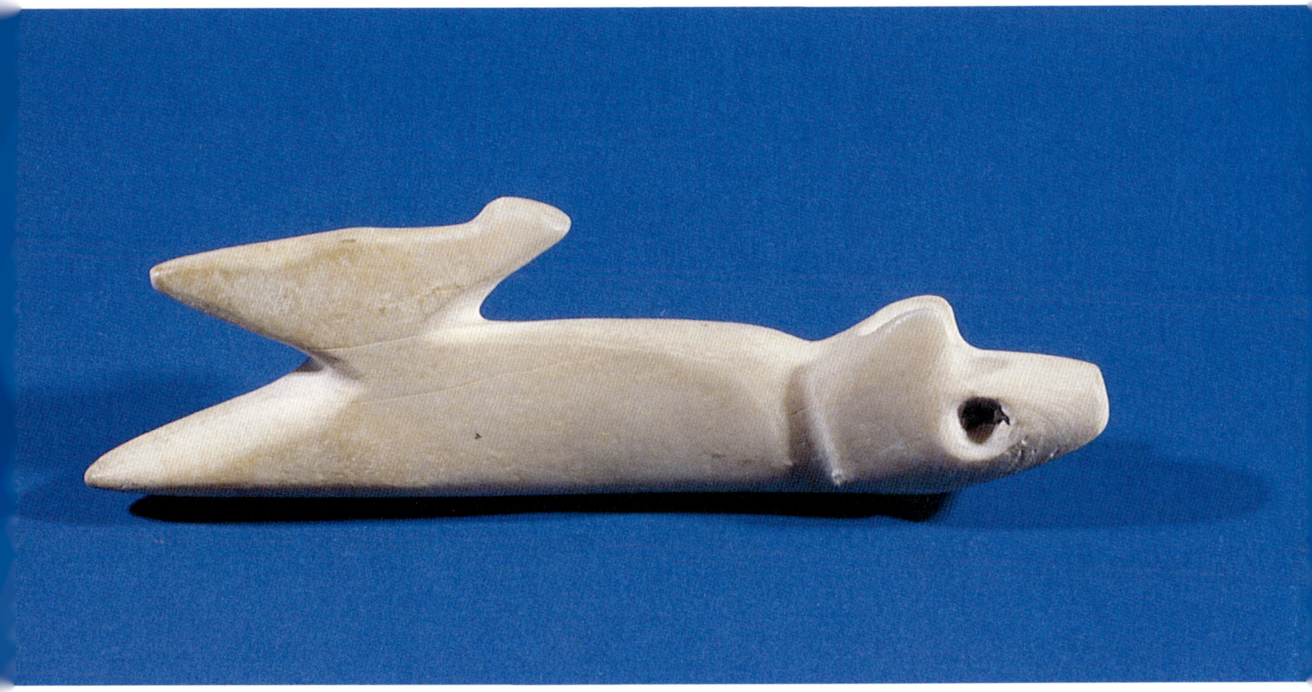

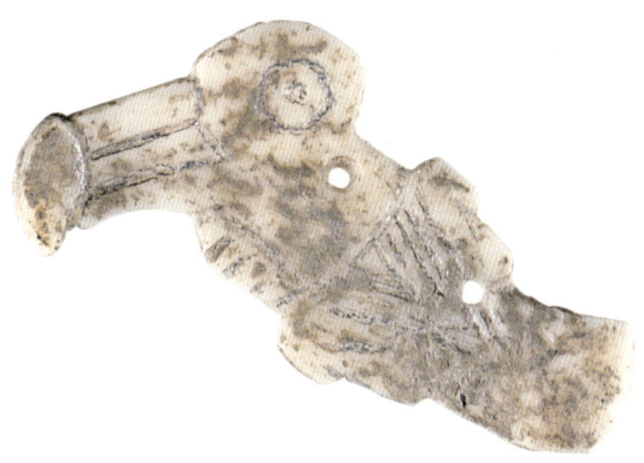

48. Carved pendant. Coleman site, Dade County (8-Da-141), a black dirt midden. Date unknown; possibly a "Buzzard Cult" effigy from about A.D. 1500. Marine shell, 1.7 cm high x 4.1 cm long by 0.3 cm thick. Historical Museum of Southern Florida, Miami, no. HASF 1992.79.2. Photograph by Joe Davis.

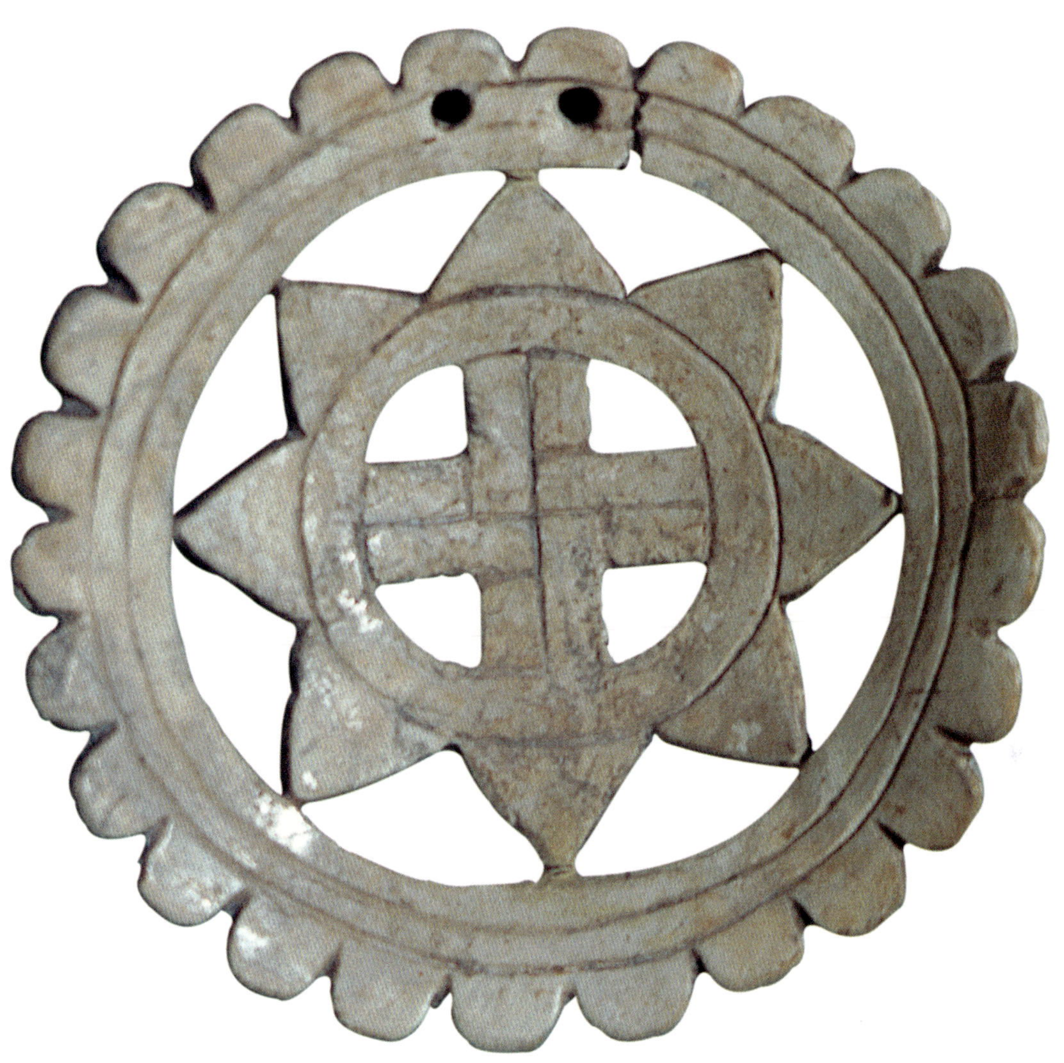

49. Gorget. Kaufmann Island, Lake Kerr, Marion County. Probably Late Mississippian, ca. A.D. 1350–1500. Marine shell, 12.8 cm diameter. Fort Caroline National Memorial, Jacksonville, no. 173-62.

51. Gorget with spider motif. Found in sandbar at Cedar Key, Levy County. Probably Late Mississippian, ca. A.D. 1350–1500. Marine shell, 4.3 cm high x 5.0 cm wide. Private collection.

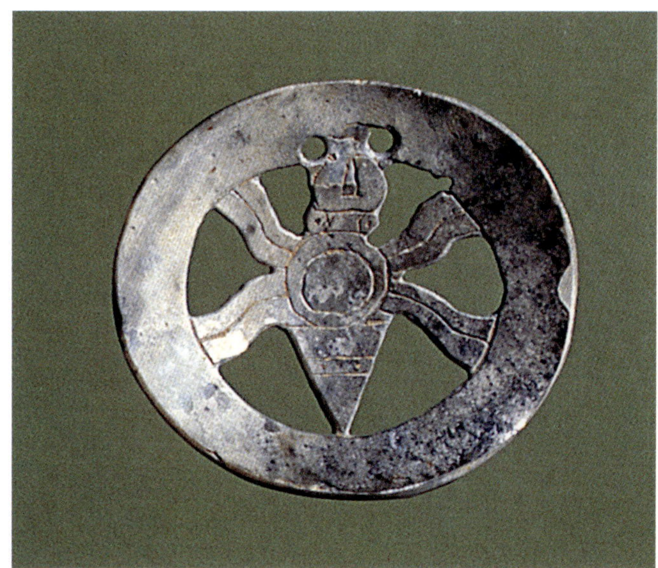

50. Gorget with cross. Key Marco, Collier County (8-Cr-49). Mississippian, ca. A.D. 1200–1500. Marine shell, 12.2 cm diameter. University Museum, Philadelphia, no. 40891.

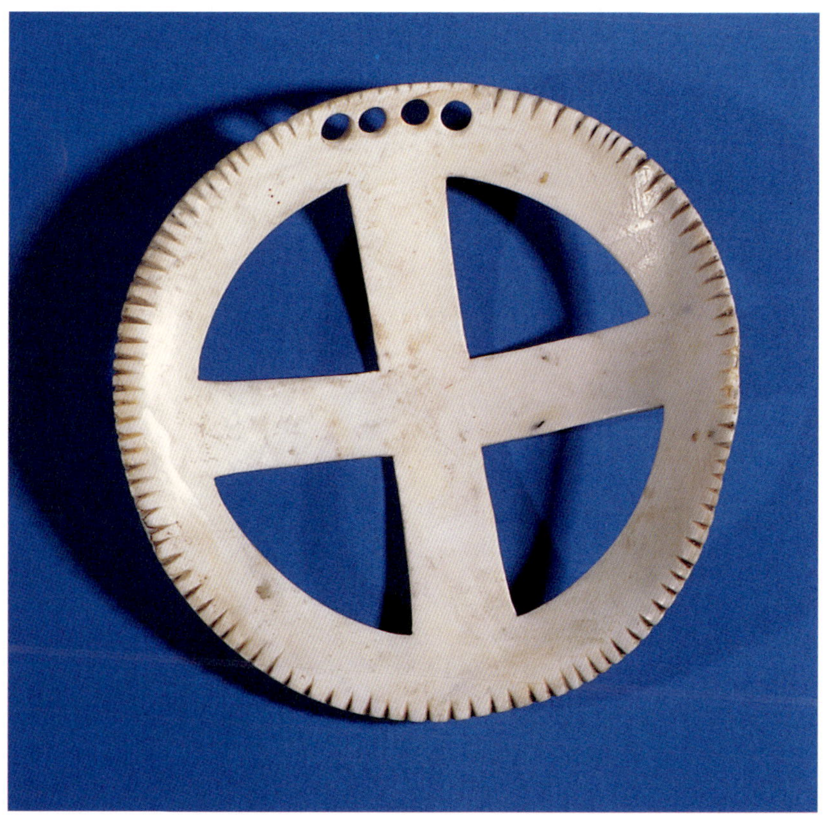

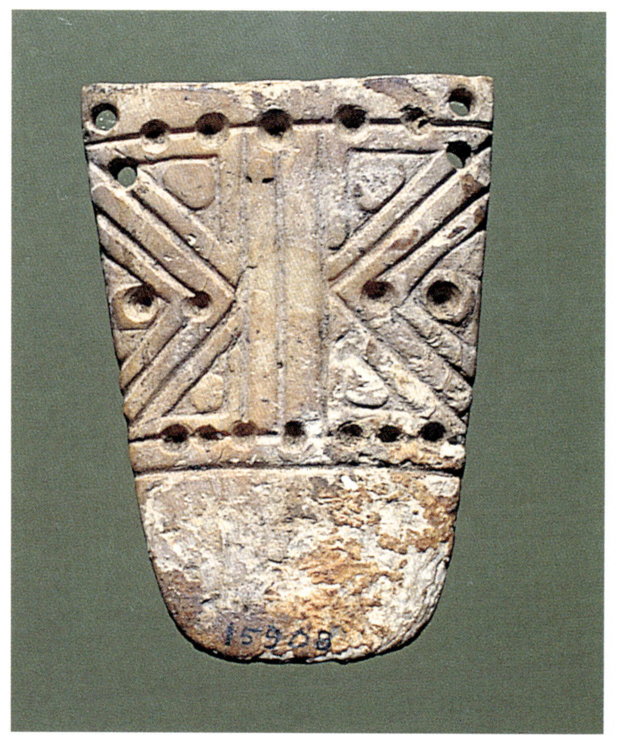

52. (right) Gorget with geometric motif. From a mound at Lake Jessup, Seminole County, collected by F. W. Bruce, Arlington, Florida. Probably Mississippian, ca. A.D. 1200–1500. Marine shell, 7.2 cm long x 5.0 cm wide. Florida Museum of Natural History, Gainesville, no. 1023. Received in 1921.

53. (below) "Fish" ornament. Alachua County, found by Judge James Bell in 1880. Date unknown. Marine shell, 10.0 cm long x 4.0 cm wide x 0.3 cm thick. Smithsonian Institution, Washington, D.C., no. A043173.

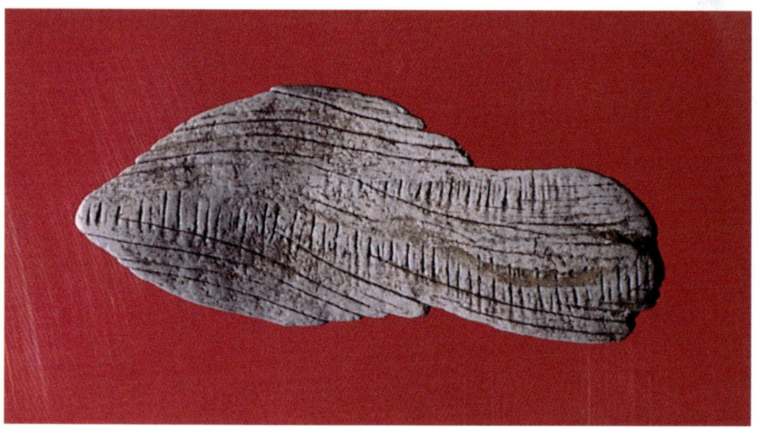

54. (facing page) Clamshell painted with human figure. Key Marco, Collier County (8-Cr-49). Date unknown, possibly Late Prehistoric. Marine shell, 9.0 cm long x 5.0 cm wide x 1.0 cm thick. University Museum, Philadelphia, no. 40796.

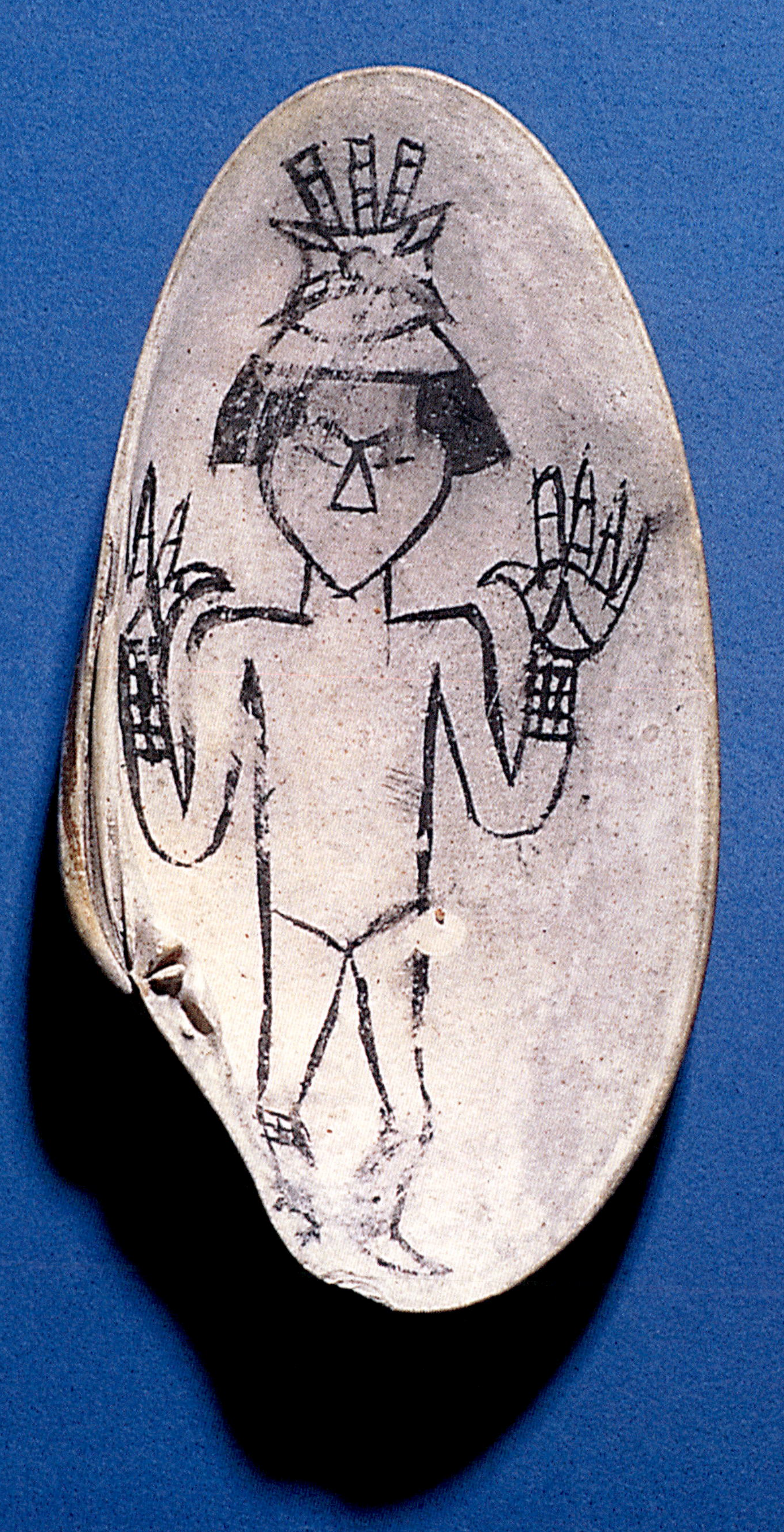

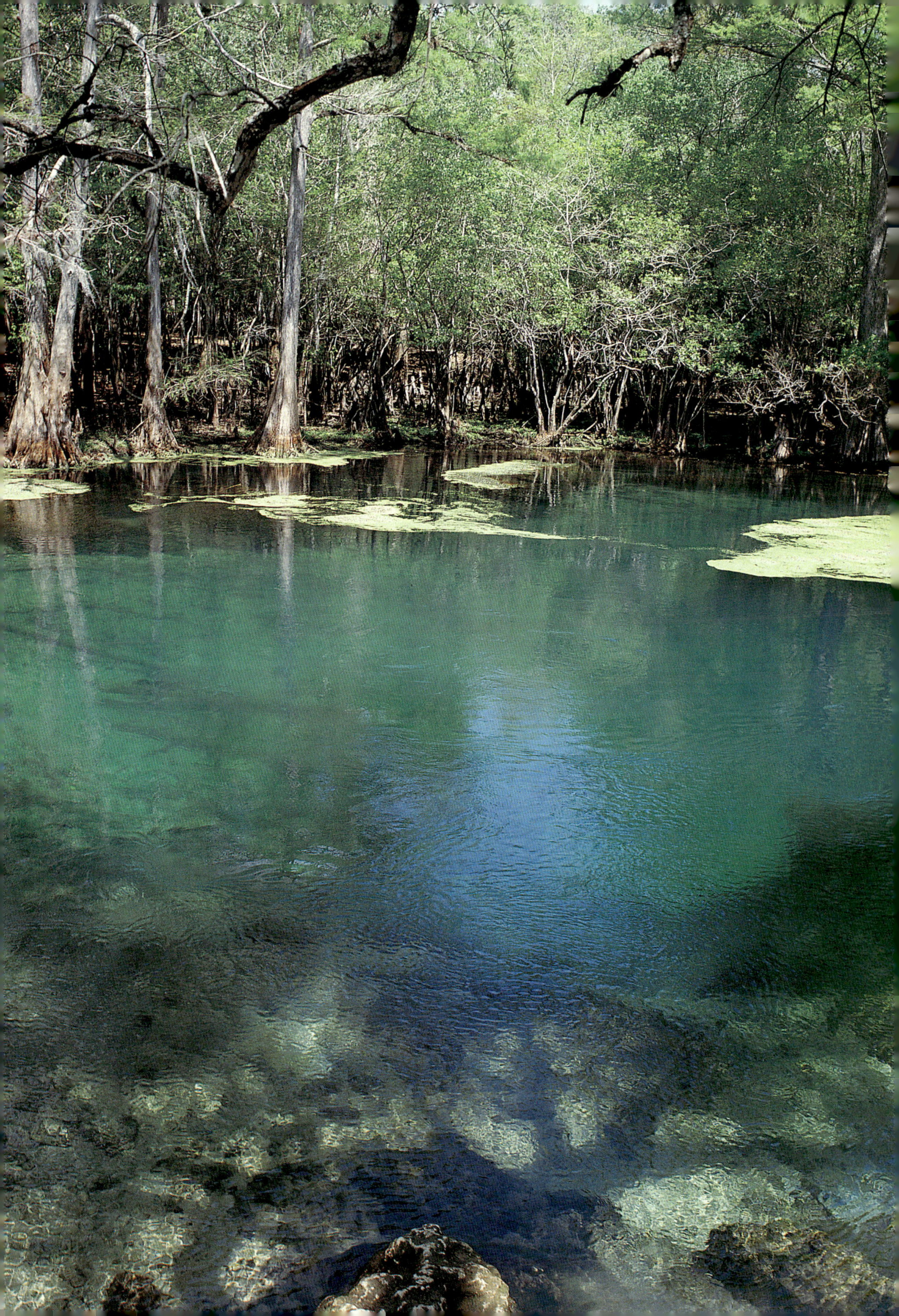

STONE

THE STONE OBJECTS shown in plates 55 through 61 are made of raw materials not native to Florida. The style of the stone pendant or plummet in plate 55 closely resembles other examples from Florida that date to the Deptford culture of 500 B.C. (Brose et al. 1985, 86, plate 68). Similar objects were fashioned using marine shell.

Bannerstones similar to the one in plate 56 are found at Late Archaic sites dating from 3000 to 1000 B.C. throughout the Midwest and Eastern Woodlands. The specimen in plate 56 was probably a trade item.

Stone pipes made their appearance in the Woodland period (called Deptford in Florida) at least by 400 B.C. and underwent general stylistic changes through time. There is such great creative diversity that it almost seems as if pipe makers were trying to outdo one another (for examples, see Fundaburk and Foreman 1957, plates 77–80, 99–106). The pipes in plates 57 and 58 resemble those from the Mississippian period dating after A.D. 1000. The pipe in plate 59 is made of micaceous brown steatite. It was recovered in 1876 by W. E. D. Scott, who excavated an Indian Mound near Panasoffkee Lake in Sumter County while on an ornithological expedition for the College of New Jersey (now Princeton University). The pipe is incised with a conventionalized animal design, apparently a raptorial bird, and is tentatively assigned to the Swift Creek or early Weeden Island period (Baird 1988, 51).

Plate 60 is a stone (steatite) discoidal carved with the hand-eye motif typical of the Mississippian period.

The bird effigy pendant in plate 61 was made of a light tan stone that was polished and incised. It has drill holes on the neck for mounting. A similar specimen made of shell came from the Spiro site in Oklahoma (Brose et al. 1985, 144, plate 104).

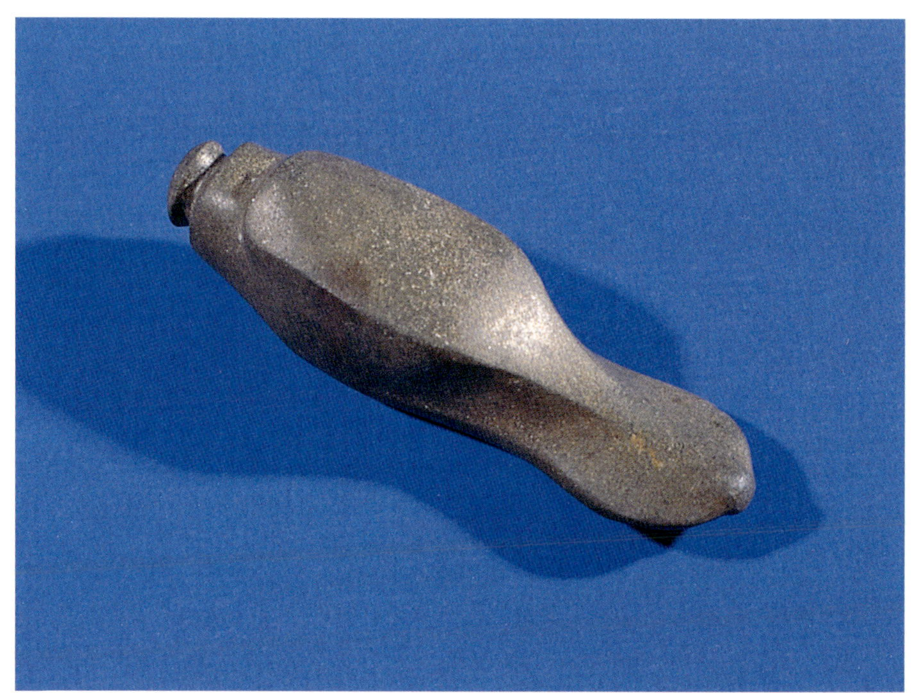

55. (above) Duck-head pendant. Cedar Key, Levy County; from the William L. Bryant Collection. Probably Hopewell (Middle Woodland), 100 B.C.–A.D. 400. Stone, 2.7 cm high x 8.5 cm long x 2.4 cm wide. National Museum of the American Indian, New York City, no. 10-4273.

56. (facing page) Bannerstone. Twelve miles west of Wauchula, Hardee County, collected by A. C. Schenck, H. M. Alexander, and O. E. Offett. Late Archaic, ca. 3000–1000 B.C. Stone, 14.2 cm diameter x 0.5–1.0 cm thick. Smithsonian Institution, Washington, D.C., no. A317061-0. Acquired by the museum on October 12, 1921.

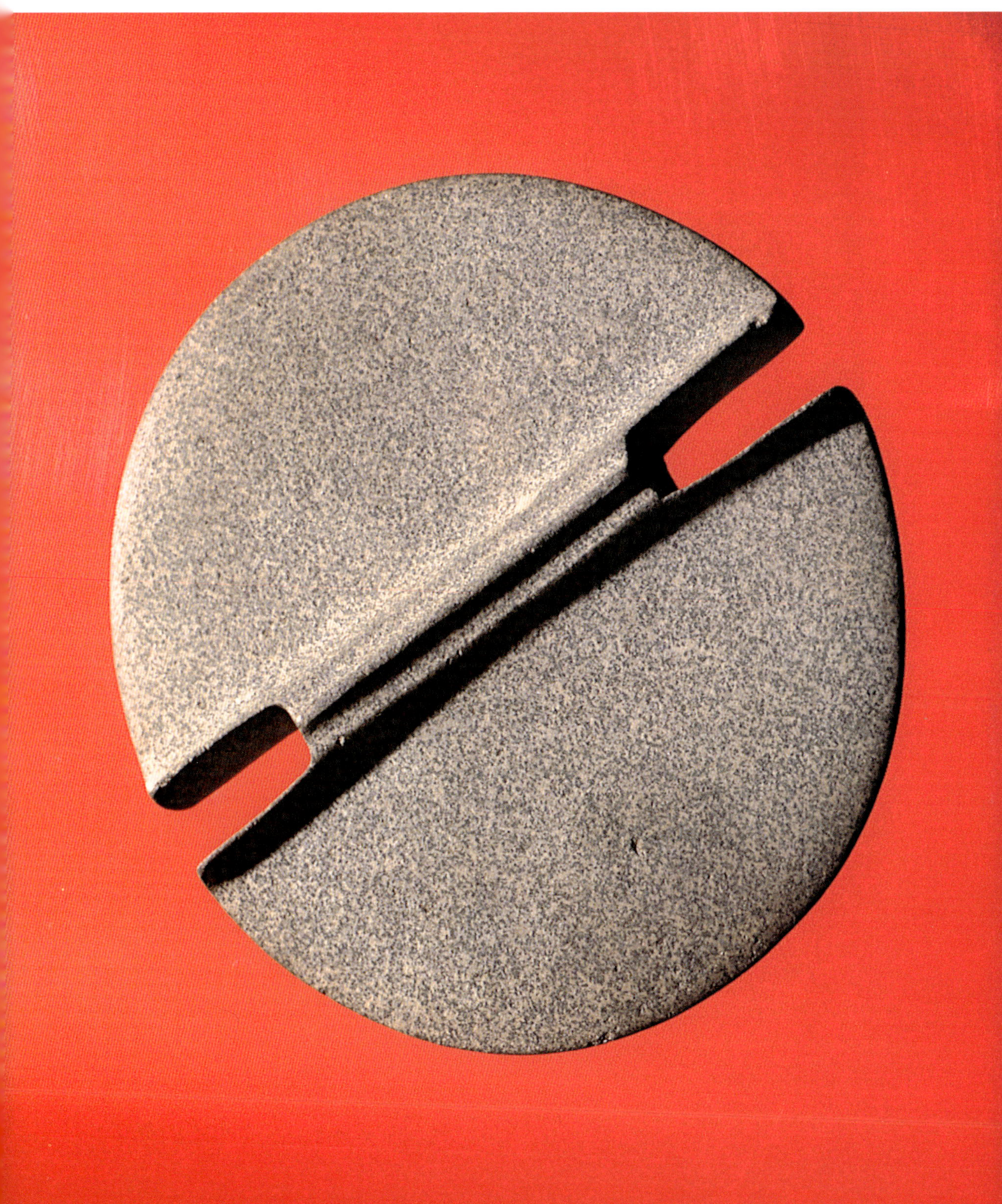

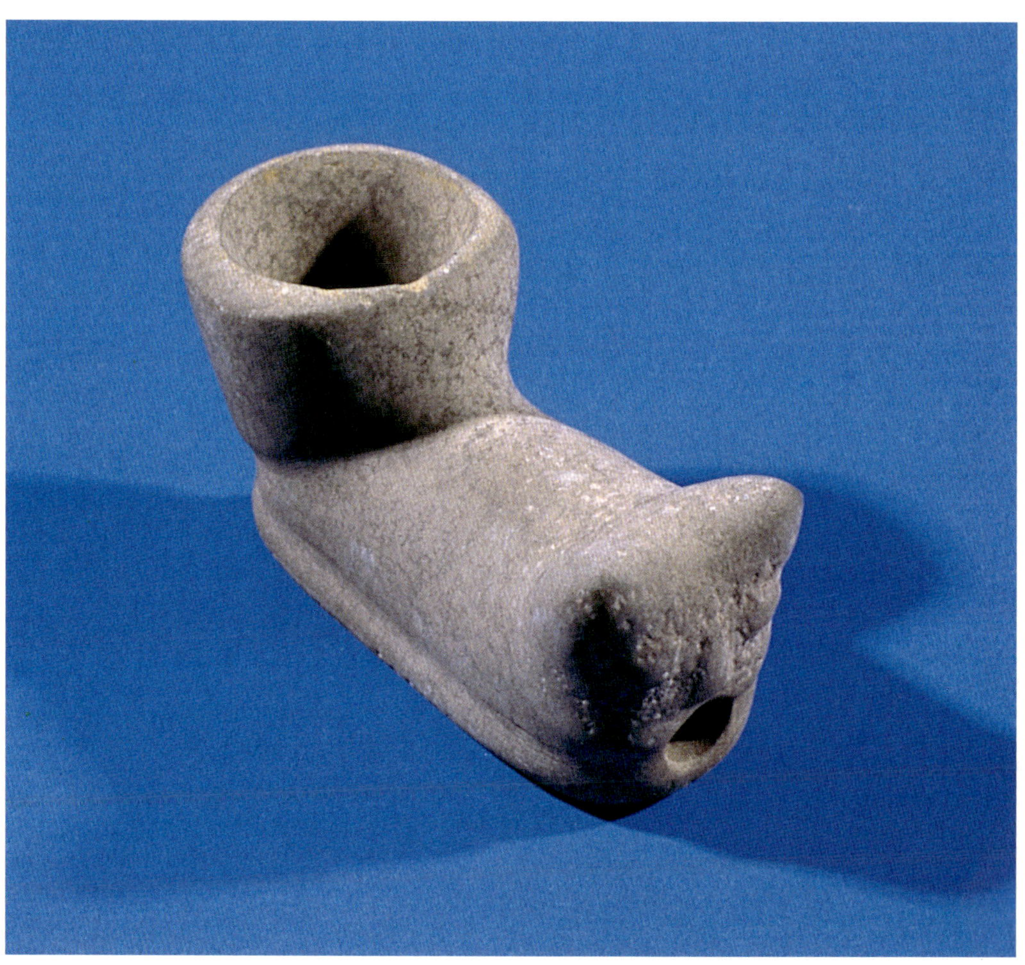

57. (above) Pipe with human face. Alachua County. Probably Mississippian period, after A.D. 1000. Stone, 5.5 cm high x 9.4 cm long x 4.2 cm wide. National Museum of the American Indian, New York City, no. 4-905. Purchased by the museum in 1915.

58. (facing page, top) Bird effigy pipe. Southwest Florida Coast. Probably Mississippian period. Stone, 3.0 cm high x 7.5 cm long x 2.5 cm wide. University Museum, Philadelphia, no. 5929. Gift of Colonel James Willcox, 1890.

59. (facing page, bottom) Elbow pipe with zoomorphic design. Panasoffkee Lake, Sumter County. Probably Swift Creek or Weeden period, A.D. 300–800. Stone (micaceous brown steatite), 10.8 cm high x 14.0 cm long x 6.2 cm across the bowl. Princeton University, no. PU 7223. Photograph by Donald Baird.

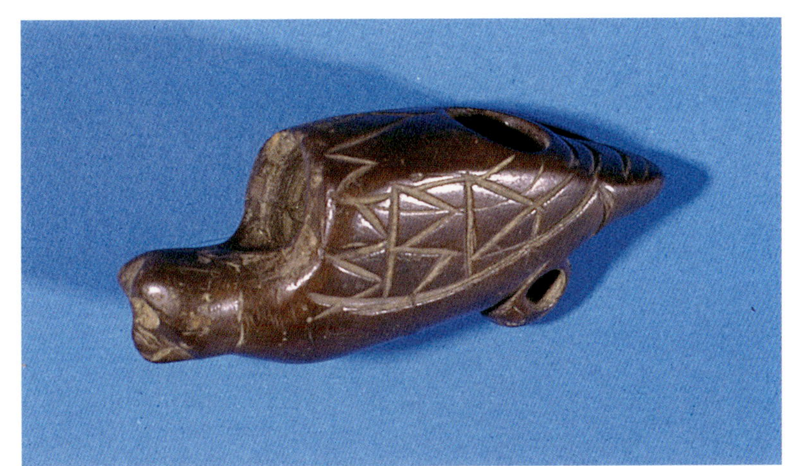

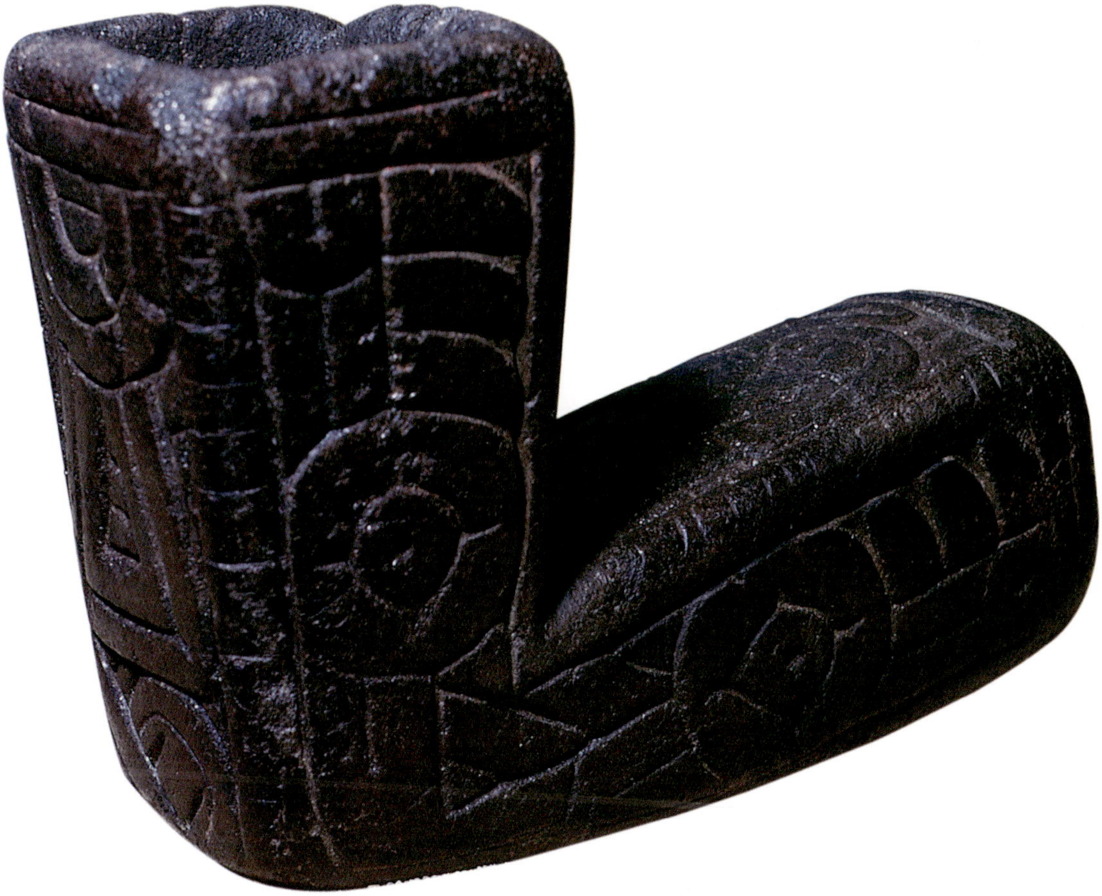

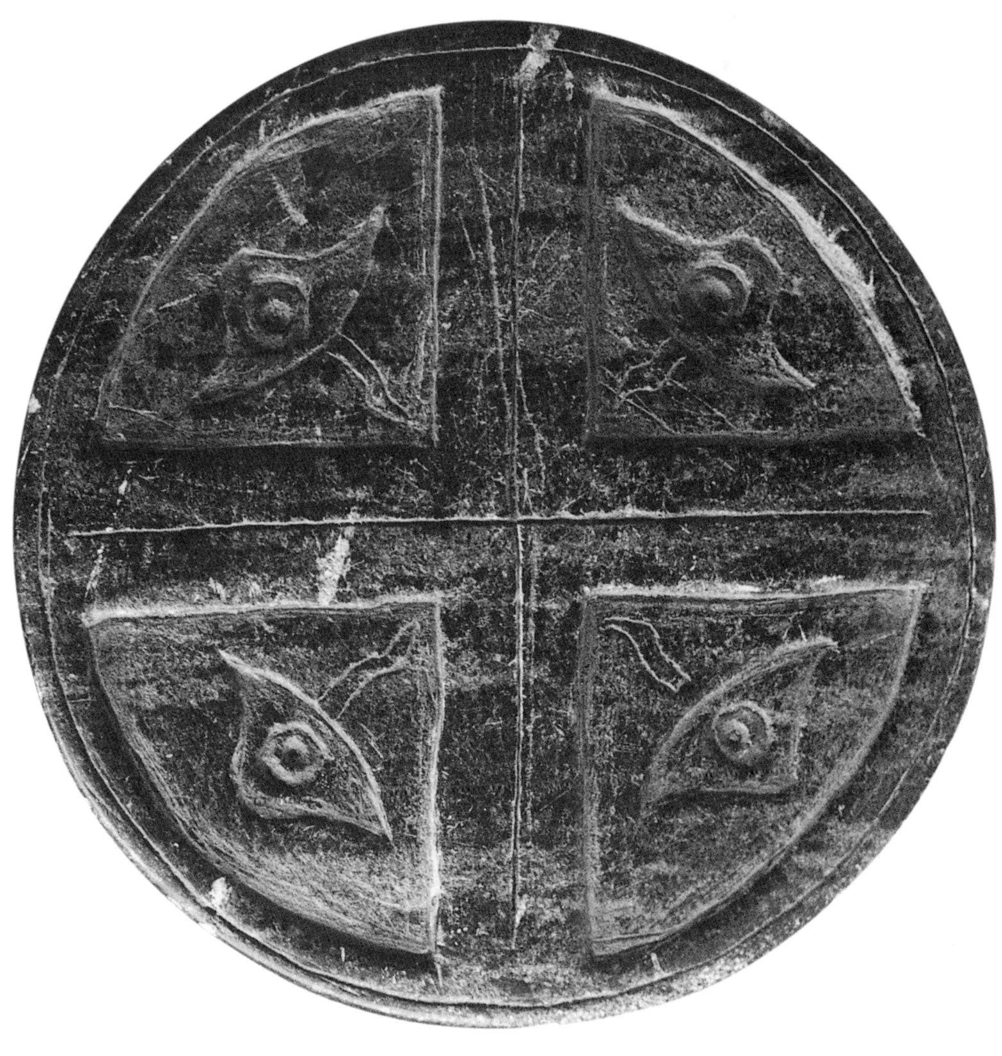

60. (above and facing page, top) Discoidal with hand-eye motif. Source unknown. Mississippian, A.D. 1200–1500. Stone, 11.9 cm diameter. Jacksonvile Museum of History and Science, no. 77-76-2. Donated in 1977 by Mr. and Mrs. Bruce Greene, Naples, Florida.

61. (facing page, bottom) Bird effigy pendant or amulet. Okaloosa County. Mississippian, ca. A.D. 1200. Stone, 6.9 cm long x 5.3 cm wide. Temple Mound Museum, Fort Walton Beach, Florida. Present location unknown; missing and presumed stolen from the museum. Photograph by Roy C. Craven, Jr., 1981.

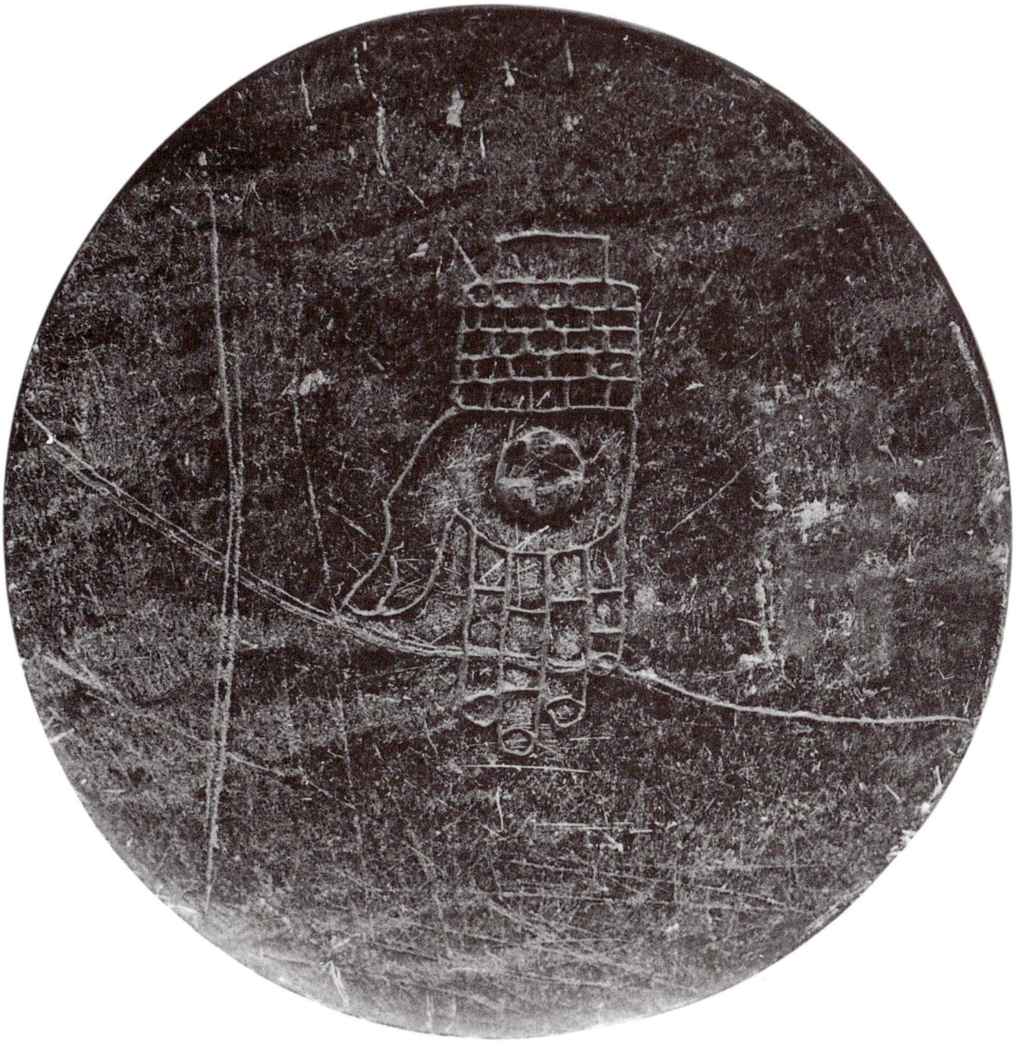

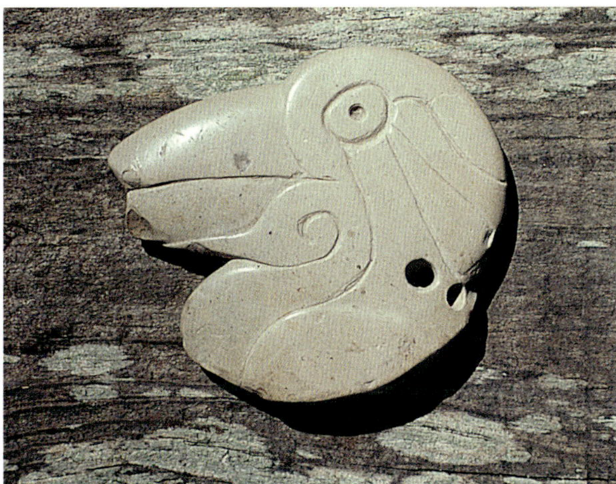

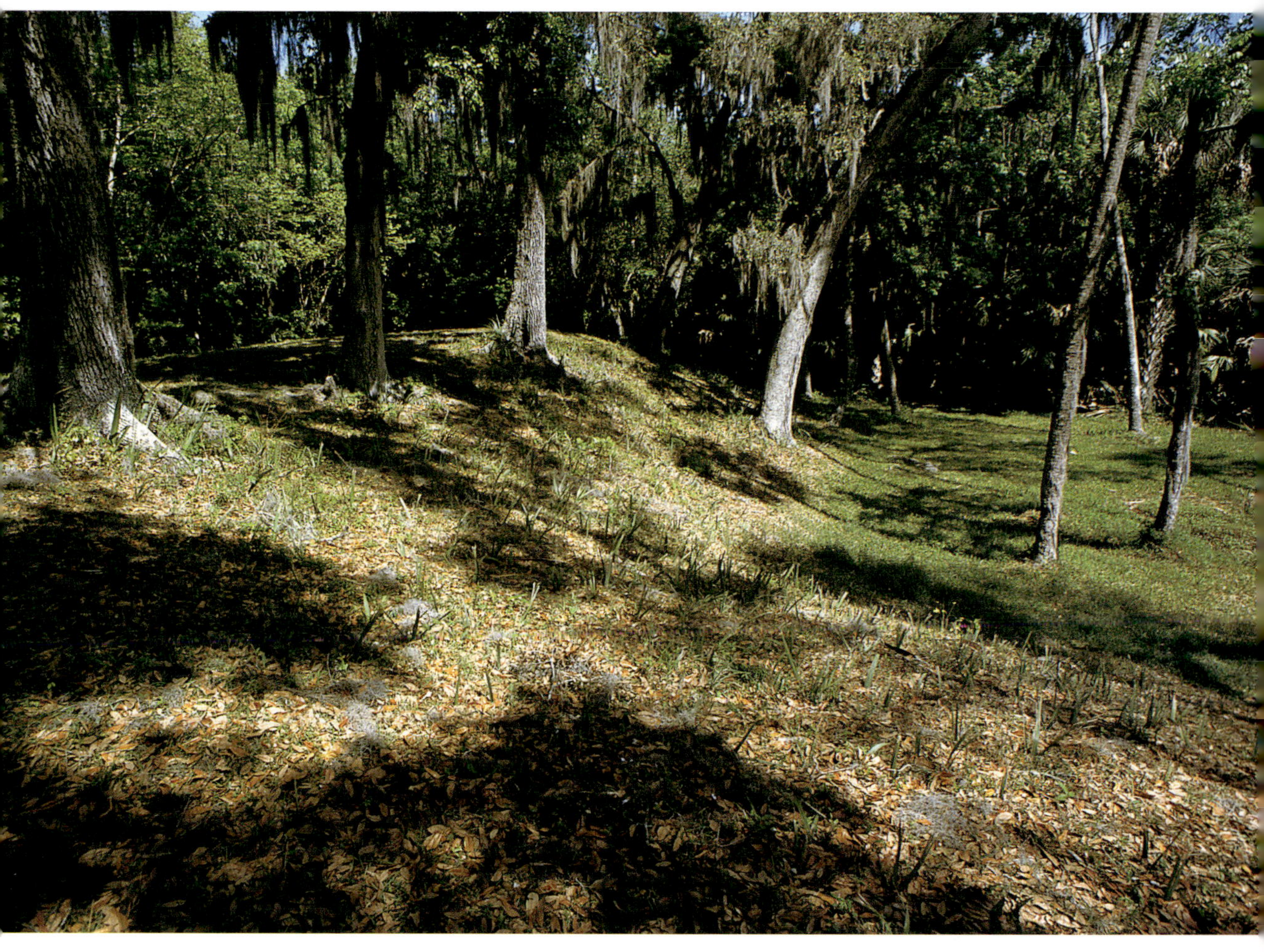

Crystal River mound

CERAMICS

THE FIRST POTTERY in North America was made before 2000 B.C. on the coast of Georgia and the northern St. Johns River region in Florida. For at least one hundred years, Orange Series ceramics have been recognized as the earliest manifestation of this industry in Florida. The name comes from a site on the St. Johns River in Orange County, but, just as commonly, these ceramics are referred to as "fiber-tempered" because fibers were added as temper to the clay before it was fired. The clay is hand molded, and the pots are usually rectangular with flat bases. The oldest pottery is not decorated, but soon pots were incised with designs, some of which resembled those on bone artifacts. Fiber-tempered pottery of the Orange period has been found around nearly the entire perimeter of Florida as well as at some inland sites. By 1000 B.C. fiber temper is replaced by sand temper or chalky (sponge spicule) temper, and hand molding gives way to coiling. Pot surfaces were undecorated for at least 500 years. In South Florida, pottery surfaces remain plain throughout most of Florida's prehistory, but the appearance of check stamping among the Deptford peoples at sites on the Gulf Coast around 500 B.C. marked the beginning of ceramic regionism in the state and also an increase in cultural complexity. Deptford, Swift Creek, Weeden Island, Safety Harbor, and Fort Walton cultures are known not only by their distinctive ceramic vessels and other artifacts but also by the appearance of burial and temple mounds, and their relationships with Hopewellian and Mississippian cultures in Midwestern and Southeastern states.

The Florida aborigines were not skilled pyrotechnologists. Their low-fired vessels broke easily and were discarded into their middens. These pieces, known as sherds, are recovered at most sites. Practically no whole or reconstructable vessels have been found prior to the time when pottery was used as gravegoods. Fortunately, the elaborate ceramic objects that were made especially for burials were usually placed gently in the mounds with the deceased and covered with dirt. Many of these mortuary pieces were "killed" by knocking a hole in the bottom either before or after firing. This practice was thought to release the spirit of the pot so that it could accompany the dead to the hereafter. Although plates 62 through 103 illustrate great diversity within Florida's ceramic industry, they also reveal that, in some cases, culturally specific styles can be recognized.

Pottery remains from archaeological sites in Florida have been studied since the mid-nineteenth century. Many interesting stories, too numerous to recount here, have been written about the sites and about the people who have recovered and devised classification systems for these artifacts.

62. Bowl with complicated stamp. Dixie County. Swift Creek (Hopewell), A.D. 100–300. Ceramic, 21.4 cm high x 24.0 cm diameter. South Florida Museum and Bishop Planetarium, Bradenton, no. SFM A6547(2380).

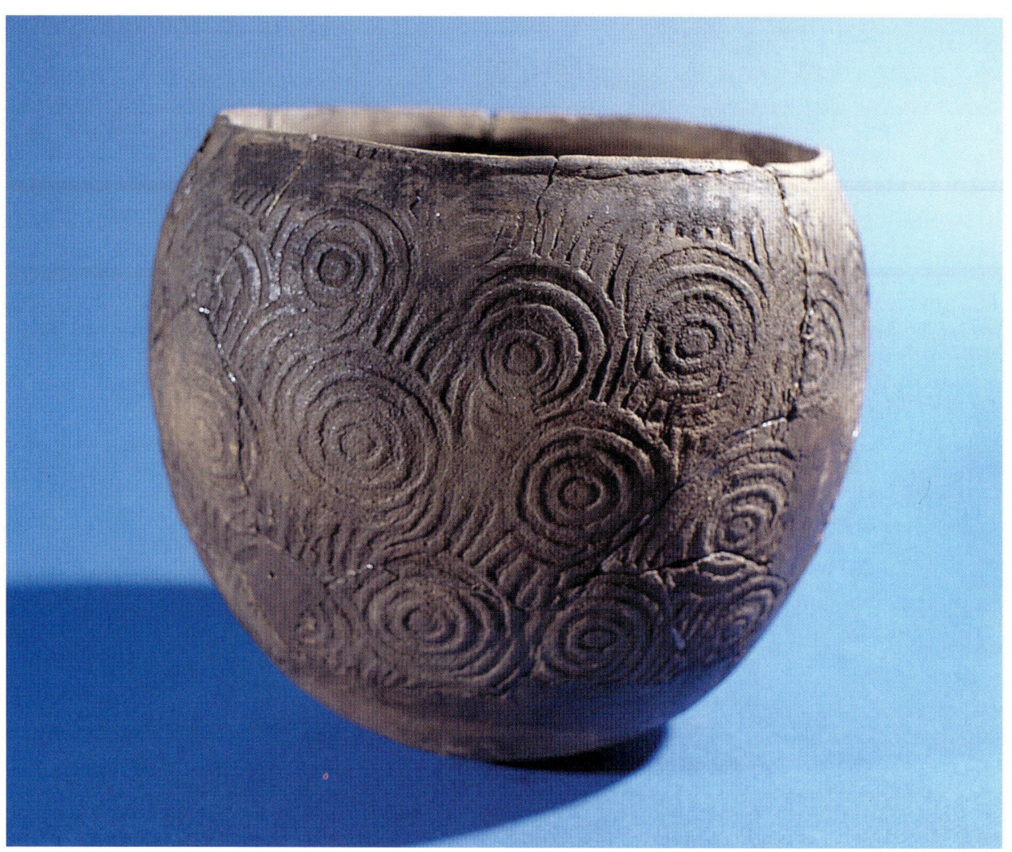

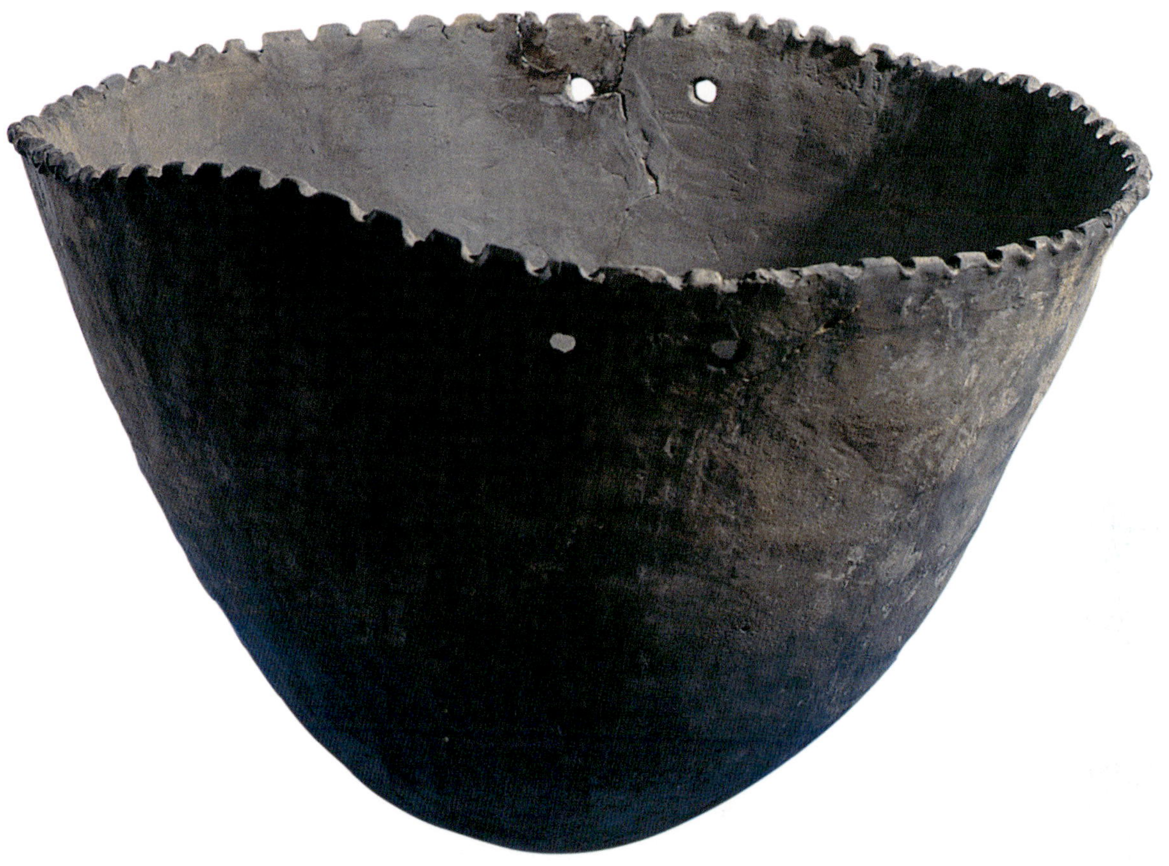

63. Large cooking pot. Dent Mound, Duval County (8-Du-68). St. Johns I (Woodland), ca. 500 B.C.–A.D. 800. Ceramic, 27.5 cm high x 40.5 cm diameter. Jacksonville Museum of Science and History, no. 88.8.

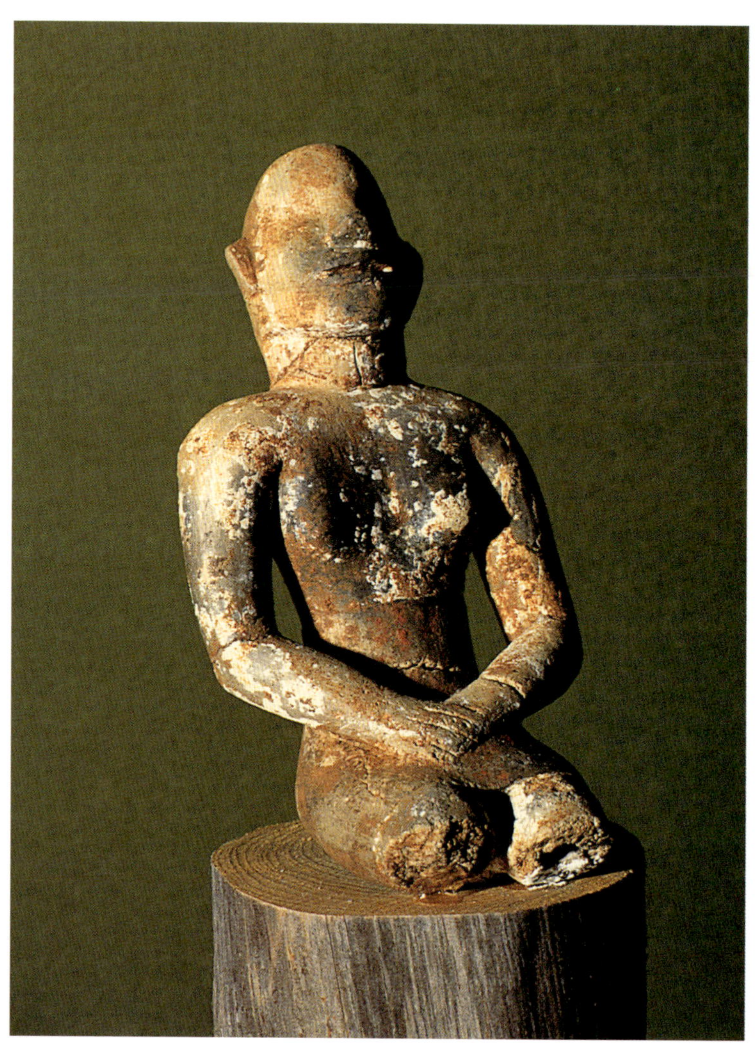

64. Seated human effigy figure. Leon County. Block Stern Mound Burial (8-Le-148). Late Swift Creek (?), ca. A.D. 400. Ceramic, 10.5 cm high x 5.5 cm wide. Florida Bureau of Archaeological Research, Tallahassee, no. 74-189-64.

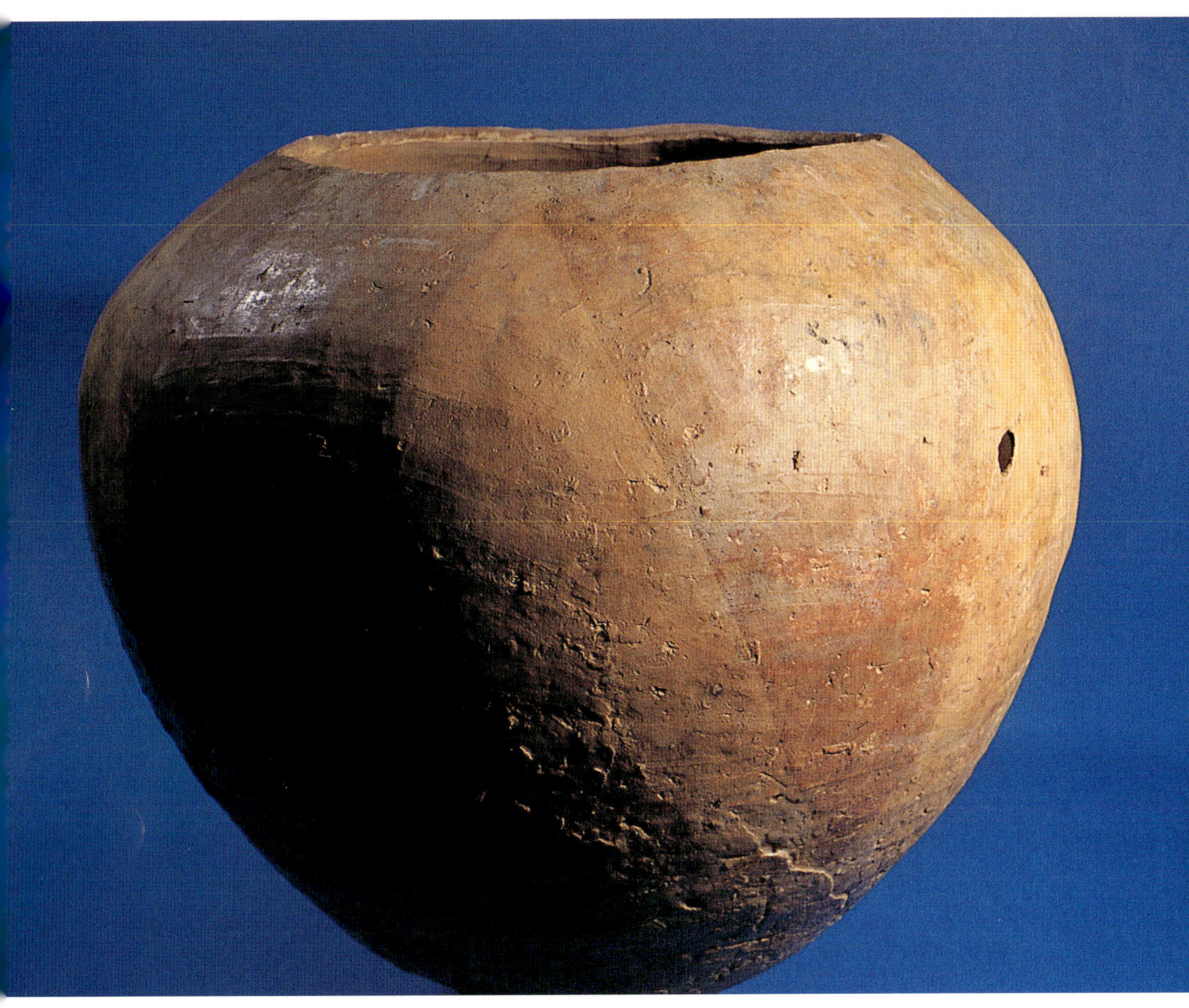

65. Red-on-buff bowl; large triangular motif in a red wash encircles the whole body of the vessel of cream paste. Marion County. St. Johns Ib, ca. A.D. 100–800. Ceramic (Dunns Creek Red?), 32 cm high x 116 cm in circumference. Private collection.

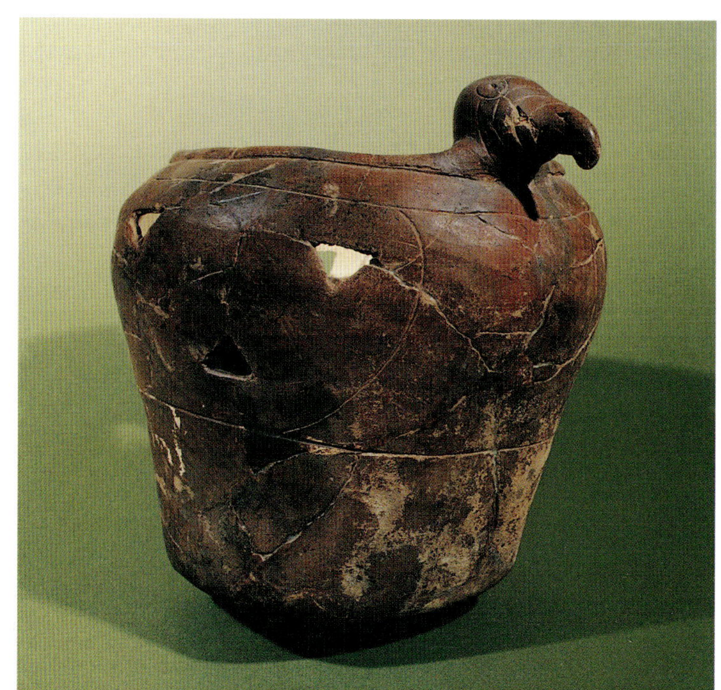

66. Turkey vulture effigy incense burner. McKeithen Site, Columbia County (8-Co-17). Weeden Island, ca. A.D. 250–700. Ceramic, 22 cm high. Florida Museum of Natural History, Gainesville, no. A-20086.

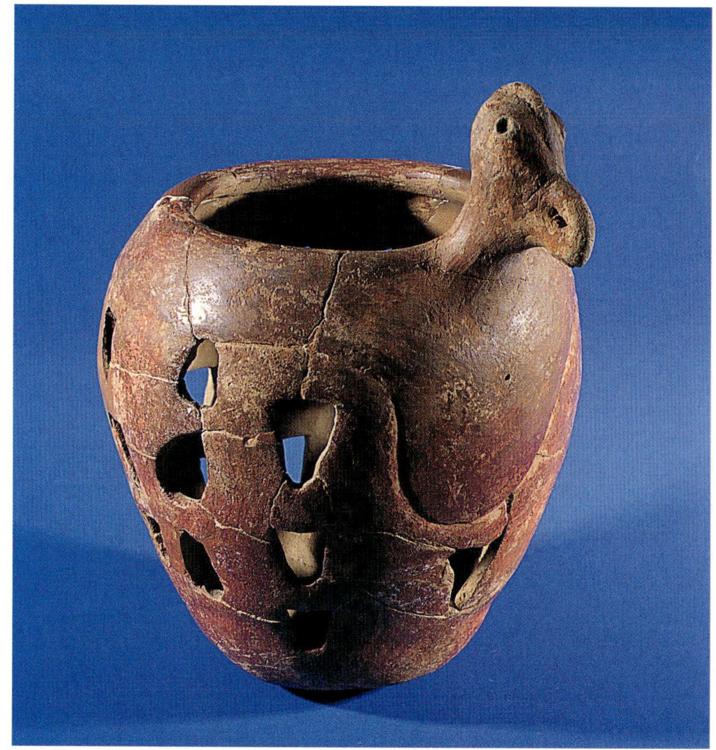

67. Turkey vulture effigy incense burner. Davis Point, St. Andrews Bay, Calhoun Co. (C. B. Moore). Weeden Island, ca. A.D. 250–700. Ceramic, 23.5 cm high x 16.0 cm wide. National Museum of the American Indian, New York City, no. 17-4020.

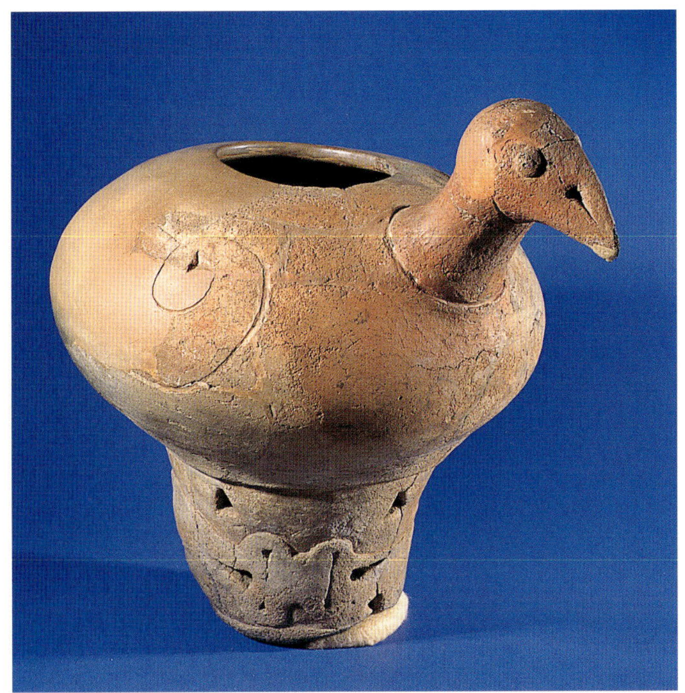

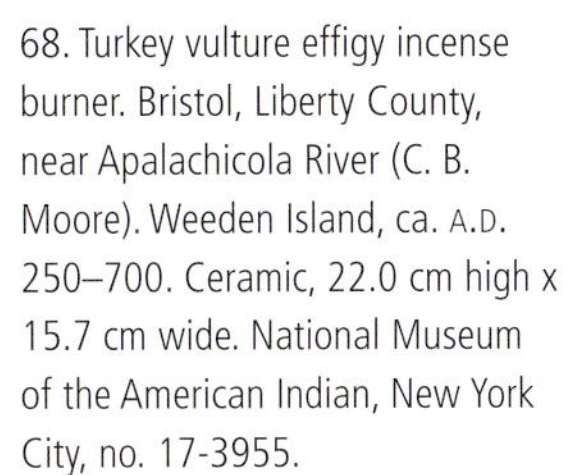

68. Turkey vulture effigy incense burner. Bristol, Liberty County, near Apalachicola River (C. B. Moore). Weeden Island, ca. A.D. 250–700. Ceramic, 22.0 cm high x 15.7 cm wide. National Museum of the American Indian, New York City, no. 17-3955.

69. Bird effigy incense burner. Taylor County near Aucilla River. Weeden Island, ca. A.D. 250–700. Ceramic, 17 cm high x 25 cm wide. Private collection.

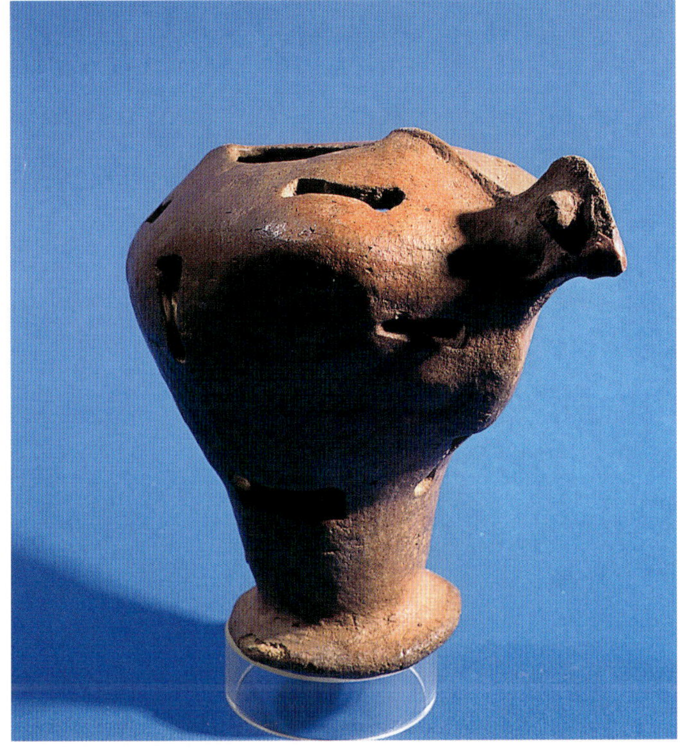

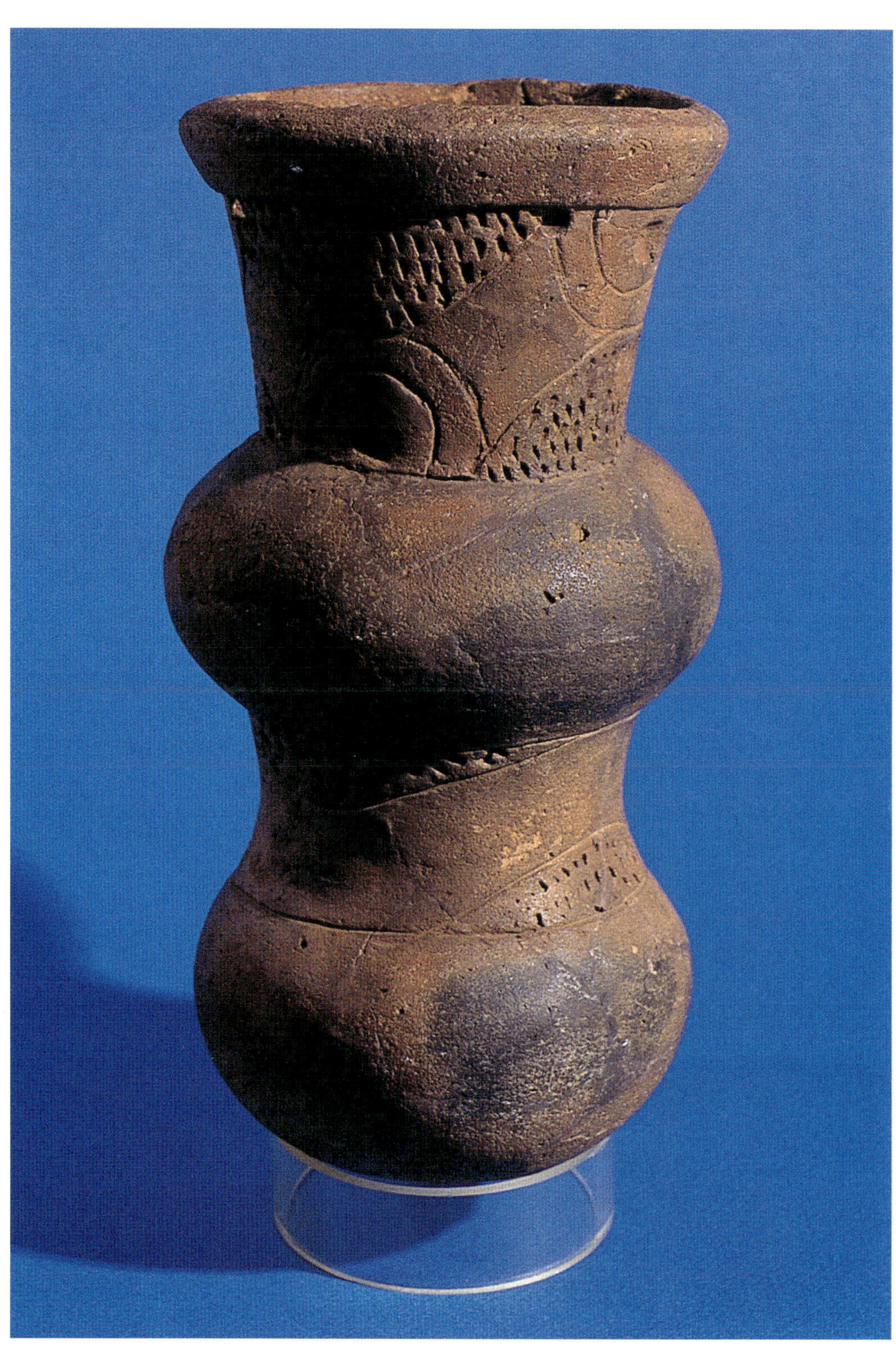

70. (facing page) Double-globed pot. Dent Mound, Duval County (8-Du-68). Weeden Island, ca. A.D. 250–700. Ceramic (Weeden Island Punctate), 22 cm high x 11 cm wide x 37 cm circumference. Jacksonville Museum of Science and History. On loan from the collection of Peter Recourt.

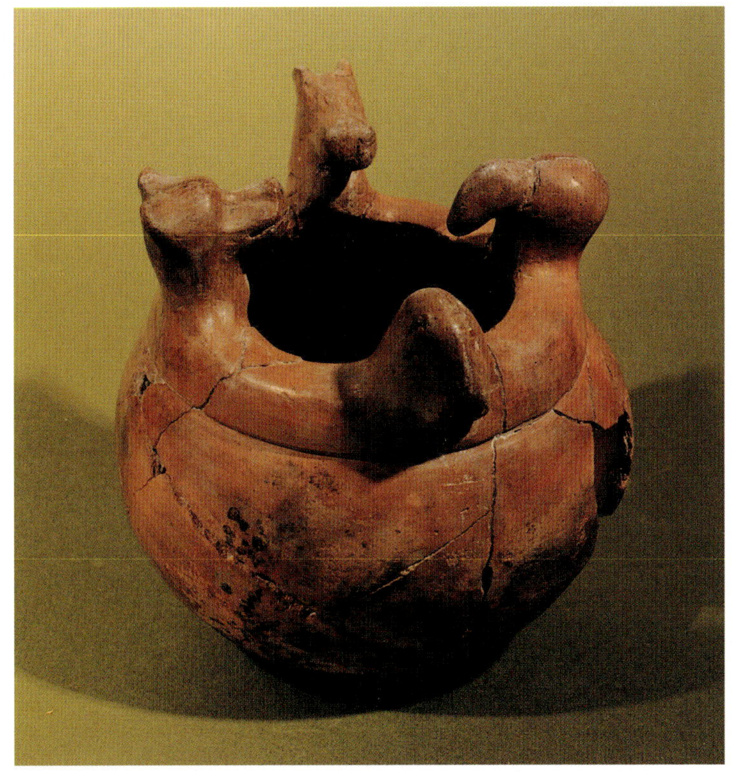

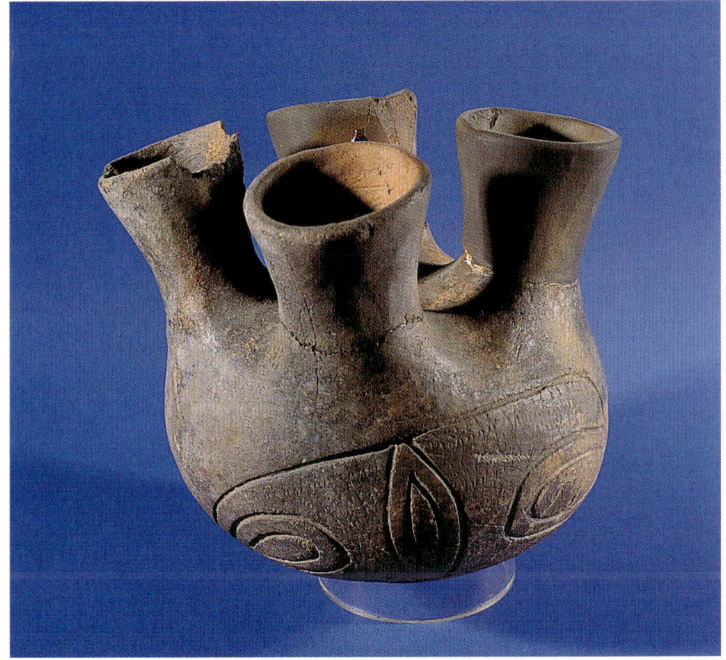

71. (above) Open-necked plain effigy vessel with four heads on rim. McKeithen Site, Columbia County (8-Co-17). Weeden Island, ca. A.D. 250–700. Ceramic, 14 cm high. Florida Museum of Natural History, Gainesville, no. A-10952.

72. (left) Vessel with four spouts. Franklin County near Apalachicola River. Weeden Island (?), ca. A.D. 250–700. Ceramic, 16.0 cm high x 15.9–18.6 cm diameter. National Museum of the American Indian, New York City, no. 17-3413.

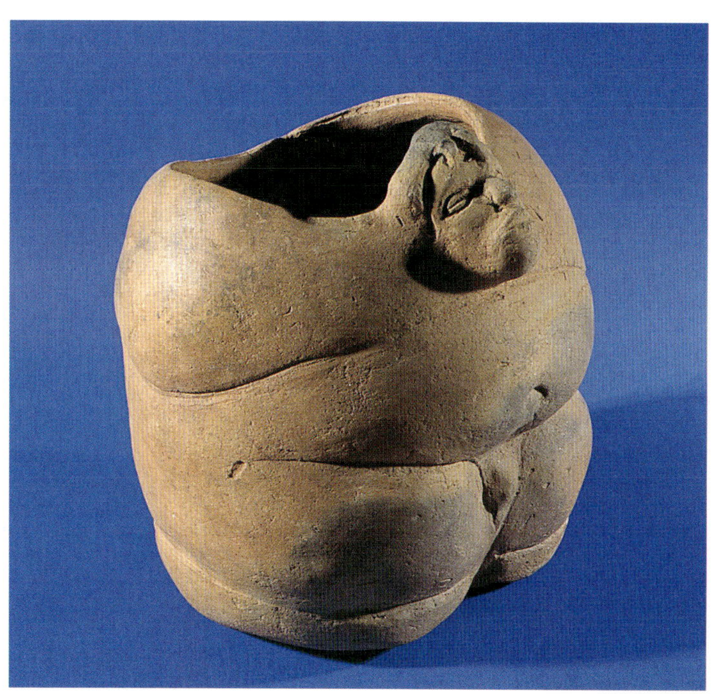

73. (left) Effigy vessel with adorno face. Davis Landing, Bay County (C. B. Moore). Weeden Island, ca. A.D. 250–800. Ceramic, 16.9 cm long x 15.9 cm wide. National Museum of the American Indian, New York City, no. 8-4159.

75. (facing page) Ware effigy urn. Okaloosa County (8-Ok-5); along the shoreline of Santa Rosa Sound adjacent to the city of Mary Esther. Weeden Island, ca. A.D. 250–800. Ceramic, 32.7 cm high x 14.0 cm wide at shoulders. Indian Temple Mound Museum, Fort Walton Beach, Florida, no. 1646.

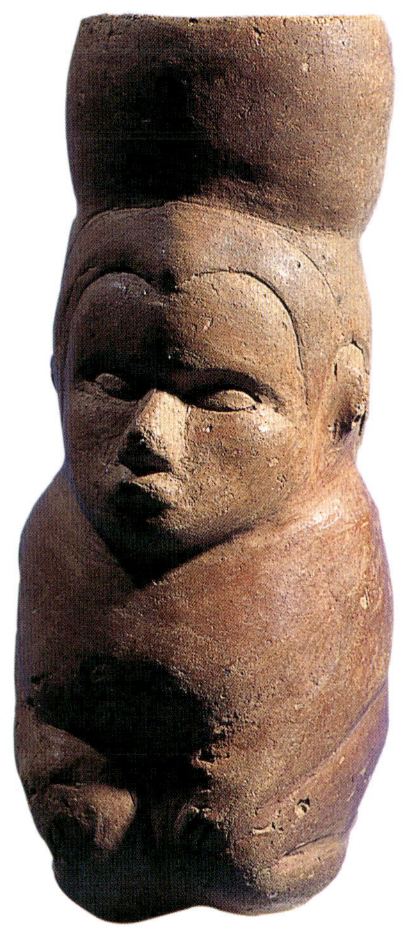

74. Human effigy vase. Mound near Jacksonville. Weeden Island (?), ca. A.D. 250–800. Ceramic, 24 cm high x 10 cm wide. Private collection.

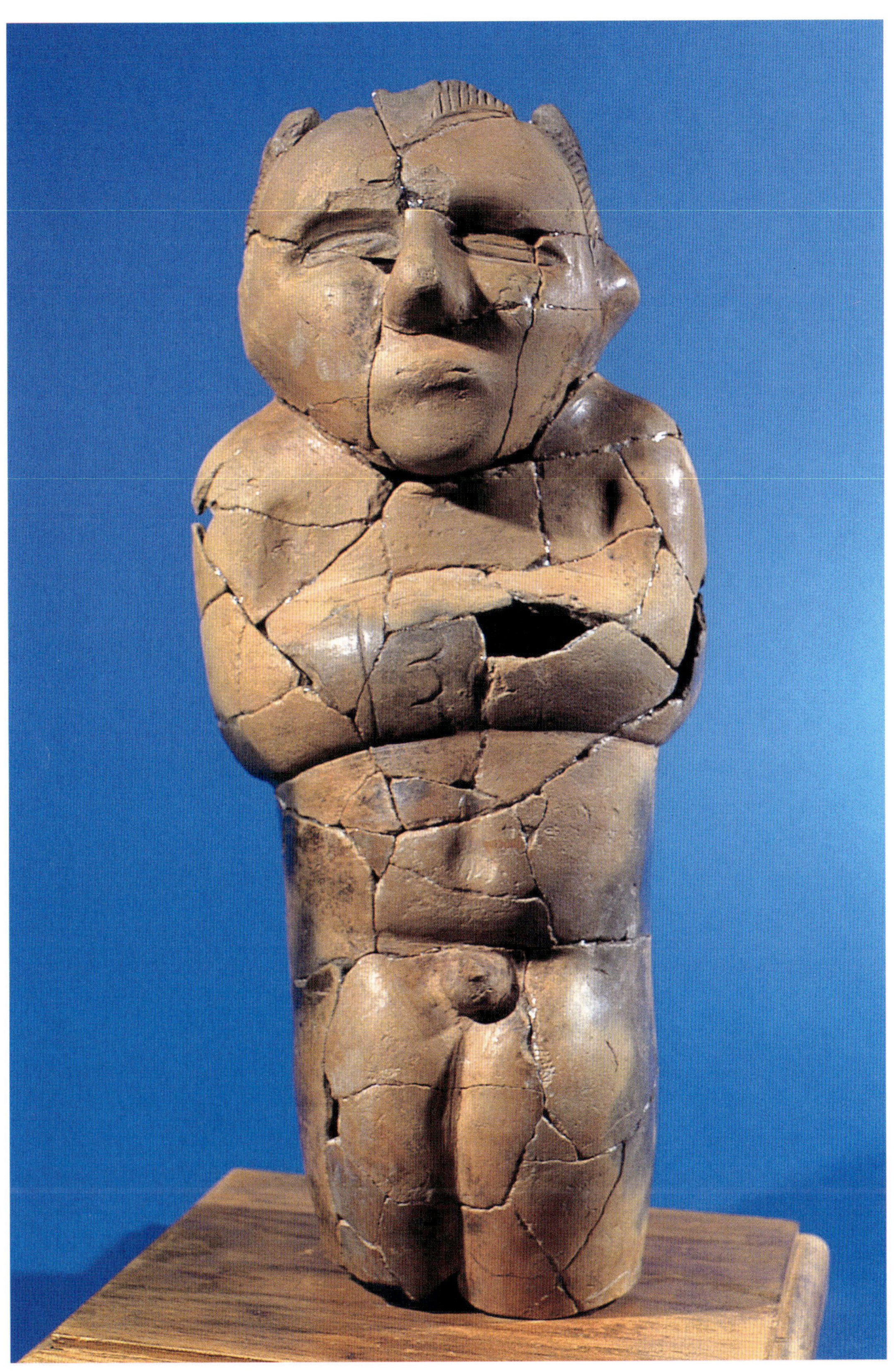

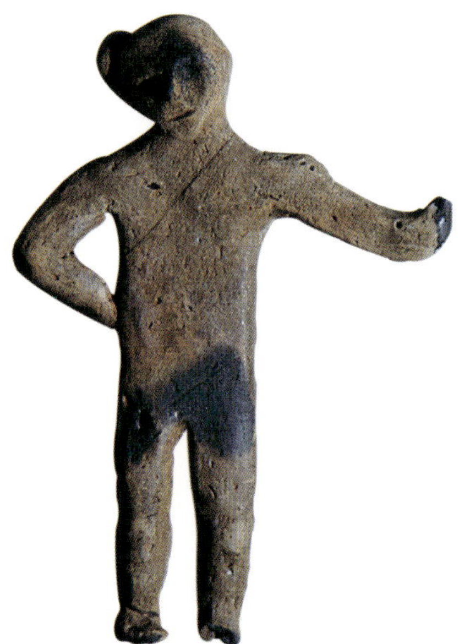

76. Fired-clay human effigy. Kauffman Island, Lake Kerr, Marion County. Date unknown. Ceramic (St. Johns paste), 19.0 cm high, 13.5 at shoulder, 4.0 cm at torso, 2.0 cm thick. Fort Caroline National Memorial, Jacksonville, no. 217-94.

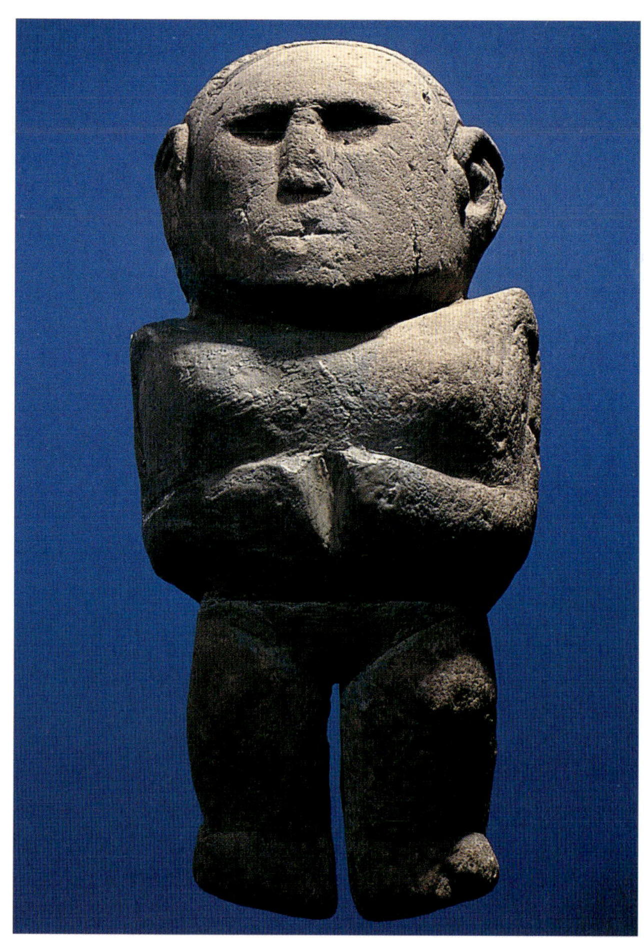

77.Human figure. Tick Island, Volusia County (8-Vo-24). Date unknown. Ceramic, 22 cm high x 10 cm wide x 6 cm deep. Private collection.

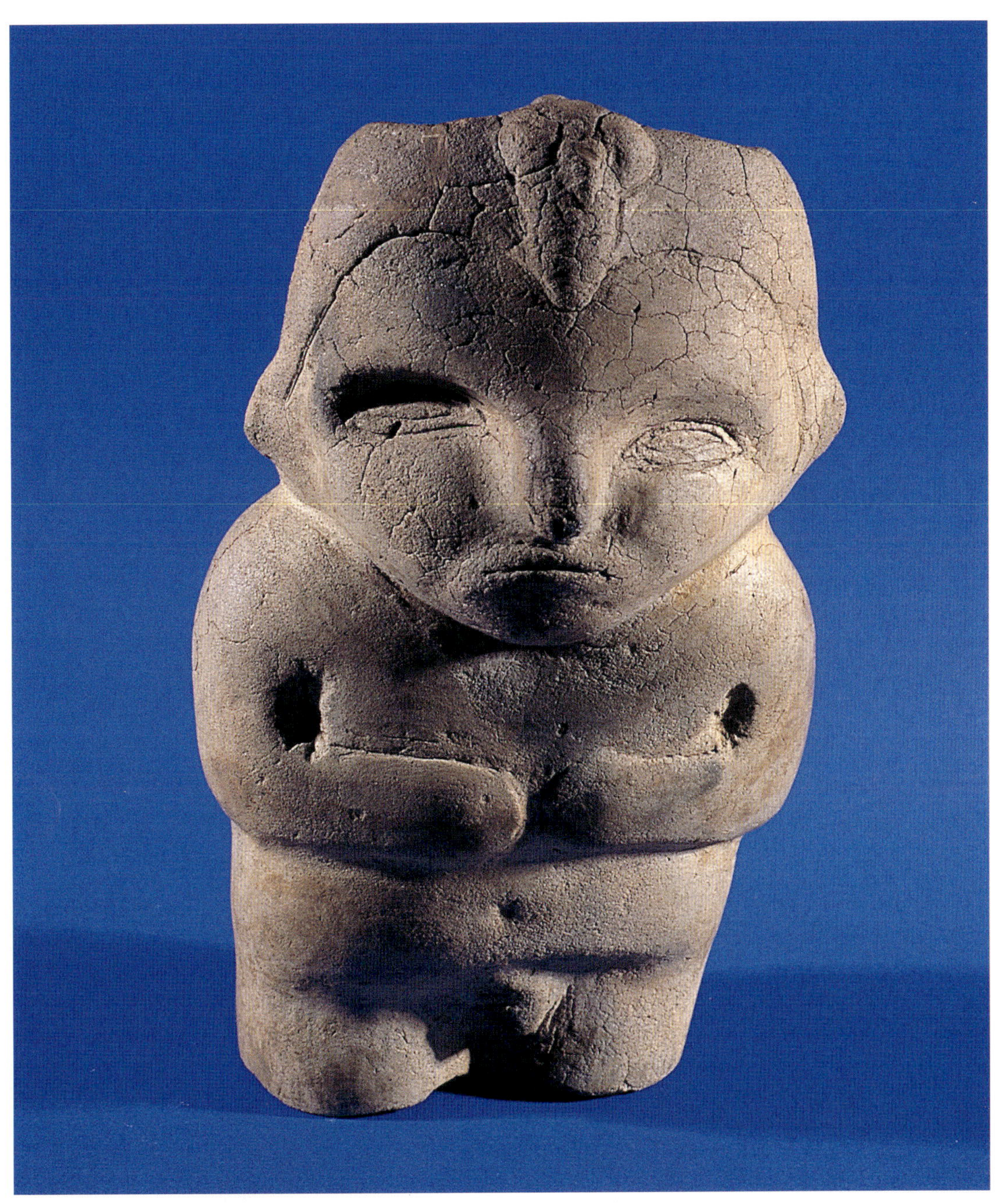

78. Human effigy vessel. Burnt Mill Creek, St. Andrews Bay, Washington County (C. B. Moore). Weeden Island, ca. A.D. 250–800. Ceramic, 19.0 cm long x 11.3 cm wide. National Museum of the American Indian, New York City, no. 17-4876.

79. Two ceramic vessels. Weeden Island, Pinellas County (8-Pi-1). Weeden Island, ca. A.D. 250–800. Ceramic, left 19.3 cm high x 16.0 cm wide; right 16.0 cm high x 20 cm wide x 64.5 circumference. Smithsonian Institution, Washington, D.C., nos. A-326976 (left), A-326972 (right).

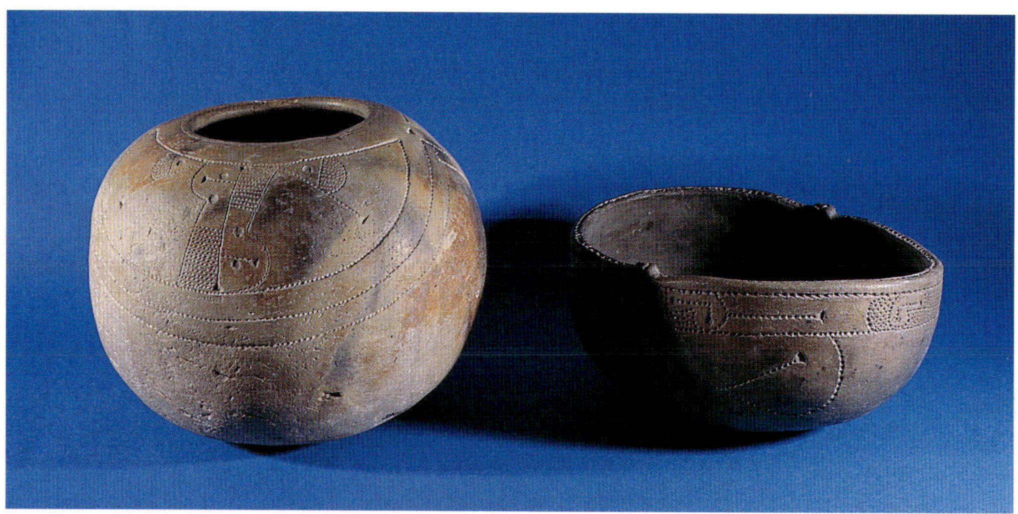

80. (facing page) Four-legged effigy urn. Buck Burial Mound, Okaloosa County (8-Ok-11). Weeden Island, ca. A.D. 250–800. Ceramic, 36.4 high x 22.9 cm wide. Indian Temple Mound Museum, Fort Walton Beach, Florida, no. 1197.

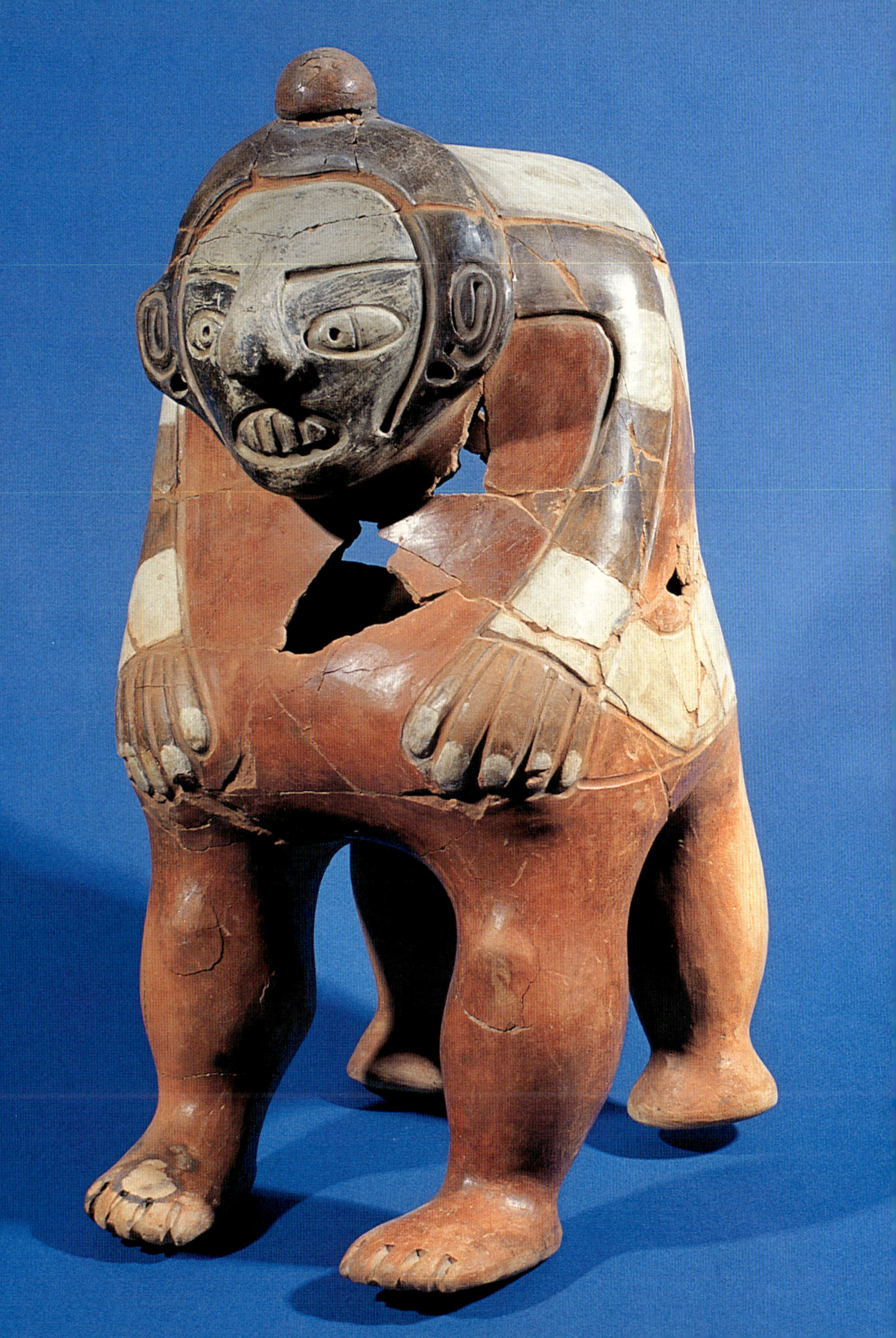

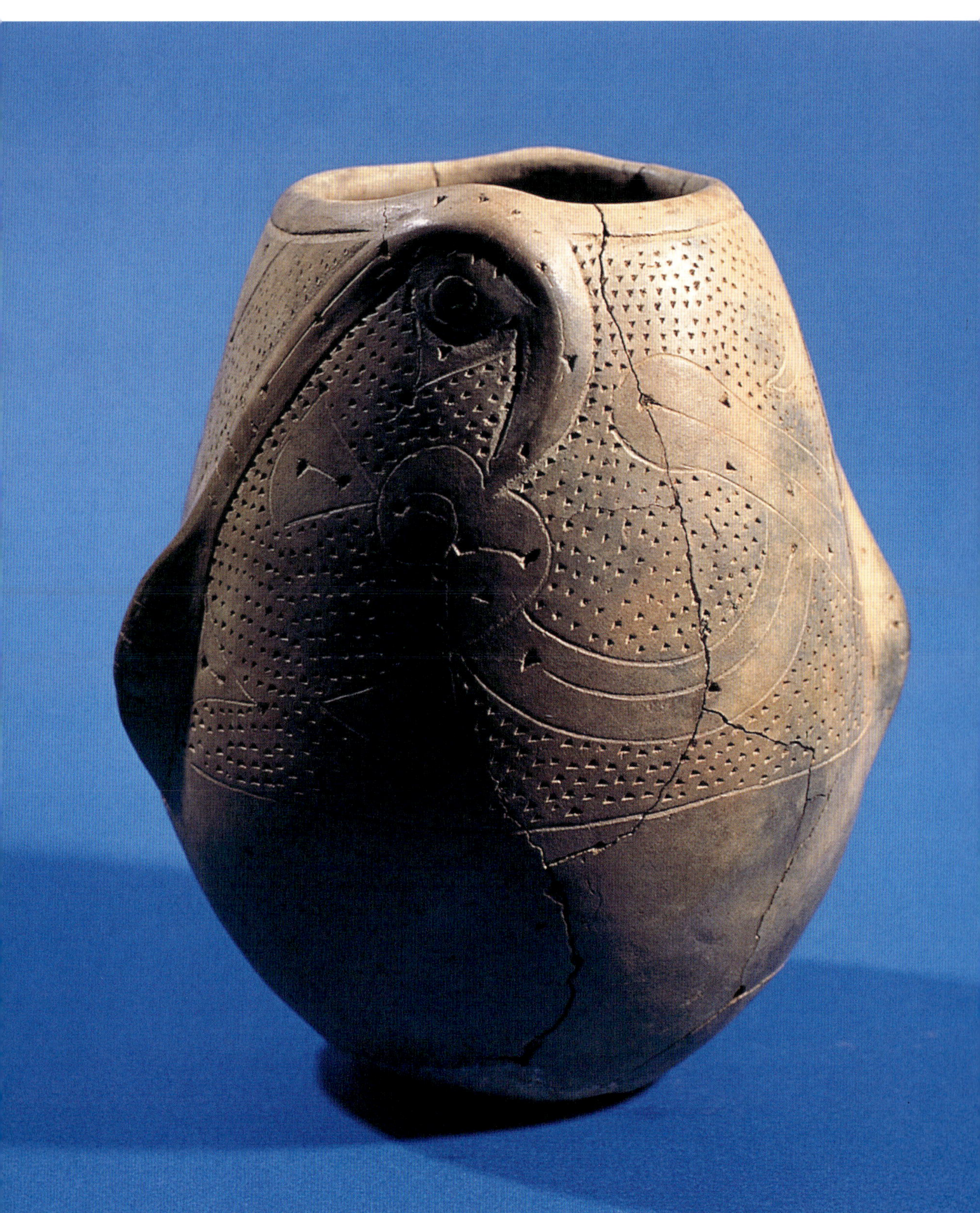

81. (facing page) Vase with waterbird design. Clearwater, Pinellas County. Weeden Island (?), ca. A.D. 250–800. Ceramic, 19.5 cm high x 44.5 cm circumference. Private collection.

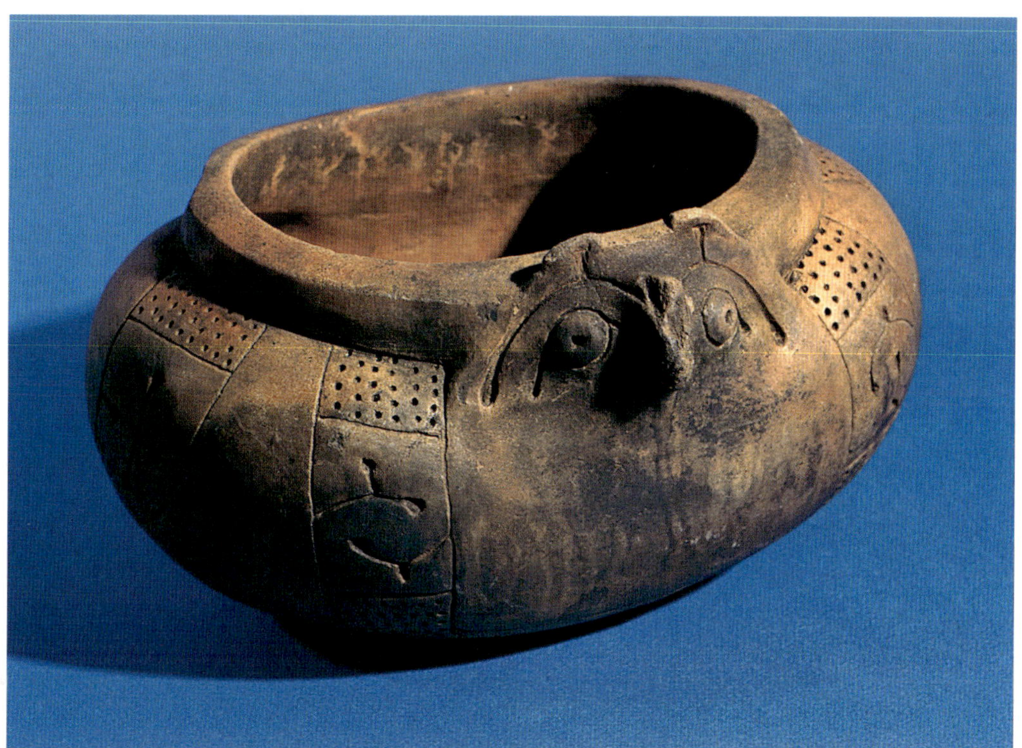

82. Owl effigy vessel. Spring Warrior Mound, Taylor County (8-Ta-2). Fort Walton (Late Mississippian), ca. A.D. 1350–1500. Ceramic, 12.8 cm high x 24 cm wide x 67.0 cm circumference. Jacksonville Museum of Science and History, no. 76441.

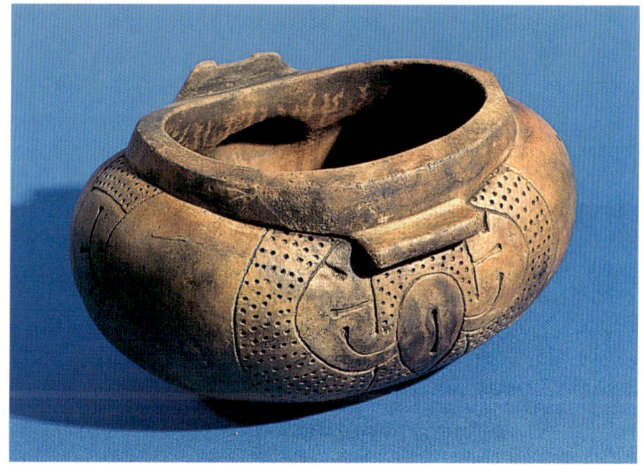

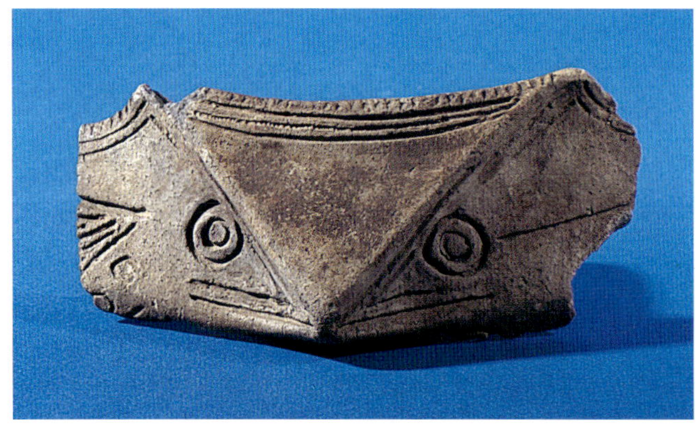

83. (left) Owl head sherd. Choctawhatchee Beach Cemetery Site, Walton County (8-Wl-33). Fort Walton (Late Mississippian), ca. A.D. 1350–1500. Ceramic, 6.9 cm high x 14.0 cm long. Indian Temple Mound Museum, Fort Walton Beach, Florida, no. 1415.

84. (below) Frog effigy vessel. Choctawhatchee Beach Cemetery Site, Walton County (8-Wl-33). Fort Walton (Late Mississippian), ca. A.D. 1350–1500. Ceramic, 7.8 cm high x 16.5 cm long. Indian Temple Mound Museum, Fort Walton Beach, Florida, no. 1305.

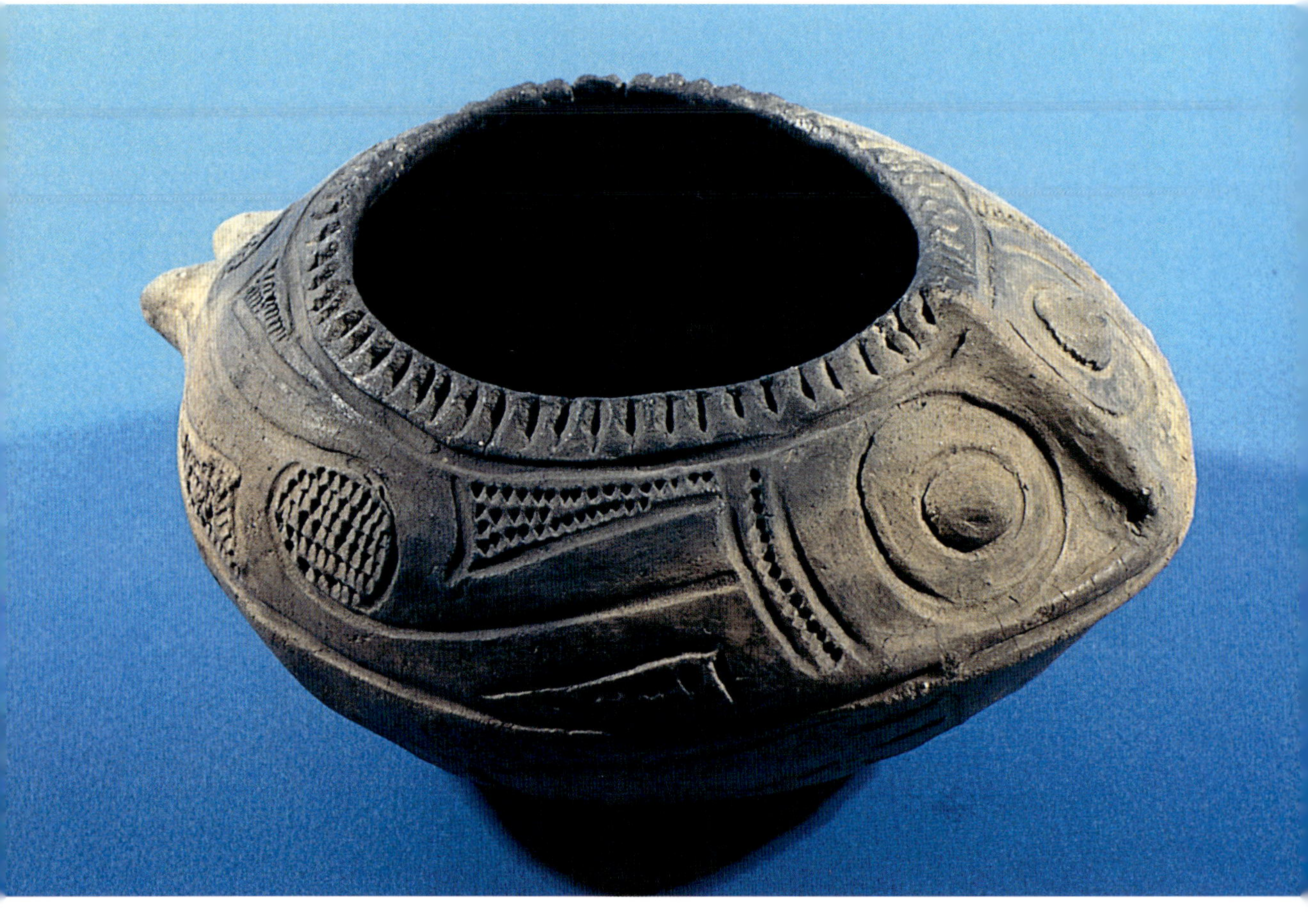

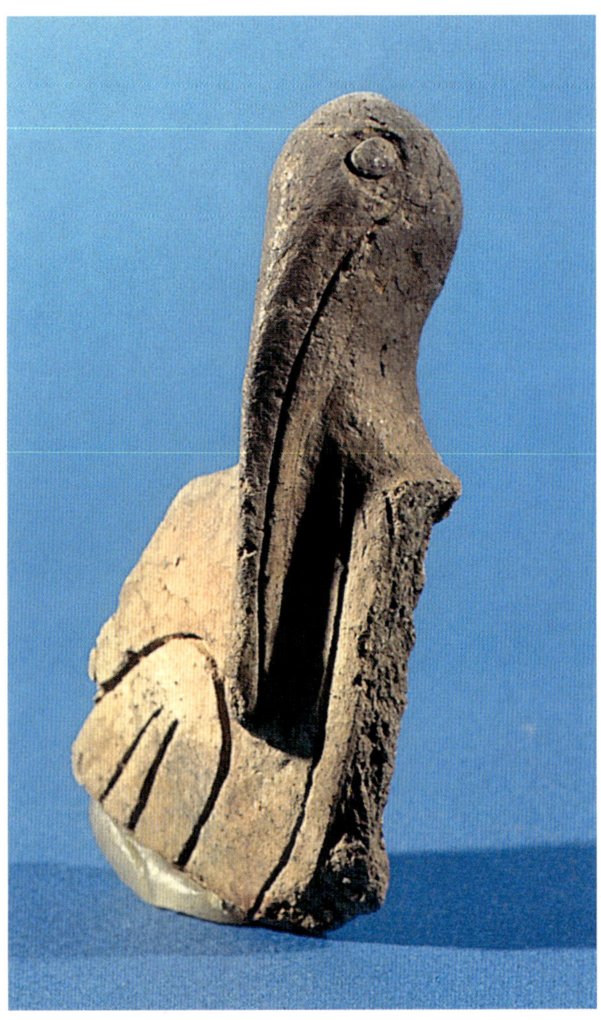

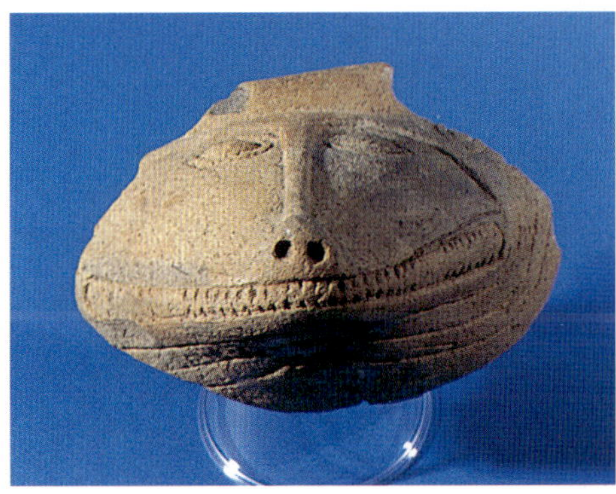

85. (above) Pelican head sherd. Choctawhatchee Beach Cemetery Site, Walton County (8-Wl-33). Fort Walton (Late Mississippian), ca. A.D. 1350–1500. Ceramic, 10.8 cm high. Indian Temple Mound Museum, Fort Walton Beach, Florida, no. 1089.

86. (left) Possum head vessel. Choctawhatchee Beach Cemetery site, Walton County (8-Wl-33). Fort Walton (Late Mississippian), ca. A.D. 1350–1500. Ceramic, 11.5 cm high x 18.0 cm wide. Indian Temple Mound Museum, Fort Walton Beach, Florida, no. 1269.

87. Six-pointed dish. Holly Branch Burial site, Okaloosa County (8-Ok-35). Fort Walton (Late Mississippian), ca. A.D. 1350–1500. Ceramic, 9.0 cm high x 41.5 cm diameter. Indian Temple Mound Museum, Fort Walton Beach, Florida, no. 1254.

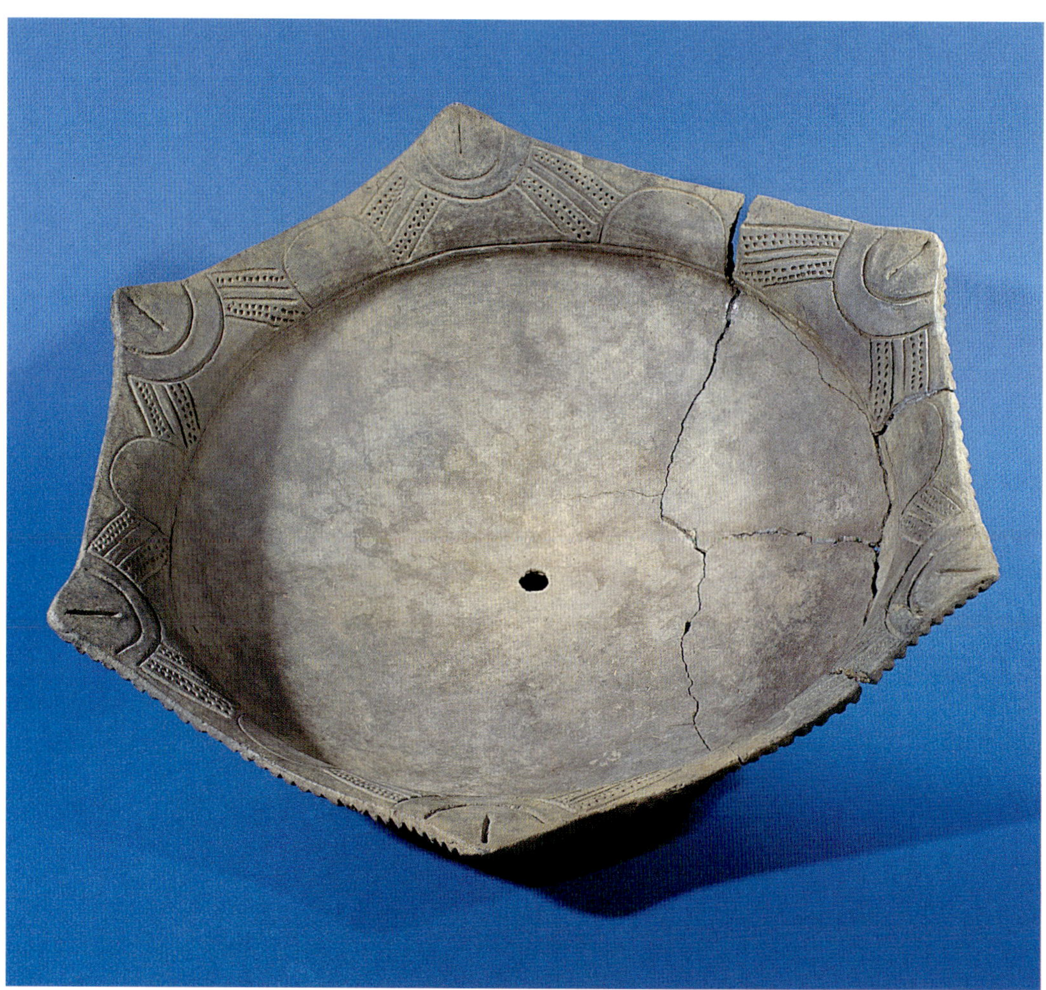

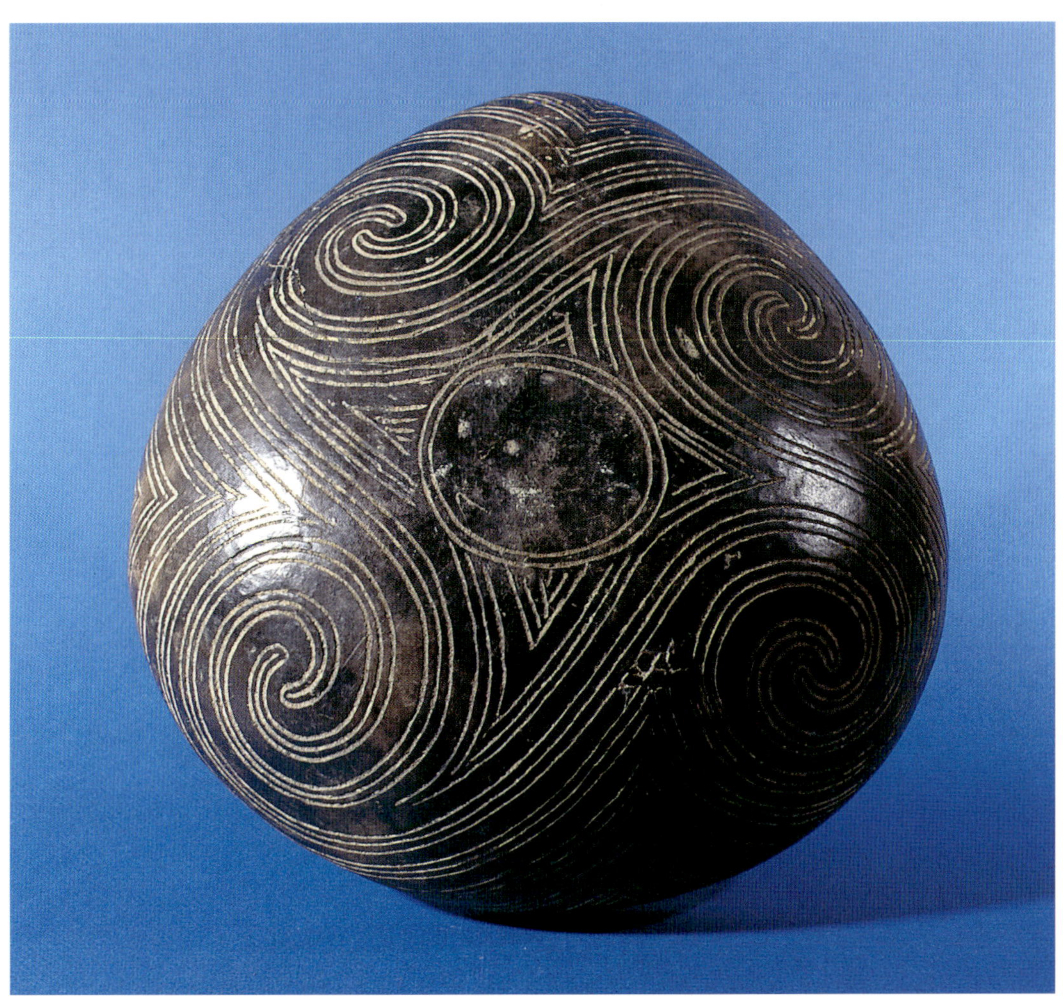

88. Incised effigy bowl in the form of a marine shell. Johnson Ceremonial Pot Breaking site, Walton County (8-Wl-30). Fort Walton (Late Mississippian), ca. A.D. 1350-1500. Ceramic, 7.6 cm high x 29.2 cm long x 26.7 cm diameter. Indian Temple Mound Museum, Fort Walton Beach, Florida, no. 1265.

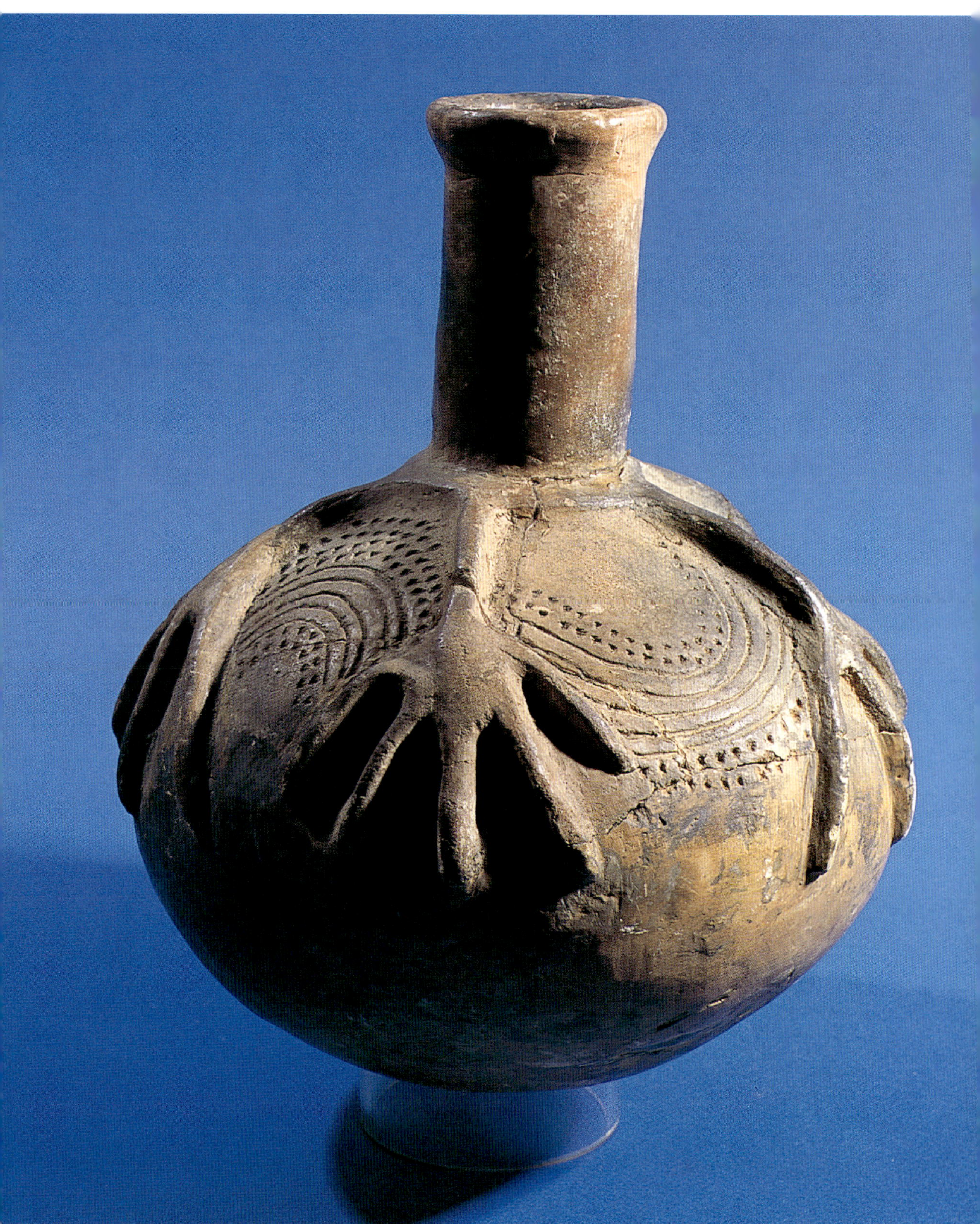

89. (facing page) Incised bottle with effigy bird feet and human hands. Wilson Mound, Old Myakka City, Sarasota County (either 8-So-70 or 8-So-77). (Found in 1934 over a skeleton near the center of the mound.) Safety Harbor (Late Mississippian), ca. A.D. 1350–1500. Ceramic, 27 cm high x 69 cm circumference. Private collection.

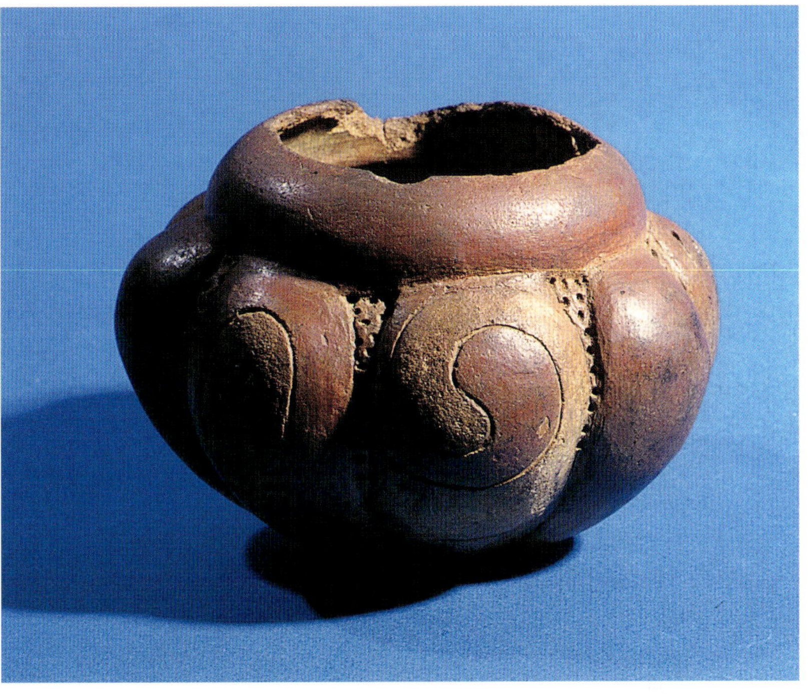

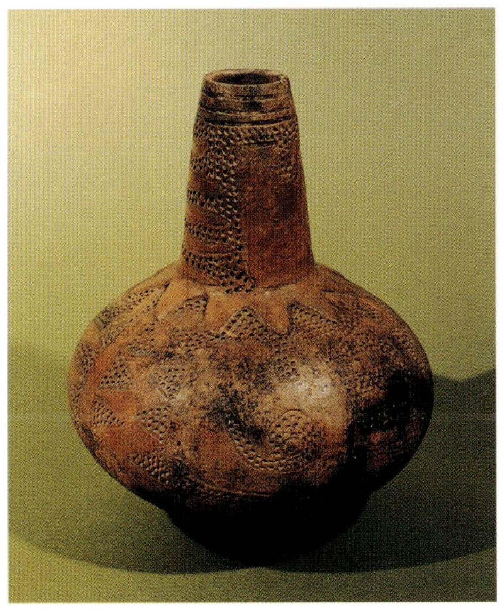

90. (above) Bowl with eight lobes (Sarinam Cherry?). Taylor County. Date unknown; probably Middle Woodland or Mississippian. Ceramic, 13 cm high x 48 cm circumference. Private collection.

91. (left) Narrow-necked incised bottle. Picnic Mound, Hillsborough County (8-Hi-3). Safety Harbor (Late Mississippian), ca. A.D. 1350–1500. Ceramic, 27 cm high x 20 cm diameter x 4.5 cm rim diameter. Florida Museum of Natural History, Gainesville, no. 76661.

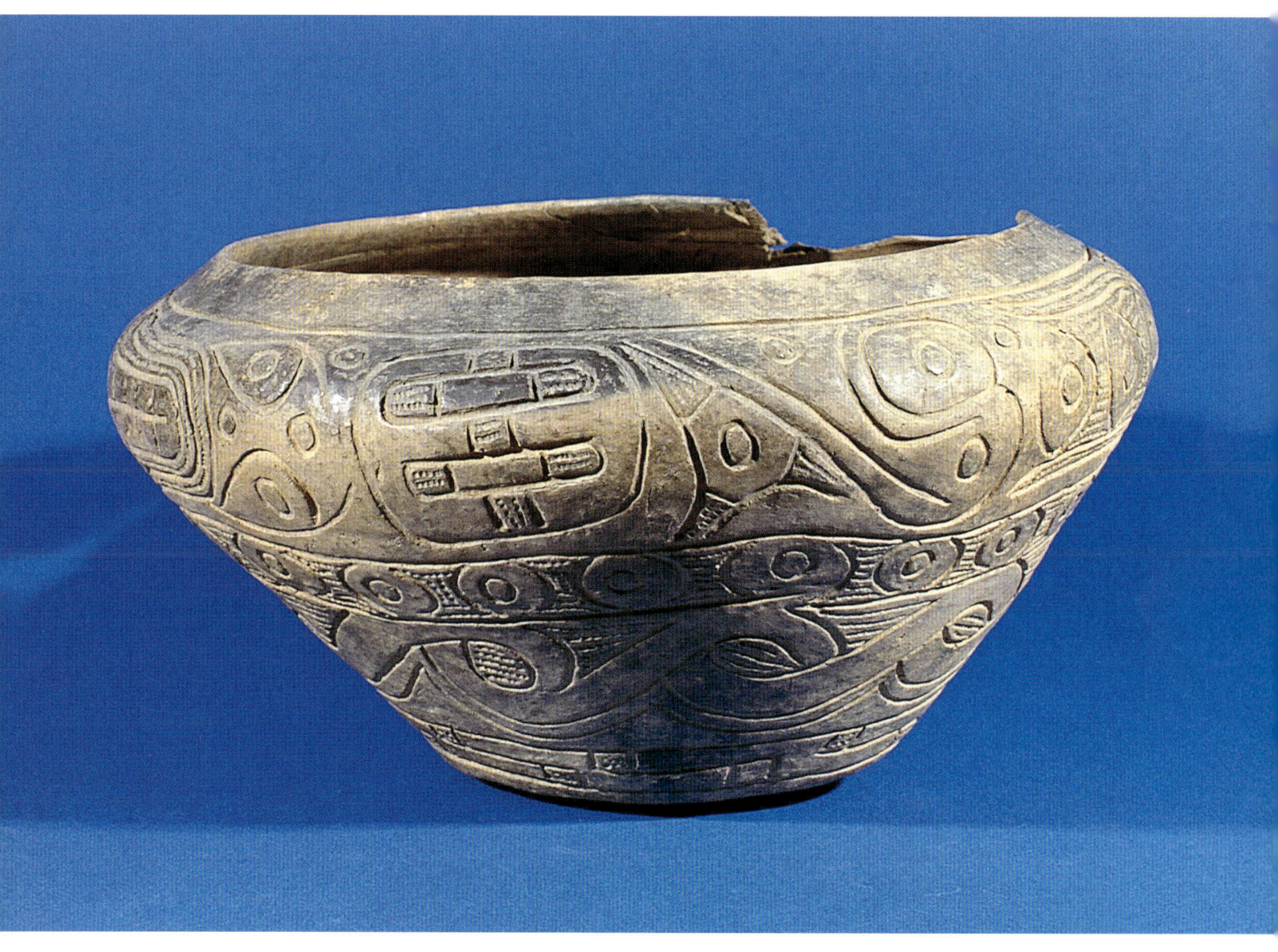

92. (above) Casuela-shaped vessel. Johnson Ceremonial Pot Breaking site, Walton County (8-Wl-30). Fort Walton (Late Mississippian), A.D. 1350–1500. Ceramic, 15.2 cm high x 30.5 cm diameter x 23.0 cm rim diameter. Indian Temple Mound Museum, Fort Walton Beach, Florida, no. 1587.

95. (facing page) Casuela-shape vessel. Fort Gadsen, Apalachicola River. Probably Mississippian, ca. A.D. 1100–1500. Ceramic, 10 cm high x 88 cm circumference. Private collection.

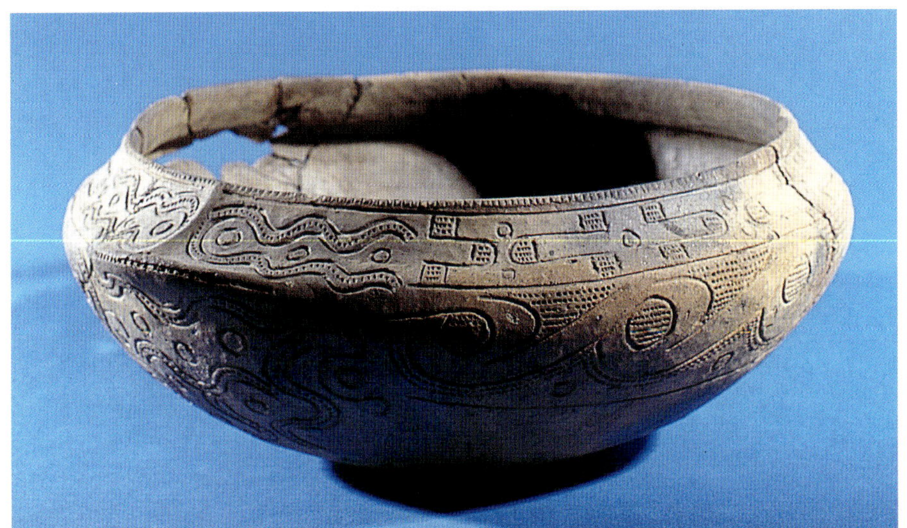

93. (above) Marriage bowl (two designs, casuela shape). Pickens-Pencak Ceremonial site, Walton County (8-Wl-50). Fort Walton and Englewood (Late Mississippian), A.D.1350–1500. Ceramic, 13.3 cm high x 32.4 cm diameter. Indian Temple Mound Museum, Fort Walton Beach, Florida, no. 1253.

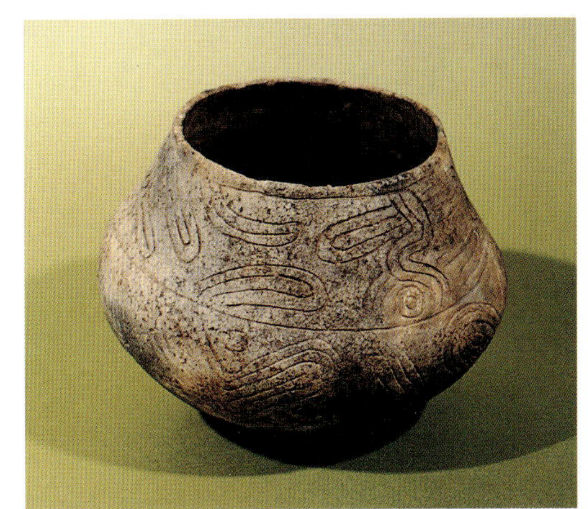

94. (right) Open-necked vessel with incised motifs. Santa Rosa Shell Mound, Walton County (collected in 1916). Mississippian, ca. A.D. 1100–1500. Ceramic (Point Washington Incised), 18 cm high x 22.5 cm diameter x 15.0 rim diameter. Florida Museum of Natural History, Gainesville, no. 5009.

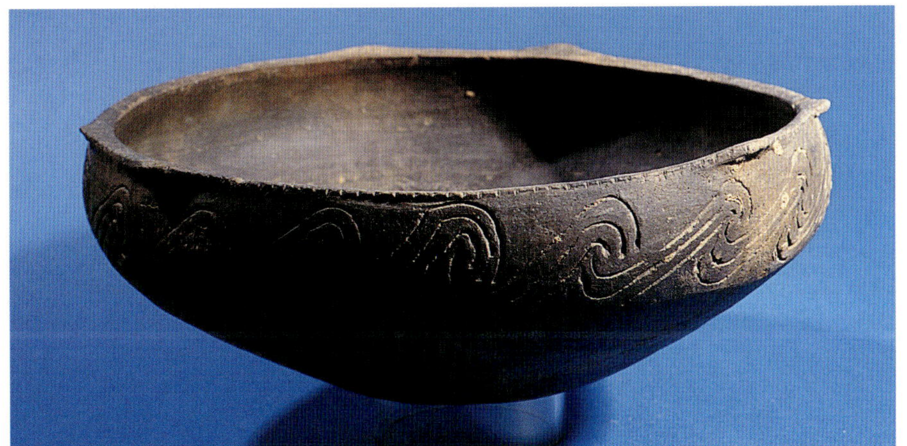

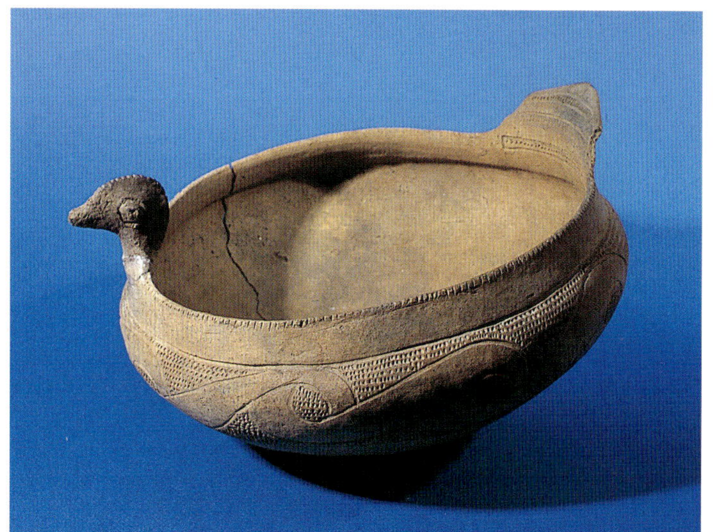

96. (left) Effigy vessel with bird head. Johnson Ceremonial Pottery Site, Walton County (8-Wl-30). Fort Walton (Late Mississippian), ca. A.D. 1350–1500. Ceramic, 10.2 cm high x 20.3 cm diameter. Indian Temple Mound Museum, Fort Walton Beach, Florida, no. 1264.

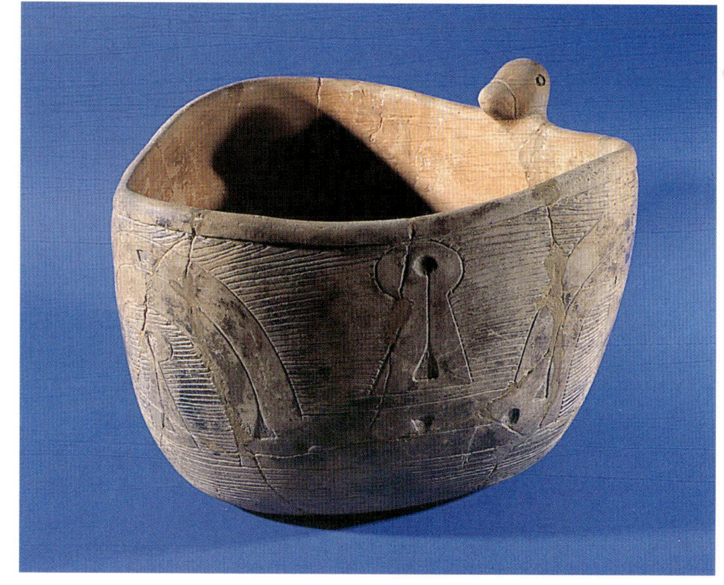

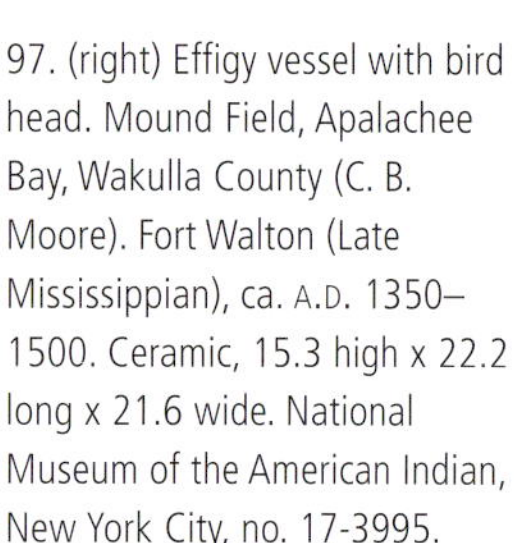

97. (right) Effigy vessel with bird head. Mound Field, Apalachee Bay, Wakulla County (C. B. Moore). Fort Walton (Late Mississippian), ca. A.D. 1350–1500. Ceramic, 15.3 high x 22.2 long x 21.6 wide. National Museum of the American Indian, New York City, no. 17-3995.

98. Effigy vessel with two bird heads and a tail. Cemetery at Hogtown Bayou, Choclawatchee Bay, Walton Co. (C. B. Moore). Fort Walton (Late Mississippian), ca. A.D. 1350–1500. Ceramic, 32.6 long x 30.3 wide x 16.9 high. National Museum of the American Indian, New York City, no. 6-2177.

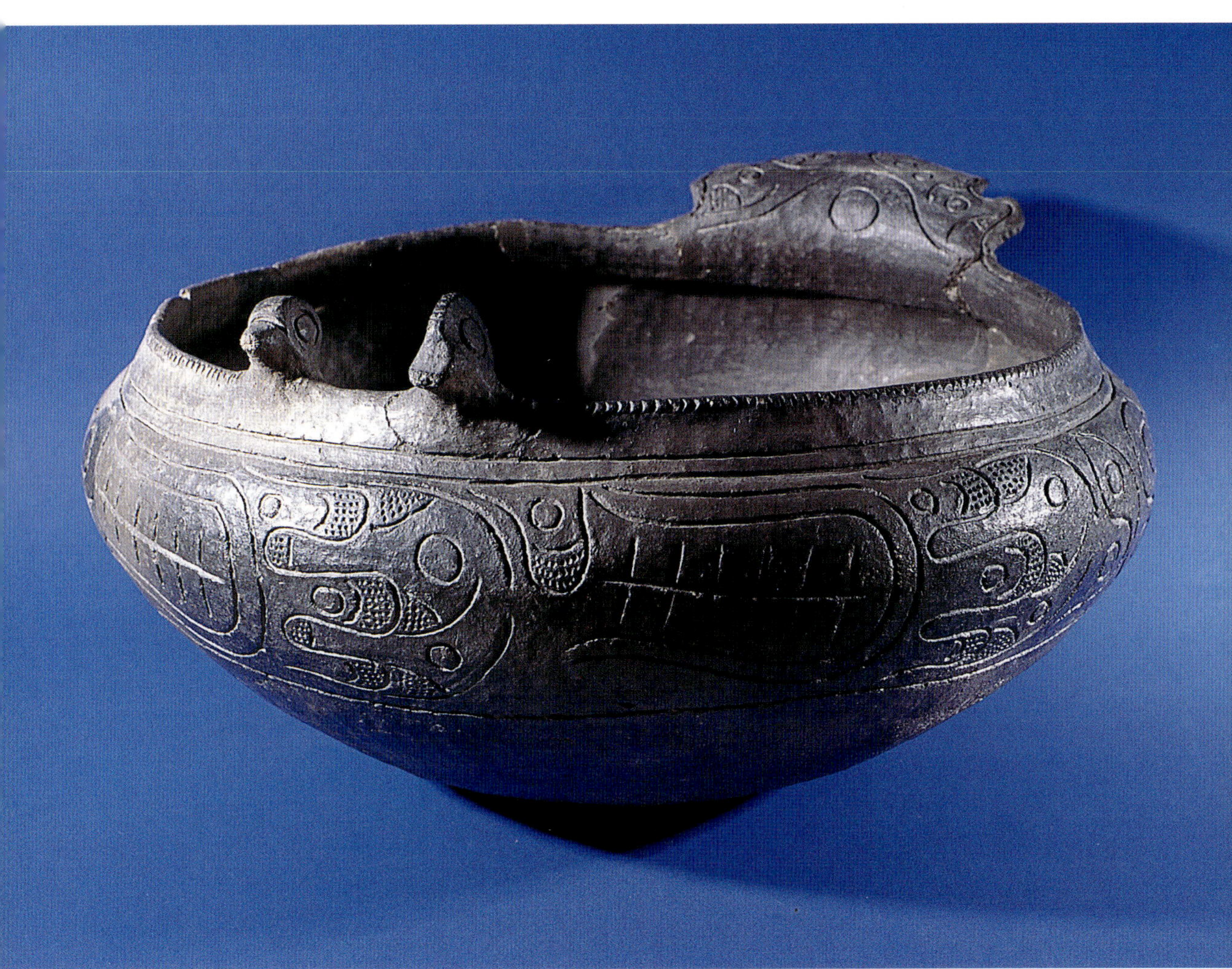

99. Incised and punctated bowl. Hernando County. Safety Harbor (Late Mississippian), ca. A.D. 1350–1500. Ceramic, 15.0 cm high x 32.5 cm diameter. South Florida Museum and Bishop Planetarium, Bradenton, no. SFM A6517 (2324).

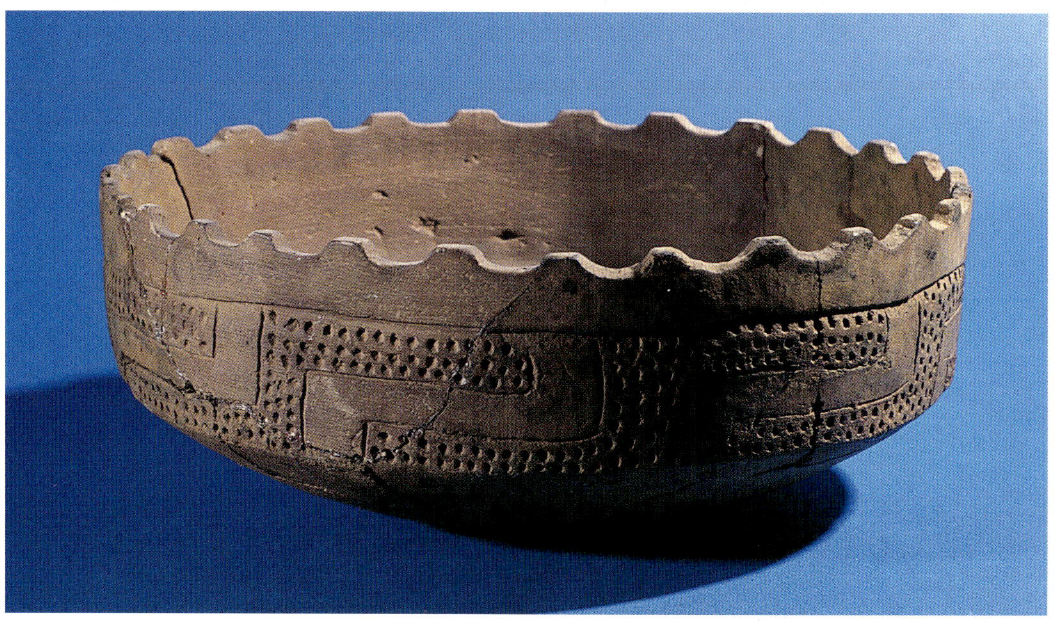

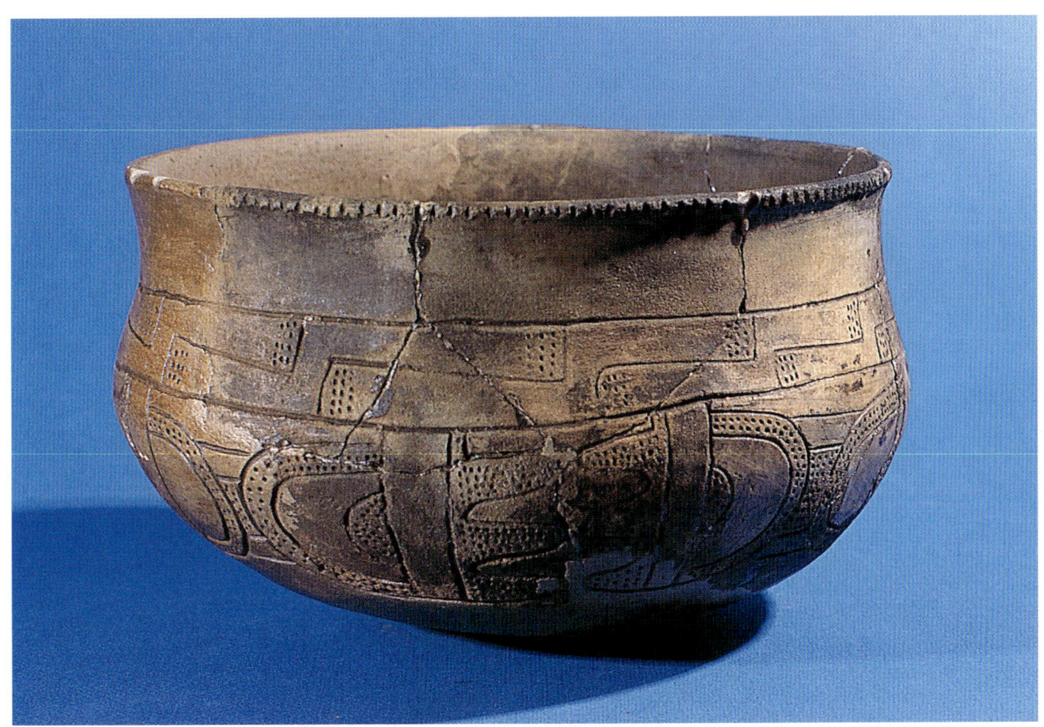

100. Incised and punctated bowl. Pasco County. Safety Harbor (Late Mississippian), ca. A.D. 1350–1500. Ceramic, 15.5 cm high x 25.0 cm diameter. South Florida Museum and Bishop Planetarium, Bradenton, no. SFM A6536 (2325).

101. (right) Human figure (Mr. Ooo). Crude figure with nose and waist band applique; eyes and mouth incised. Astor, Lake County. Date unknown, probably Late Prehistoric or Early Historic. Ceramic, 17 cm high x 8 cm wide x 3.0 cm thick. Private collection.

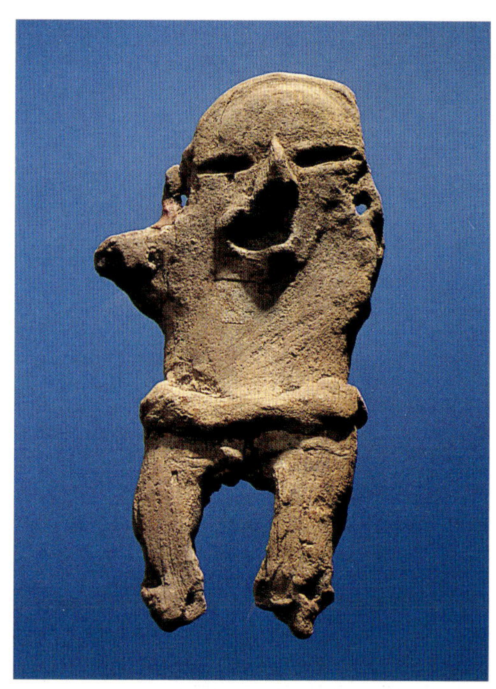

102. (below) Two ceramic dog figurines and one small bird bowl. *A and B,* Thursby Midden, Volusia County (8-Vo-35); *C,* Shields Mound, Duval County (C. B. Moore). Date unknown, probably Late Prehistoric to Early Historic. Ceramic, *A,* 4.4 cm high x 7.0 cm long x 3.3 cm wide; *B,* 5.0 cm high x 8.2 cm long x 3.3 cm wide; *C,* 3.8 cm high x 7.5 cm long x 4.2 cm wide. National Museum of the American Indian, New York City, nos. 17/2211 (A and B); 17/3404 (C).

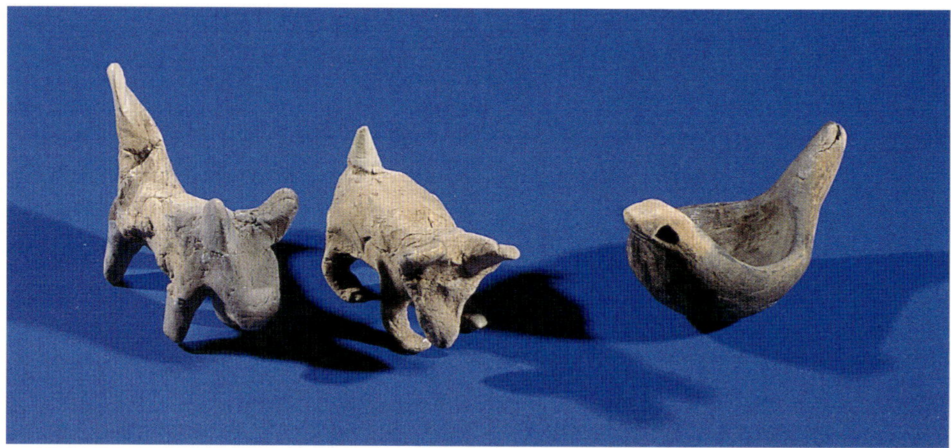

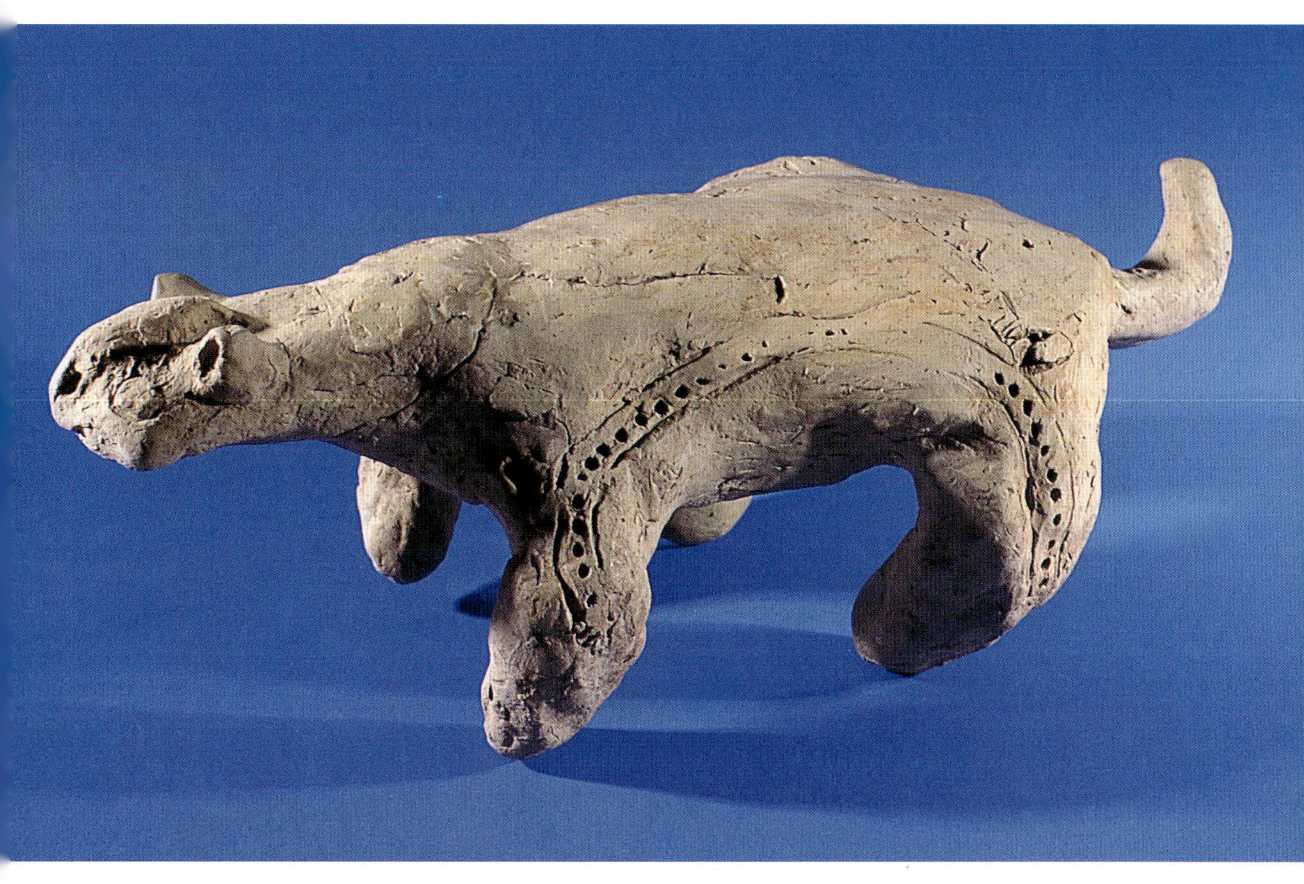

103. (above) Cat figure. Mound, one mile west of Duvals, Lake County (C. B. Moore). Date unknown, probably Late Prehistoric to Early Historic. Ceramic, 10.5 cm high x 29.5 cm long x 14.0 cm wide. National Museum of the American Indian, New York City, no. 17-3959.

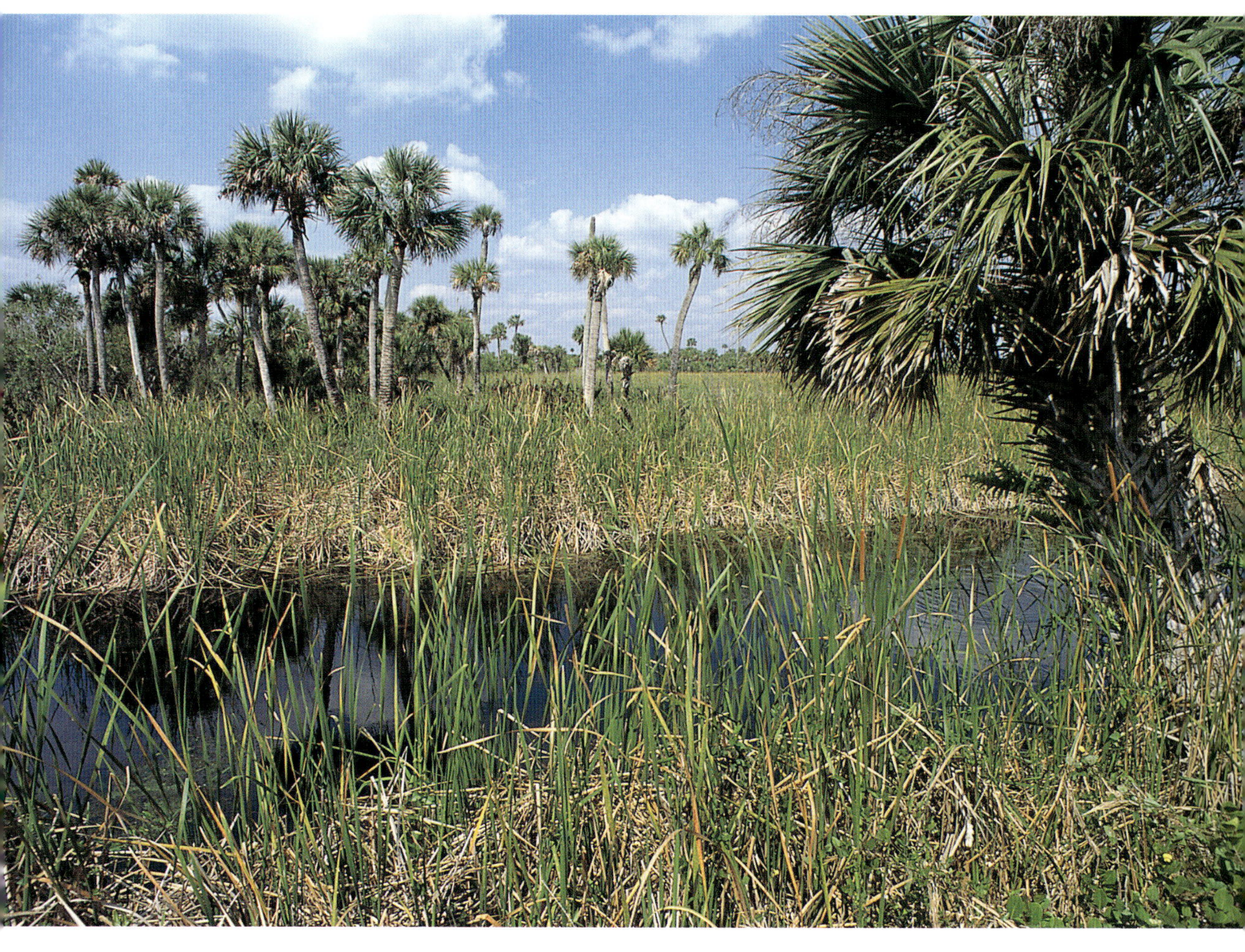

Everglades

METAL

ALTHOUGH METALS are not native to Florida, copper was brought into the state by the first century A.D. as part of an exchange network called the Hopewell Interaction Sphere, in which most cultural groups throughout the Midwest and Eastern Woodlands participated. For example, copper celts, pendants, ear spools, and animal cutouts from the Crystal River site date from this period (Moore 1903). The sturdy celts and pendants are corroded but remain in good condition; the thin cutouts are very corroded and fragmentary. Many of these artifacts are in the National Museum of the American Indian.

During the Mississippian period, about A.D. 1200–1400, some extremely elaborate copper artifacts were made. A drawing of a copper repoussé breast plate representing a hawkman dancer is shown on the next page. It and other specimens were recovered from burials at the Lake Jackson Mound Complex in Leon County (Jones 1994). These once magnificent pieces were in an advanced state of degradation when found and are very fragile. Gold shines forever but copper does not; because of its composition it is subject to all kinds of corrosive activity.

The artifacts shown in plates 104 through 114 were reworked from gold and silver that had originated in Central or South America and was seized by the Indians from ships wrecked off the Florida coasts. A solid gold crested bird figure (ivory-billed woodpecker?), identical to the silver ones in plate 104, was found in Manatee County. A brass replica of it is in storage at the Smithsonian Institution. Only eight of these figures (possibly hair or clothing ornaments) are known to exist, and these are unique to Florida. Plaques or ceremonial tablets similar in style to those in plates 106 and 107 are known in wood, stone, and metal. They vary greatly in size and decoration (Allerton et al. 1984; Sears 1982, 60–63; Branstetter 1991).

The pendant in plate 115 was not modified. It represents an anthropomorphic crocodile god and is similar to objects from Costa Rica that were manufactured between A.D. 800 and 1500 (Detroit Institute of Art 1991, 222, items 252–54).

The Indians treasured shiny things, like hard-to-get mica and copper; the easy-to-get metals from shipwrecks must have been a bonanza to them. Fontaneda reports:

> I desire to speak of the riches found by the Indians of Ais, which perhaps were as much as a million dollars, or over, in bars of silver,

> in gold, and in articles of jewelry. These things Carlos divided with the caciques of Ais, Jeaga, Guacata, Mayajuaco, and Mayaca, and he took what pleased him, or the best part. (True 1944, 20)

The Spanish and French were aware that the Indians were in the possession of much gold and silver. They attempted to trade cheap trinkets to the Indians in exchange for these precious metals.

Slaving expeditions, warfare, and disease introduced by the Europeans following A.D. 1492 brought an end to the aboriginal way of life in Florida and throughout the Americas. A world full of familiar things, 11,000 years of evolving traditions, suddenly ceased. The final photograph (plate 116) of gold doubloons in the surf symbolically depicts this demise.

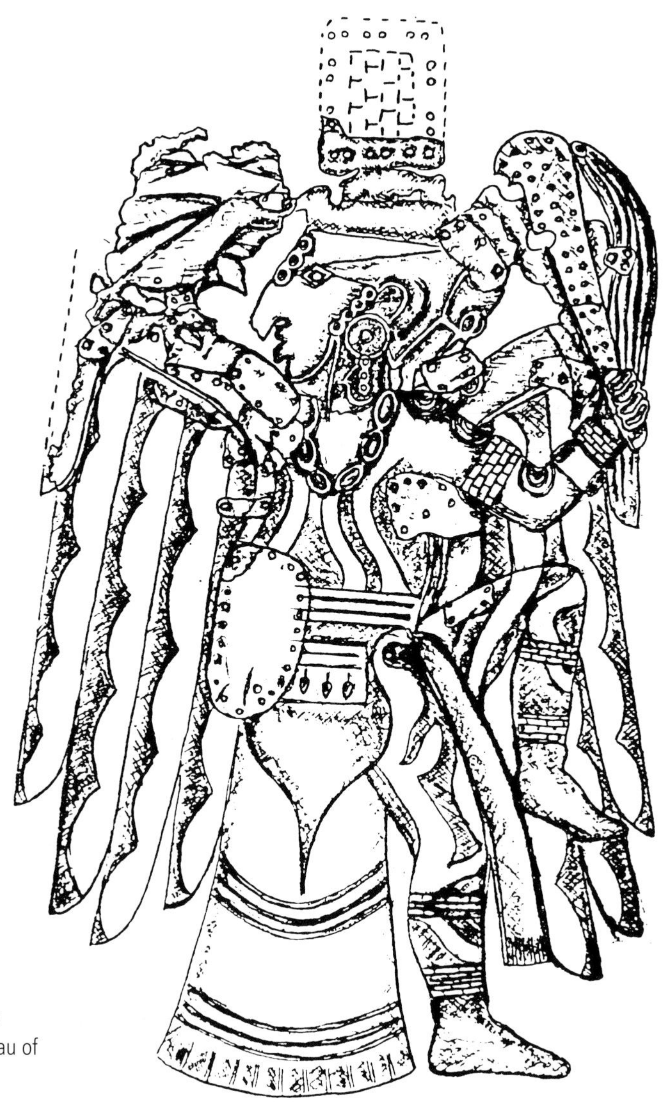

Drawing of a copper repoussé breastplate from Lake Jackson. By permission of Bureau of Archaeological Research, Tallahassee.

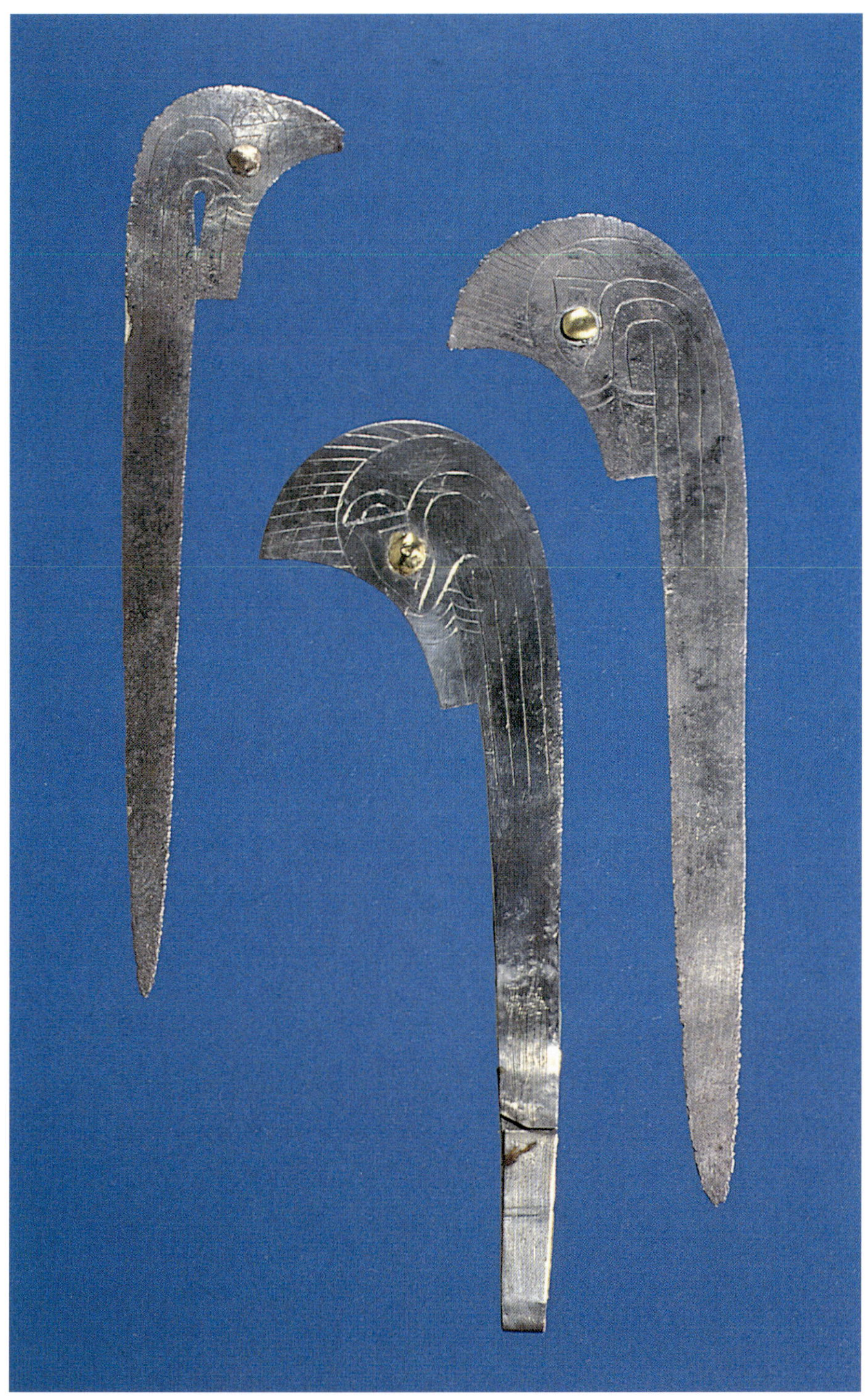

104. Three silver crested bird hairpins with gold or copper inset eyes. From the Tallant Collection. *Left,* Gopher Gully, Glades. County (8-Gl-28); *middle,* Nicodemus Mound, Glades County (8-Gl-19); *right,* Bee Branch, Highlands County (formerly Glades County), (8-Hg-17). Early Historic, after A.D. 1500. Silver and gold; specimen on right is 24.3 cm long x 6.9 cm wide. South Florida Museum and Bishop Planetarium, Bradenton, nos. SFM 4512, SFM 8552, SFM 6184 (left to right).

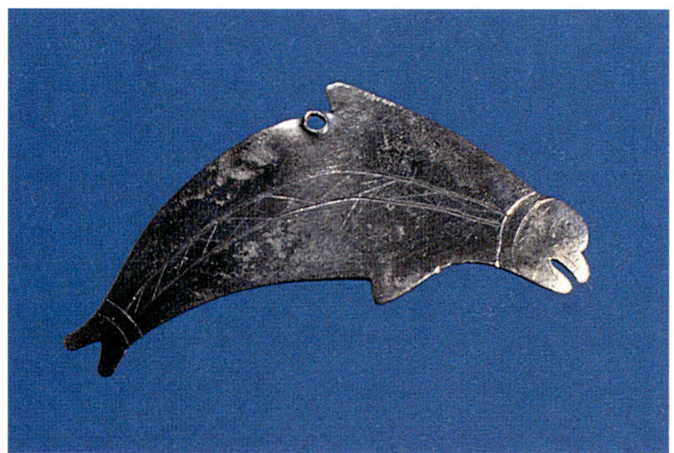

105. (above) Porpoise pendant. Thomas Mound, Highland County (8-Hg-7), Tallant Collection. Early Historic, after A.D. 1500. Silver, 6.8 cm long x 3.8 cm wide x 0.1 cm thick. South Florida Museum and Bishop Planetarium, Bradenton, no. SFM A5650.

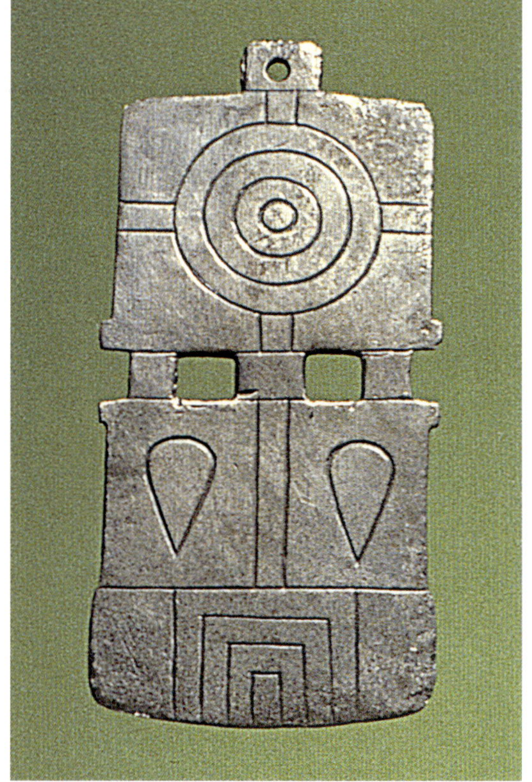

106. (right) Medallion or tablet of uncertain symbolism. Fort Center, Glades County (8-Gl-13). Early Historic, after A.D. 1500. Silver, 9.3 cm long x 5.6 cm wide x 0.2 cm thick; made from heavy slab of silver. Florida Museum of Natural History, Gainesville, no 82-17-74.

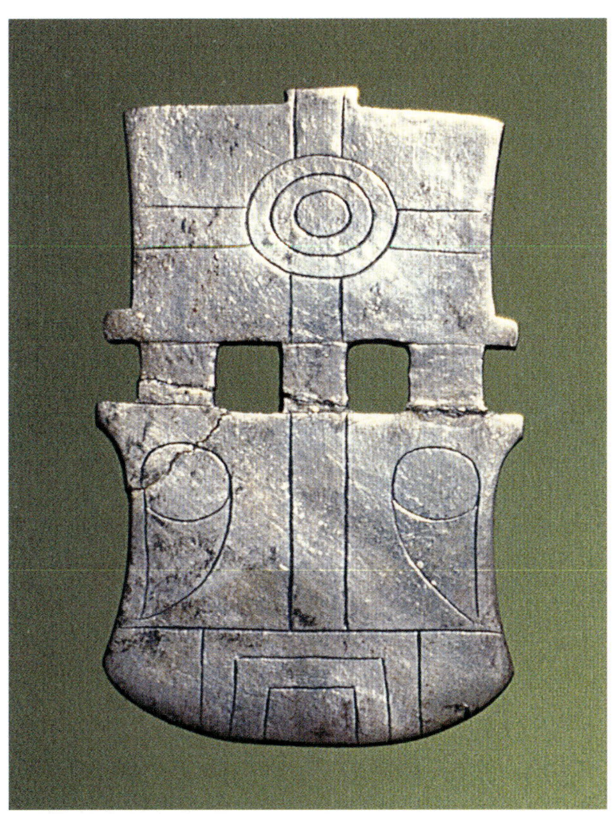

107. Medallion or tablet with uncertain symbolism. Fort Center, Glades County (8-Gl-13). Early Historic, after A.D. 1500. Silver, 8.3 cm long x 4.0 cm wide, very thin. Florida Museum of Natural History, Gainesville, no. 82-17-73.

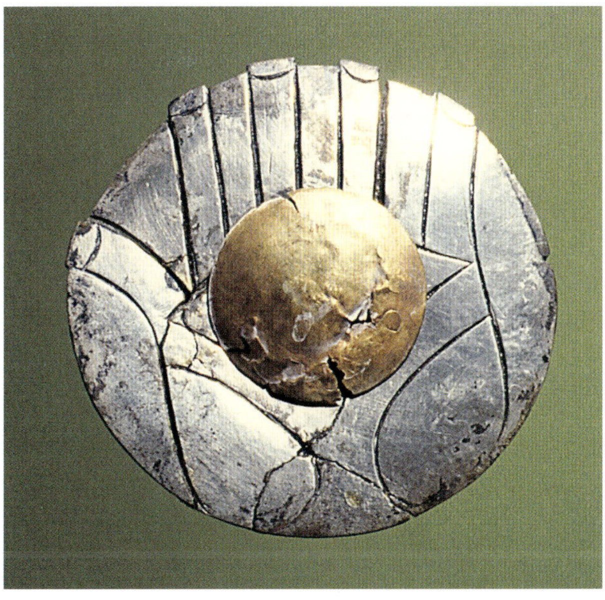

108. Disc with hand-and-eye motif. Fort Center, Glades County (8-Gl-13). Early Historic, after A.D. 1500. Heavy cast silver with gold inset, disc 8.3 cm diameter x 0.1 cm thick; button 3.67 cm diameter. Florida Museum of Natural History, Gainesville, no. 82-17-73/82-17-10 (button).

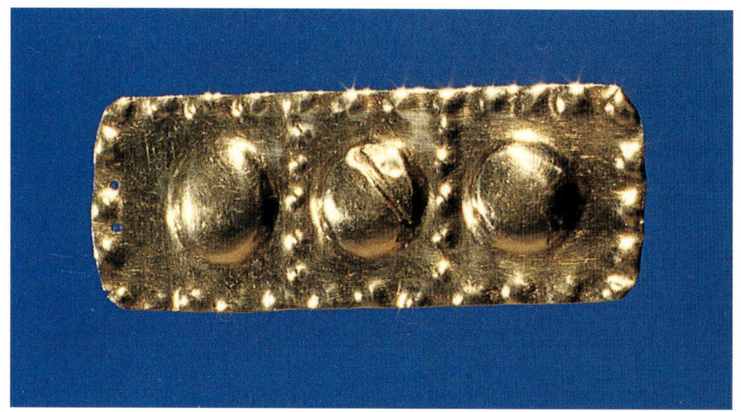

109. (above) Rectangular pendant. Bee Branch, Highlands County (8-Hg-17) formerly Glades County, Tallant Collection. Early Historic, after A.D. 1500. Gold, 9.8 cm long x 3.7 cm wide x 0.3 cm thick. South Florida Museum and Bishop Planetarium, Bradenton, no. SFM A6706.

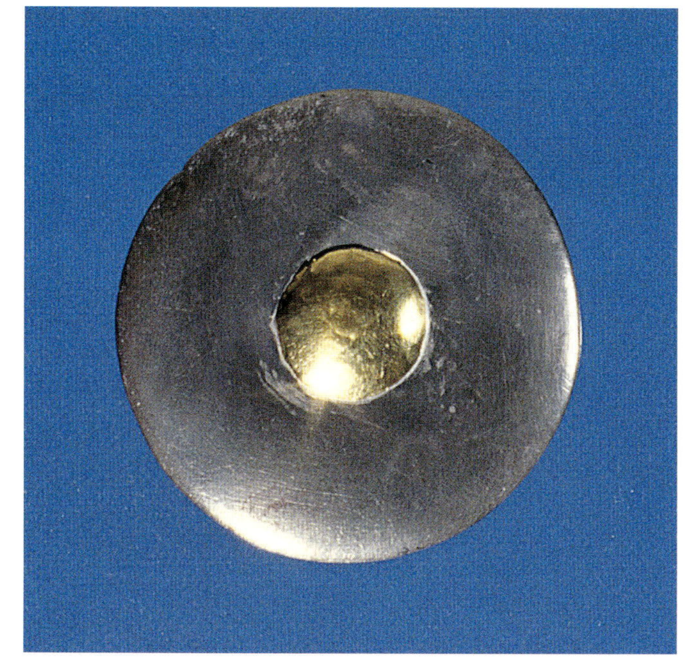

110. (right) Silver disc with gold button. Nicodemus Mound, Glades County (8-Gl-19), Tallant Collection. Early Historic, after A.D. 1500. Silver and gold, 8.4 cm diameter. South Florida Museum and Bishop Planetarium, Bradenton, no. SFM 8497.

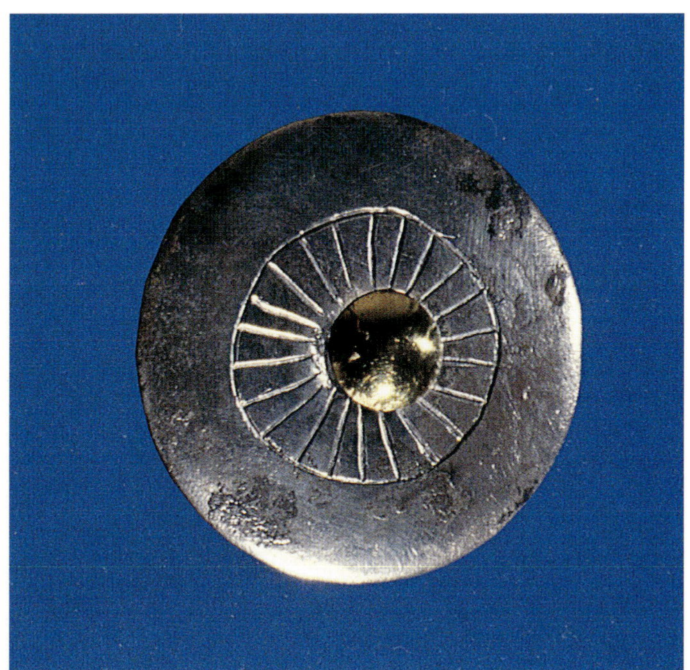

111. (left) Incised silver disc with gold button. Ortona Mound, Glades County (8-Gl-35), Tallant Collection. Early Historic, after A.D. 1500. Silver and gold, 5.5 cm diameter. South Florida Museum and Bishop Planetarium, Bradenton, no. SFM A1959.

112. (below) Silver disc with silver button. Gopher Gully, Glades County (8-Gl-28), Tallant Collection. Early Historic, after A.D. 1500. Silver (petal motif), 7.0 cm diameter. South Florida Museum and Bishop Planetarium, Bradenton, no. SFM 4508 (disc); SFM 8510 (button).

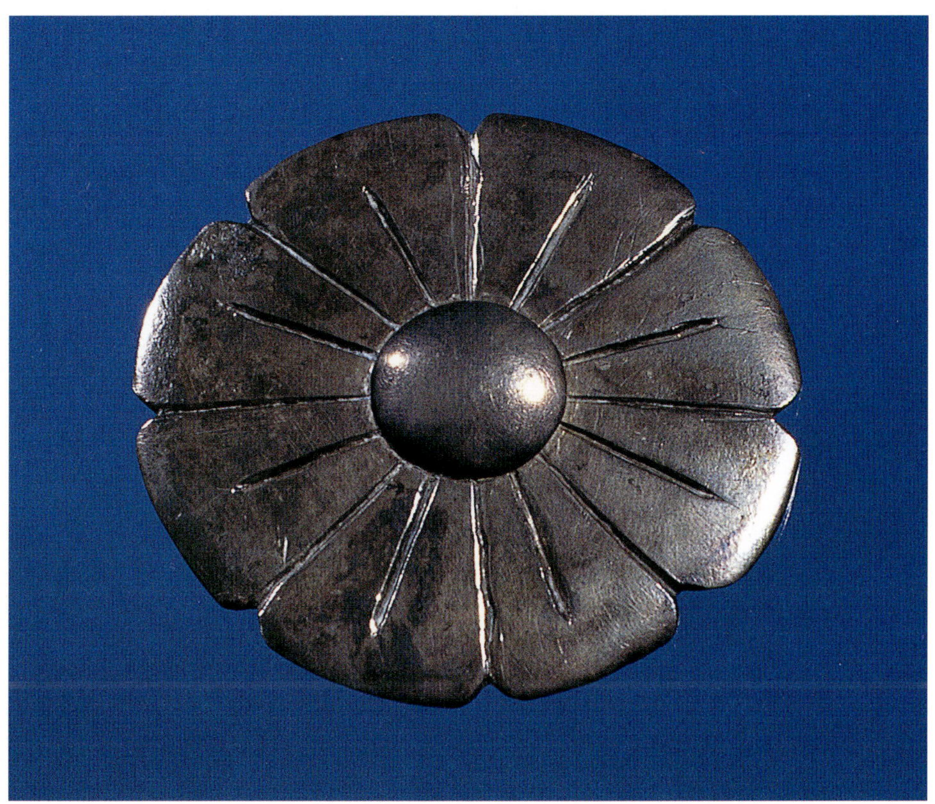

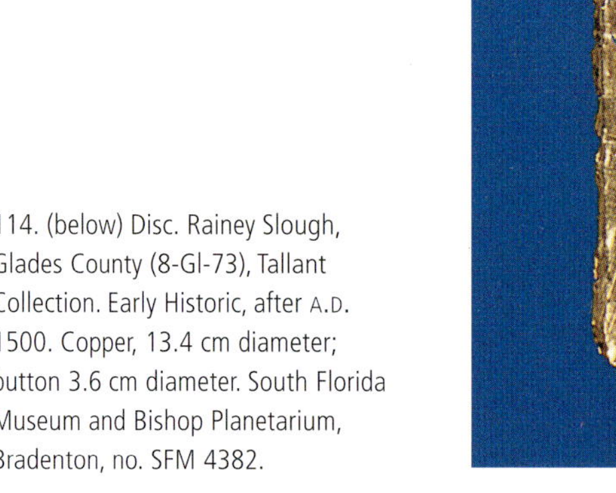

113. (right) Plaque. Rainey Slough, Glades County (8-Gl-73), Tallant Collection. Early Historic, after A.D. 1500. Gold, 8.1 cm long x 4.5 cm wide; very thin. South Florida Museum and Bishop Planetarium, Bradenton, no. SFM A6734.

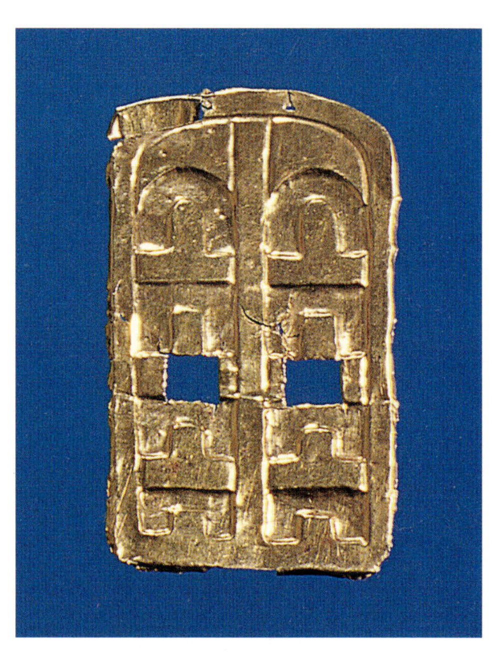

114. (below) Disc. Rainey Slough, Glades County (8-Gl-73), Tallant Collection. Early Historic, after A.D. 1500. Copper, 13.4 cm diameter; button 3.6 cm diameter. South Florida Museum and Bishop Planetarium, Bradenton, no. SFM 4382.

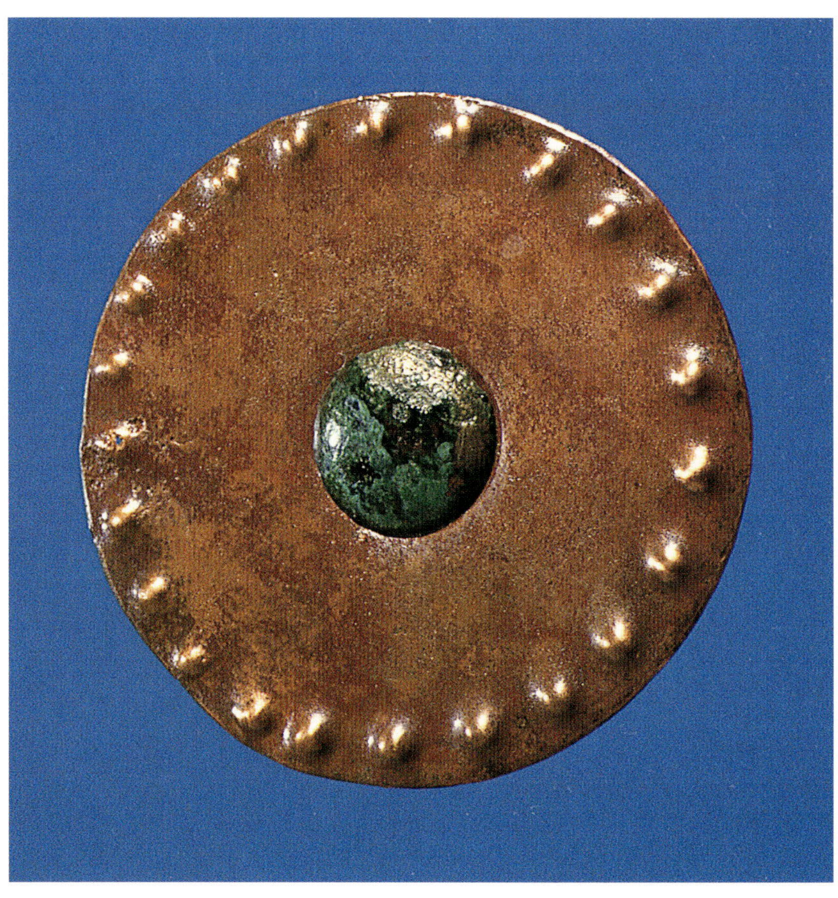

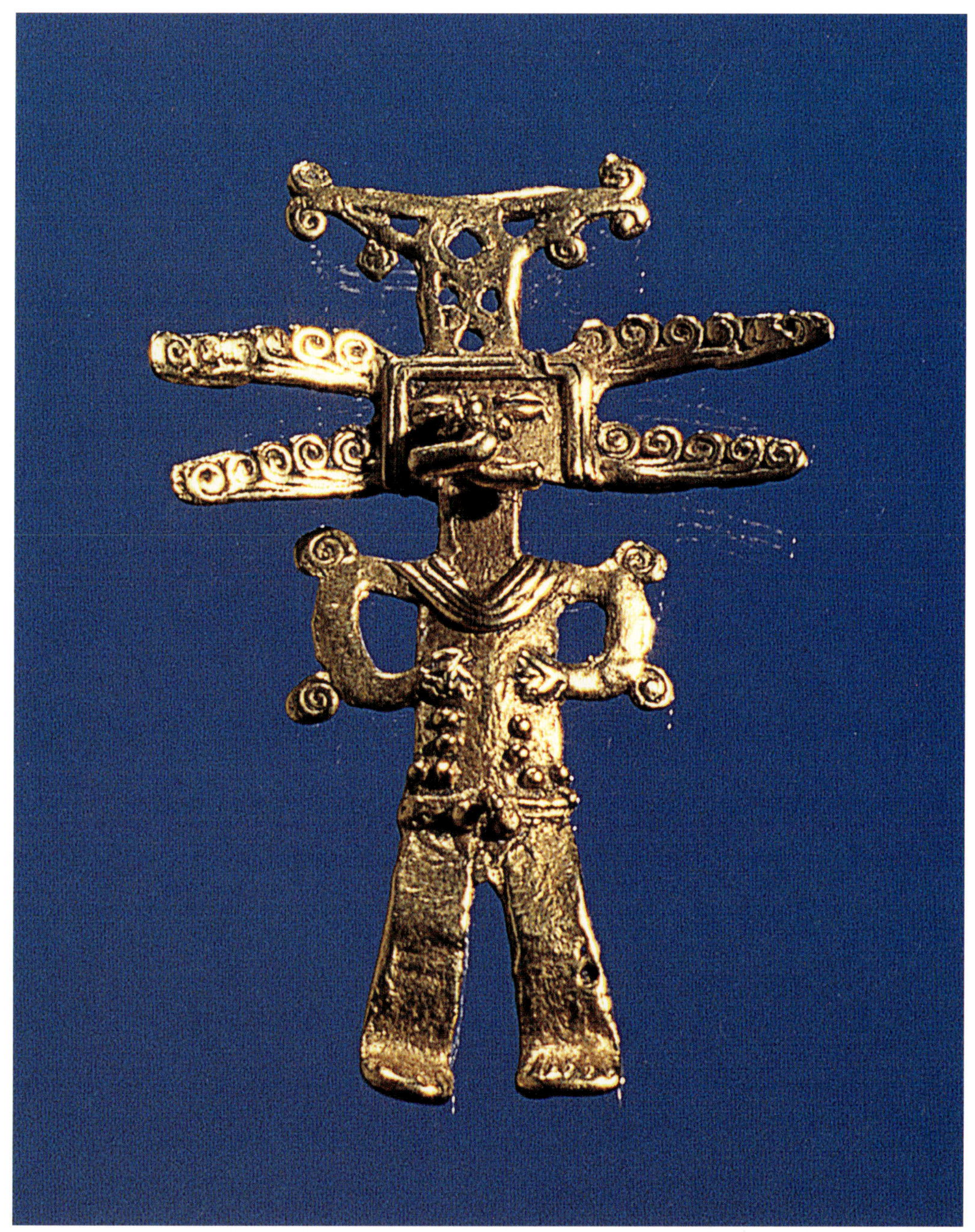

115. Anthropomorphic crocodile-god pendant. St. Marks, Wakulla County (8-Wa-15), Tallant Collection. Early Historic, after A.D. 1500 (unmodified, similar to specimens from Costa Rica dating from A.D. 800–1500. Gold, 8.7 cm high x 6.1 cm wide x 0.2 cm thick. South Florida Museum and Bishop Planetarium, Bradenton, no. SFM A6952.

BIBLIOGRAPHY

Alexander, Michael, ed.
1976 *Discovering the New World: Based on the Works of Theodore de Bry.* New York: Harper and Row.

Allerton, David, George M. Luer, and Robert S. Carr
1984 Ceremonial Tablets and Related Objects from Florida. *Florida Anthropologist* 37/1:5-54.

Andrews, E. W., and C. M. Andrews, eds.
1945 *Jonathan Dickinson's Journal, or, God's Protecting Providence* [1699]. New Haven: Yale University Press.

Baird, Donald
1988 The Princeton Dig at Panasoffkee Lake, Florida, 1876. *Bulletin of the Archaeological Society of New Jersey* 43:51-56.

Bartram, John
1875 Antiquities of Florida. *Smithsonian Institution Annual Report, 1874,* 393.

Bartam, William
1791 *Travels through North and South Carolina, Georgia, East and West Florida.* New York: James and Johnson.

Bennett, Charles E.
1968 *Settlement of Florida.* Gainesville: University Presses of Florida.

Benson, Carl A.
1967 A Unique Wood Carving from Tick Island. *Florida Anthropologist* 20/3-4:178-79.

Bourne, Edward Gaylord, ed.
1922 *Narratives of the Career of Hernando de Soto.* 2 vols. New York: Allerton Book Co.

Boyd, Mark F., Hale G. Smith, and John W. Griffin
1951 *Here They Once Stood: The Tragic End of the Apalachee Missions.* Gainesville: University Presses of Florida.

Branstetter, Laura

1991 The Tallant Collection: Metal Artifacts from Florida's Historic Period. Master's thesis, University of South Florida.

Brinton, Daniel G.

1859 *Florida Peninsula: Its Literary History, Indian Tribes, and Antiquities.* Philadelphia: J. Sabin.

Brose, David S., James A. Brown, and David W. Penney

1985 *Ancient Art of the American Woodland Indians.* Photographs by Dirk Bakker. New York: Abrams.

Bullen, Ripley P.

1955 Carved Owl Totem, DeLand, Florida. *Florida Anthropologist* 8/3:61-73.

Carr, Robert S.

1985 Prehistoric Circular Earthworks in South Florida. *Florida Anthropologist* 38/4:288-301.

Chatelain, Verne E.

1941 *The Defenses of Spanish Florida, 1565-1763.* Washington, D.C.: Catholic University Press.

Coleman, Wesley, James McCullin, and Jeanie McGuire

1983 A Carved Shell Pendant from Dade County, Florida. *Florida Anthropologist* 36/3-4:140-41.

Crosby, Alfred W., Jr.

1972 *The Colombian Exchange: Biological and Cultural Consequences of 1492.* Contributions in American Studies, No. 2. Westport, Conn.: Greenwood Press.

Cushing, Frank Hamilton

1897 Exploration of Ancient Key Dwellers' Remains on the Gulf Coast of Florida. *Proceedings of the American Philosophical Society* 25/153:329-448.

Detroit Institute of Art

1991 Precolumbian Art of Costa Rica: Between Continents, Between Seas. New York: Abrams.

Doran, Glen H., and David N. Dickel

1988 Multidisciplinary Investigations at the Windover Site. In *Wet Site Archaeology,* edited by Barbara A. Purdy, 263-89. West Caldwell, N.J.: Telford Press.

Fewkes, J. Walter

1924 Preliminary Archaeological Explorations at Weeden Island, Florida. *Smithsonian Miscellaneous Collections* 73/13:1-26.

Fundaburk, Emma Lila, and Mary Douglass Foreman, eds.

1957 *Sun Circles and Human Hands: The Southeastern Indians—Art and Industries.* Luverne, Ala.: Emma Lila Fundaburk.

Gannon, Michael V.

1967 *The Cross in the Sand: The Early Catholic Church in Florida, 1513-1870.* Gainesville: University Presses of Florida.

Gatschet, Albert Samuel.

1877–78 The Timucua Language. *Proceedings of the American Philosophical Society* 16:626-42; 17:490-504.

Gilliland, Marion Spjut

1975 *The Material Culture of Key Marco, Florida.* Gainesville: University Presses of Florida.

1989 *Key Marco's Buried Treasure.* Gainesville: University Presses of Florida.

Goggin, John M.

1940 The Tekesta Indians of Southern Florida. *Florida Historical Quarterly* 18:278.

1952 *Space and Time Perspective in Northern St. Johns Archeology, Florida.* Yale University Publications in Anthropology, No. 47. New Haven: Yale University Press.

Granberry, Julian

1993 *A Grammar and Dictionary of the Timucua Language.* Tuscaloosa: University of Alabama Press.

Hann, John H.

1987 *Apalachee: The Land between the Rivers.* Gainesville: University Presses of Florida.

Hemming, John

1978 *Red Gold: The Conquest of the Brazilian Indians, 1500-1760.* Cambridge, Mass.: Harvard University Press.

Hudson, Charles

1990 *The Juan Pardo Expedition: Spanish Explorers and the Indians of the Carolinas and Tennessee, 1566-1568.* Washington, D.C.: Smithsonian Institution Press.

Hulton, Paul H.

1977 *The Work of Jacques le Moyne de Morgues: A French Huguenot Artist in France, Florida, and England.* 2 vols. London: British Museum Publications.

Jahn, Otto L., and Ripley P. Bullen

1978 The Tick Island Site, St. Johns River, Florida. *Florida Anthropologist* 31/4:II:25.

Jones, Calvin

1981 Excavations of an Archaic Cemetery in Cocoa Beach, Florida. *Florida Anthropologist* 34/2:81-89.

1994 The Lake Jackson Mound Complex (8-Le-1): Stability and Change in Fort Walton Culture. *Florida Anthropologist* 47/2:120-46.

Kennedy, W. Jerald

1993 Archaeological Survey and Excavations at the Jupiter Inlet I Site (8Pb34), Dubois Park, Palm Beach County, Florida. Report on file at Florida Atlantic University, Department of Anthropology.

Laudonnière, René

1975 *Three Voyages.* Translated by Charles E. Bennett. Gainesville: University Presses of Florida.

Lanning, John Tate

1935 *The Spanish Missions of Georgia.* Chapel Hill: University of North Carolina Press.

Lawson, Edward W.

1946 *The Discovery of Florida and Its Discoverer, Juan Ponce de Leon.* St. Augustine, Fla.

Leader, Jonathan

1985 Metal Artifacts from Fort Center: Aboriginal Metal Working in the Southeastern United States. Master's thesis, Department of Anthropology, University of Florida.

1988 Technological Continuities and Specialization in Prehistoric Metalwork in the Eastern United States. Ph.D. diss., Department of Anthropology, University of Florida.

Lorant, Stefan

1946 *The New World: The First Pictures of America.* New York: Duell, Sloan, and Pearce.

Lowery, Woodbury

1905 *The Spanish Settlements within the Present Limits of the United States: Florida, 1562-74.* New York: Putnam's.

Lyon, Eugene

1976 *The Enterprise of Florida: Pedro Menéndez de Avilés and the Spanish Conquest of 1565-1568.* Gainesville: University Presses of Florida.

Matter, Robert Allen

1975 Missions in the Defense of Spanish Florida, 1566-1710. *Florida Historical Quarterly* 54:33.

Milanich, Jerald T.

1994 *Archaeology of Precolumbian Florida.* Gainesville: University Press of Florida.

Milanich, Jerald T., and Susan Milbrath, eds.

1989 *First Encounters.* Gainesville: University Presses of Florida.

Milanich, Jerald T., and Samuel Proctor, eds.

1978 *Tacachale.* Gainesville: University Presses of Florida.

Moore Clarence B.

1893a Certain Sand Mounds of the St. John's River, Florida, Part I. *Journal of the Academy of Natural Sciences of Philadelphia* 2nd series, 10.

1893b Certain Shell Heaps of the St. Johns River, Florida, Hitherto Unexplored. *American Naturalist* 27:8-13, 113-17, 605-24, 709-33.

1894 Certain Sand Mounds of the St. John's River, Florida, Part II. *Journal of the Academy of Natural Sciences of Philadelphia* 2nd series, 10.

1900 Certain Antiquities of the Florida West-Coast. *Journal of the Academy of Natural Sciences of Philadelphia* 11:349-94.

1902 Certain Aboriginal Remains of the Northwest Florida Coast, Part 2. *Journal of the Academy of Natural Sciences of Philadelphia* 11:42-97.

1903 Aboriginal Mounds of the Central Florida West-Coast, Aboriginal Mounds of the Apalachicola River. *Journal of the Academy of Natural Sciences of Philadelphia* 12:361-94.

1907 Crystal River Revisited, Mounds of the Lower Chattahoochee and Lower Flint Rivers, Notes on the Ten Thousand Islands, Florida. *Journal of the Academy of Natural Sciences of Philadelphia* 16:406-56, 459-76.

1918 The Northwestern Florida Coast Revisited. *Journal of the Academy of Natural Sciences of Philadelphia* 16:513-79.

Morison, Samuel Eliot

1974 *The European Discovery of America: The Southern Voyages, a.d. 1492-1616.* New York: Oxford University Press.

Priestly, Herbert I., trans. and ed.

1928 *The Luna Papers: Documents Relating to the Expedition of Don Tristán de Luna y Arellano for the Conquest of La Florida in 1559-1561.* 2 vols. Florida State Historical Society Publication No. 8.

Purdy, Barbara A.

1991 *The Art and Archaeology of Florida's Wetlands.* Boca Raton, Fla.: CRC Press.

Rau, Charles

1878 Observation on a Gold Ornament from a Mound in Florida. *Annual Report of the Smithsonian Institution for 1877,* 3-6.

Ribaut, Jean

1964 *The Whole and True Discouerye of Terra Florida* [1563; facsimile]. Gainesville: University Presses of Florida.

Robertson, James A., trans. and ed.

1933 *True Relation of the Hardships Suffered by Governor Hernando de Soto and Certain Portuguese Gentlemen during the Discovery of the Province of Florida, Now Newly Set Forth by a Gentleman of Elvas.* 2 vols. Florida State Historical Society Publication.

Rouse, Irving

1951 *A Survey of Indian River Archeology, Florida.* Yale University Publications in Anthropology, No. 44.

Sears, William H.

1956 *Excavations at Kolomoki, Final Report.* University of Georgia Series in Anthropology, No. 5.

1982 *Fort Center: An Archaeological Site in the Lake Okeechobee Basin.* Gainesville: University Presses of Florida.

Smith, Hale G.

1956 *The European and the Indian, European-Indian Contacts in Georgia and Florida.* Florida Anthropological Society Publications, No. 4.

Solis de Merás

1964 *Pedro Menéndez de Avilés.* Translated by J. T. Connor. Gainesville: University Presses of Florida.

Swanton, John R.

1922 *Early History of the Creek Indians and Their Neighbors.* Bureau of American Ethnology Bulletin, No. 73.

1946 *The Indians of the Southeastern United States.* Bureau of American Ethnology Bulletin, No. 137.

True, David O., ed.

1944 *Memoir of Dº d'Escalante Fontaneda Respecting Florida* [1854]. Translated by Buckingham Smith. Reprint, with revisions, Coral Gables, Fla.: University of Miami Press.

Varner, John Grier, and Jeannette Varner, trans. and eds.

1951 *Garcilaso de la Vega, the Florida of the Inca.* Austin: University of Texas Press.

Waring, A. J., Jr., and Preston Holder

1945 A Prehistoric Ceremonial Complex in the Southeastern United States. *American Anthropologist* 47/1:1-34.

Wenhold, Lucy L.

1936 A Seventeenth-Century Letter of Gabriel Diaz Vara Calderon, Bishop of Cuba. *Smithsonian Miscellaneous Collections* 95/16:1-14.

Wharton, Barry R., George R. Ballo, and Mitchell E. Hope

1981 The Republic Groves Site, Hardee County, Florida. *Florida Anthropologist* 34/2:59-80.

Willey, Gordon R.

1949a *Excavations in Southeast Florida.* Yale University Publications in Anthroology, No. 42. New Haven: Yale University Press.

1949b *Archaeology of the Florida Gulf Coast.* Smithsonian Miscellaneous Collections, No. 113.

Wyman, Jeffries

1875 *Fresh-Water Shell Mounds of the St. Johns River, Florida.* Peabody Academy of Science Memoirs, No. 4.

(overleaf) Gold doubloons in sand. Mexico and South America. Early Historic, after A.D. 1500. Private collection.

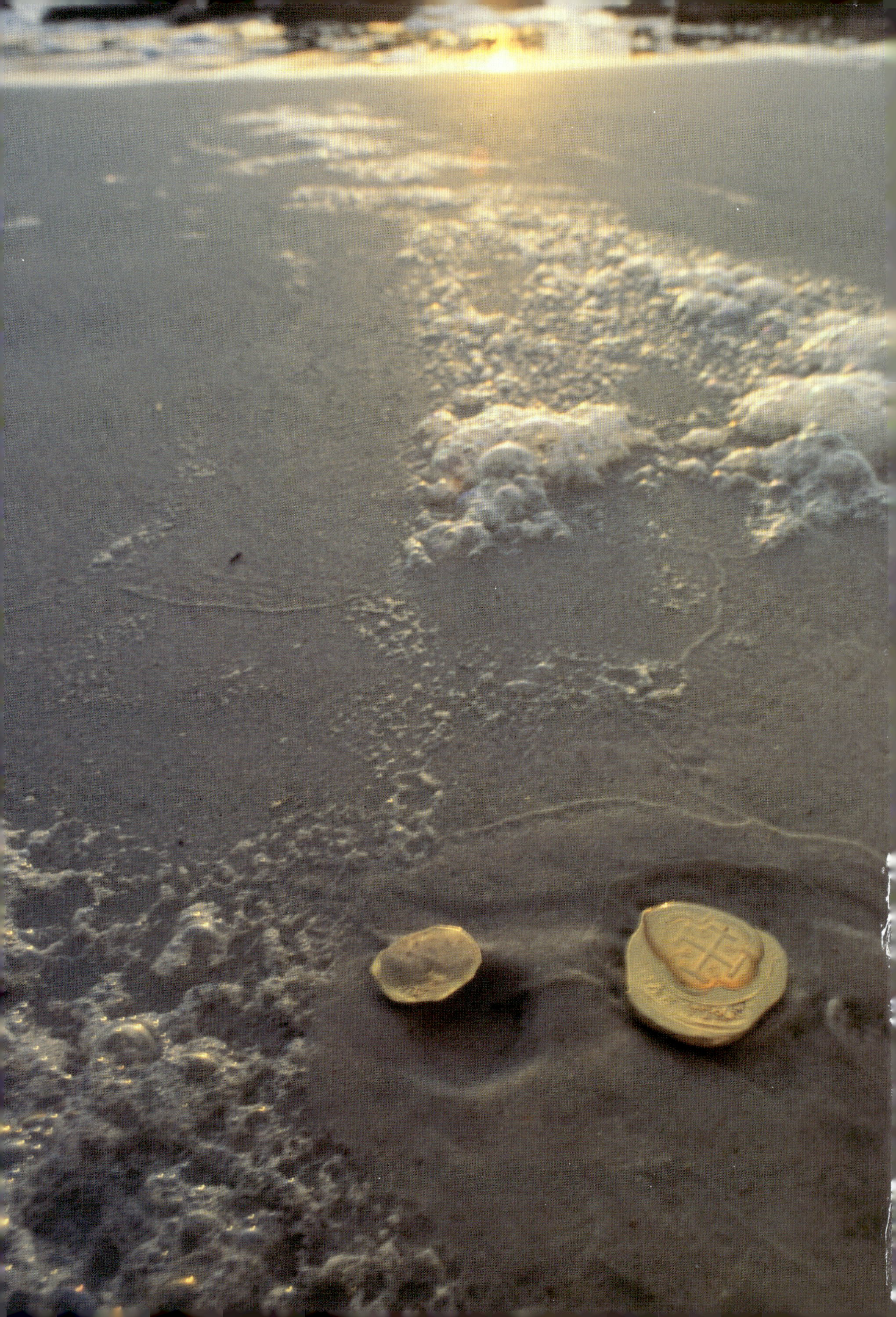